Public Governance Paradigms

POLICY, ADMINISTRATIVE AND INSTITUTIONAL CHANGE

Series Editors: Giliberto Capano, *Professor of Political Science, Scuola Normale Superiore, Italy* and Edoardo Ongaro, *Professor of Public Management, The Open University, UK*

Change is the main explanatory challenge for the social sciences. Stability and persistence are simpler to understand and explain than change; at the same time, change is not separated from stability, and, from this point of view, any approach to change (in whatever field) should be able to account for both 'constancy and change'.

Change is of significance, both for explanatory reasons, and from a more normative/prescriptive standpoint. To address, lead, control and implement change is a key task for policy-makers who, to adjust to or improve reality, constantly strive to cope with reality through designed changes in the institutional structure, in the organizational and processual dimensions of public administration, and in the governance arrangements of policies.

Following up on the above premises, this series is aimed at publishing books offering new, original, and enlightening views on change in action. The series is committed to overcoming the borders between scholars in public policy, public administration and management, and political institutions. Change happens at the crossroads where political institutions, policies and public administrations constantly interact and influence each other.

This broad perspective is highly relevant and innovative, both from the scientific and the applied perspective. The series, with its multi-dimensional and multi-theoretical commitment, is designed to offer significant information and high-quality practical knowledge for both scholars and policy-makers alike.

Public Governance Paradigms

Competing and Co-Existing

Jacob Torfing

Professor, Roskilde University, Denmark and Nord University, Norway

Lotte Bøgh Andersen

Professor, Department of Political Science, Aarhus University, Denmark

Carsten Greve

Professor, Department of Organization, Copenhagen Business School, Denmark

Kurt Klaudi Klausen

Professor, Department of Political Science and Public Management, University of Southern Denmark, Denmark

POLICY, ADMINISTRATIVE AND INSTITUTIONAL CHANGE

Edward Elgar
PUBLISHING

Cheltenham, UK • Northampton, MA, USA

Published by
Edward Elgar Publishing Limited
The Lypiatts
15 Lansdown Road
Cheltenham
Glos GL50 2JA
UK

Edward Elgar Publishing, Inc.
William Pratt House
9 Dewey Court
Northampton
Massachusetts 01060
USA

Paperback edition 2021

A catalogue record for this book
is available from the British Library

Library of Congress Control Number: 2019956522

This book is available electronically in the **Elgar**online
Social and Political Science subject collection
DOI 10.4337/9781788971225

ISBN 978 1 78897 121 8 (cased)
ISBN 978 1 78897 122 5 (eBook)
ISBN 978 1 80220 218 2 (paperback)

Printed and bound by CPI Group (UK) Ltd, Croydon, CR0 4YY

Contents

About the authors

Jacob Torfing is MA, PhD and Professor in Politics and Institutions at the Department of Social Sciences and Business, Roskilde University, Denmark and Professor at Nord University in Norway. He is Director of the Roskilde School of Governance at Roskilde University. His research interests include public sector reforms, public management, political leadership, collaborative innovation and co-creation. He has published several books and scores of articles on these topics. His latest single-authored monograph is *Collaborative Innovation in the Public Sector*, which was published by Georgetown University Press in 2016.

Lotte Bøgh Andersen is MA, PhD and Professor in Public Management and Leadership at the Department of Political Science, Aarhus University, Denmark. She is director of the Crown Prince Frederik Center for Public Leadership. Her research interests include leadership and performance in public and private organizations, employee motivation and leadership development. She has published numerous articles in *Journal of Public Administration Research and Theory*, *Public Administration Review*, *International Review of Administrative Sciences*, *Public Management Review*, *International Public Management Journal* and other publications.

Carsten Greve is MA, PhD and Professor in Public Management and Governance at the Department of Organization, Copenhagen Business School. He is co-director of the Center for Public Organization, Value and Innovation at the Department of Organization. His main research interests are public management reform and public-private partnerships. He recently published *The Logic of Public–Private Partnerships: The Enduring Interdependency between Politics and Markets* (co-author Graeme Hodge) with Edward Elgar in 2019.

Kurt Klaudi Klausen is MA and PhD in History and Organizational Theory and Professor in Public Management at the Department of Political Science and Public Management, University of Southern Denmark. His research interests include public management reform, strategic management and local government studies. He has published extensively in these areas. He recently published the article 'Still the Century of Government?' in *Public Management Review*, 2014.

Series preface

Giliberto Capano and Edoardo Ongaro

Change is the main explanatory challenge for social sciences. Stability and persistence are easier to understand and explain than change; at the same time, change is not separated from stability and, from this point of view, any approach to change (in whatever field) should be able to account for both 'constancy and change' (Hernes 1976).

Change is of significance both for explanatory reasons and from a more normative/prescriptive standpoint. To address, lead, control and implement change is the key task of policy-makers who, to adjust or improve reality, constantly strive to cope with reality through designed changes in the institutional structure, in the organizational and processual dimensions of public administration, and in the governance arrangements of policies.

Thus, change is an inescapable focus both for scholars and for policy-makers.

Following up on the above premises, this series is programmatically aimed at publishing books offering new, original and enlightening views on change of politics in action. The series is committed to overcoming borders between scholars in public policy, public administration and management, and political institutions. Change happens at the crossroads where political institutions, policies and public administrations constantly interact with and influence each other.

This broad perspective is quite relevant, and innovative we would say, both from the scientific and the applied point of view.

On the one hand, in fact, the theoretical enlargement proposed by the series can be quite fruitful for increasing the necessary conversation between different theoretical approaches, that very often are based on the same theoretical assumptions although belonging to different sub-disciplines and theoretical schools. Furthermore, this strategy could also be the bearer of positive and cumulative theoretical hybridizations capable of grasping the complexity of the mechanisms behind policy, administrative and institutional change.

On the other hand, the series – with its multi-dimensional and multi-theoretical commitment – will be capable of offering significant information and high-quality practical knowledge for policy-makers.

The series will publish both monographs and edited books.

Four main categories of publications are hosted in the series:

1. *Theory building stream*: Theoretical works explaining societal, political and institutional continuity and change. Books here may be broadly theoretical, thus proposing theories, frameworks, models for explaining continuity and change in the social sciences, with a view on applicability to policy, administration and institutions.
2. *Policy change stream*: Works explaining policy change. Works on policy analysis, providing new theoretical frames and new insights into policy change, rather than descriptions of policies in one or another sector. However, it could be that theoretically driven books, on change in specific policy fields, are also included.
3. *Public management reform stream*: Works explaining administrative change and public management reform. Various areas may be considered; on a purely illustrative basis: public management reforms; local government reforms; the pendulum of centralization/ decentralization in administrative reforms; liberal-democracy and accountability change and reform.
4. *Institutional change stream*: Works explaining institutional change, notably on governance: e.g. changing European governance; constitutional reforms dynamics and outputs; institutional change in federal governance.

Preface

Giliberto Capano and Edoardo Ongaro

This is the first book of the newly launched Edward Elgar series *Policy, Administrative and Institutional Change*, which we have the pleasure to direct. It represents an absolutely magnificent way of starting up such an editorial project. This work – written by leading international scholars Lotte Bøgh Andersen, Carsten Greve, Kurt Klaudi Klausen and Jacob Torfing – weaves together with utmost competence and brilliance a wide range of the topics and themes the series aims to address.

The book addresses directly two of the three areas covered by this series, namely administrative and institutional change, through the notion of the *public governance paradigms*. It does so in a very sophisticated way and at the same time with an ease and grace of touch which only scholars who have mastered the topic by means of their studies and research over decades, and who have been not just beholders but active shapers of some of those paradigms, can achieve.

This work is about change, which is the key explanandum of this book series, aimed at deepening the social scientific understanding of the dynamics of change processes in public administration, policy and institutions in a very profound way. It is about the *ideational bases of change*, and as such it sheds light on a hugely important yet often overlooked driver of transformative processes in the public sector. It also ties in key issues of legitimacy of public governance, a topic which calls for a deepening of our understanding and furthering our grasp over the ideational bases of public governance (Ongaro 2017, Chapter 5).

This is also a rare example of a book which is able to talk to scholars and practitioners alike, and does so seamlessly, guiding readers though the turns and bumps of the road that leads to understanding and appreciating public governance paradigms, with a competent hand on the substance and the rare clarity and capacity to get straight to the point in style.

It is an honour to start up this series on *Policy, Administrative and Institutional Change* with *Public Governance Paradigms: Competing and Co-Existing*. This book sheds light on large swathes of the literature and opens up paths of integration of strands of inquiry which have so far too often not been able to talk to each other. Scholars can discover in this book a treasure trove of knowledge gathered through decades of conceptualizations about 'reform models', 'doctrines' and 'paradigms' in public governance and management, and practitioners will find much-needed guidance on how to navigate the complexity of contemporary public governance.

1.   Introduction

Our increasingly globalized world economy is marked by increasing emphasis on systemic competition, and the development of the public sector has become an important parameter in this competition. Public sector reforms are further stimulated by new technological opportunities and new demands from citizens and private stakeholders. At the same time, both public administration research and public service organizations are becoming more evidence-based. The search for both 'best practices' and 'next practices' is accelerated by the development of public innovation units and by the growth of think tanks and other research-based organizations at the interface between academia and public policy, and the result is a more rapid selection process for what works in public governance and management (Margetts and Dunleavy 2013: 2). As such, we get more and different responses to the problems encountered in the existing approaches to managing the public sector. While the response to the alleged problems of public bureaucracy in the 1980s and 1990s was the introduction of market mechanisms and new forms of managerialism, the last two or three decades have seen the emergence of a host of competing understandings of what constitutes good public governance and management. While previous public sector reforms were narrow and technical, the new understandings of public governance give rise to profound changes and are subject to political contestation and public debate. A systematic way of analysing how public sector reforms aim to respond to emerging governance problems is urgently needed. In particular, we need to better understand the similarities and differences between the different underlying logics that inform public sector reforms.

STUDYING PUBLIC GOVERNANCE PARADIGMS

This book aims to scrutinize, compare and discuss the shifting and co-existing governance paradigms that inspire public administration reforms, and shape and reshape the general functioning and daily operation of public organizations. It provides a research-based account of the governance paradigms that are relevant for understanding what is going on in the public sector today. As such, our ambition is neither to scrutinize specific administrative processes and procedures nor to study the form, functioning and performance of particular public service organizations, but rather to uncover and describe the underlying policies, strategies, programmes and institutional templates that govern the particular manner in which the public sector is structured, functioning and operating. We refer to these policies, strategies, programmes and institutional templates as *public governance paradigms* in order to highlight the existence of relatively coherent and comprehensive norms and ideas about how to govern, organize and lead the public administration. Governance paradigms may be formed through an eclectic combination of ideas from different intellectual strands, but these ideas are re-articulated and integrated within a relatively coherent storyline that typically provides a diagnosis of current problems and challenges and a strategy for solving them. Adopting a governance paradigm may be partial in the sense of favouring some components over others and it will often involve adaptation of these elements to the context in which they are implemented. Hence, in reality the contours of a particular governance paradigm may be blurred, although at the level of discourse it provides a clear and distinct public sector approach to governing.

A particular governance paradigm may come to dominate the overall perception of the appropriate ways of structuring and operating the public sector in a particular country at a particular point in time. Nevertheless, it will compete and co-exist with old, institutionally embedded governance paradigms that continue to influence its daily operations and with new, embryonic paradigms that aspire to become the fad and fashion of tomorrow. The competing and co-existing governance paradigms may appeal to different political parties and different groups of public leaders and employees, and their support may be task-related and vary across different parts and levels of the public sector. As such, the official government discourse may be contradicted by ideas and practices at the level of local or regional government or in conflict with entrenched governance routines pervading the public school system or employment service. Indeed, the competing public governance paradigms will exist side by side within and across public organizations and create tensions and unintended effects.

The co-existing governance paradigms will enjoy different degrees of overall political and administrative support, and their relative popularity waxes and wanes over time. Hence, in retrospect, we may see that the overall design of public organizations, governance processes and forms of leadership at a particular point in time will be determined by a particular governance paradigm that promises to solve yesterday's problems and achieve desirable future results. Moreover, the predominant public governance paradigm, which enjoys firm support from central government officials and those in control of central budget allocations, will tend to exert coercive pressure on lower-level agencies to adopt and implement its core ideas (DiMaggio and Powell 1983); the local decoupling from those core ideas may appear to be a risky and short-sighted strategy (Meyer and Rowan 1977).

A key argument in this book is that the predominant governance paradigm will not succeed in eliminating the other competing governance paradigms. They will all continue to co-exist, somewhat like layers in a layer cake. The recently added top layer and the most recent addition of cream and berries placed on top will obviously tend to be the most visible layers, but the lower layers deeper down formed by the older governance paradigms may continue to provide a solid foundation. Moreover, particular aspects of the competing and co-existing governance paradigms will sometimes be merged to produce hybrid forms of public governance with more or less ambiguous effects. As such, we can conclude that the competing and co-existing governance paradigms will both form a layer cake with relatively separate public governance regimes and a marble cake with mixed and hybrid forms of public governance.

How the public administration is governed, organized and led is characterized by a high degree of stability. The path-dependence based on self-reinforcing feedback mechanisms between structures, norms, skills and behaviour tends to turn the stability of public organizations into inertia, thereby creating a remarkable resistance to change. Nevertheless, the public sector is surprisingly susceptible to influence from fashionable ideas about how to govern and be governed (DiMaggio and Powell 1983; Røvik 2011). The Weberian bureaucracy model triumphantly swept the world many years ago and constitutes one of the most widespread and institutionally entrenched fashion waves to ever hit the public sector. The global diffusion and massive impact of new public management (NPM), which in many ways goes against the grain of public bureaucracy, provides a more recent example of a successful fashion wave. Today, there are several contenders to the fashion prize as new discourses on neo-Weberianism, public value management, digitalization and network governance exert a growing influence on how the public sector should be designed and governed.

Now while the search for legitimate and desirable ways of governing the public sector in general, and the public administration in particular, is influenced by new and shifting fashions, this does not mean that the new paradigmatic reform programmes are a result of irrational moods and whims on the part of elected politicians and executive civil servants. New governance paradigms are developed and attract political and administrative attention and support because they appear to provide a plausible response to problems that the current thinking and practice in the public sector either fail to address or cannot provide an appropriate answer to. The proliferation and accumulation of problems and challenges within the predominant governance paradigm that informed the last round of public administration reforms spur critical reflection, pragmatic experimentation and mutual learning within and across public organizations. In addition, political and administrative entrepreneurs will look for inspiring solutions and positive experiences from other organizations, sectors and countries. Out of the learning-based search and development activities will eventually emerge a more or less coherent set of reform strategies that researchers, consultants and idea brokers will pick up, systematize, name and promote as a new and exciting governance paradigm that helps to answer pressing problems and challenges and promises to provide a viable path for the future development of the public sector.

New and emerging governance paradigms play an important role as they restructure and reorganize the public sector, change its interactions with the citizens and the private for-profit and non-profit sectors, and transform how public policies, regulations and services are produced, delivered and evaluated. Public administration researchers, political commentators and the mass media spend considerable time and energy analysing particular aspects of public governance, including the impact of new tax laws, the failure to provide adequate social housing or the efforts to meet ambitious goals for CO_2 emissions reductions. However, the detailed discussions about these important issues must not overshadow the more fundamental question about how we govern, organize and lead the public sector so that we are able to solve pressing societal problems in accordance with our overall goals and objectives and to support the development of the kind of society in which we want to live. There are many ways to structure, design and operate the public sector, and they have different effects on its processes, outputs and outcomes, which, in turn, affect the development of society and the economy. As public administration researchers, we want to clarify the differences between the relatively coherent public governance paradigms, scrutinize their strengths and weaknesses, and reflect on how it is possible to manoeuvre in the complex institutional terrain of conflicting and co-existing governance paradigms.

THE RECENT REVIVAL OF ADMINISTRATIVE REFORM POLICY

Our focus on the analysis and evaluation of public governance paradigms takes us far into the realm of administrative reform policy in which recommendations drawn from particular governance strategies are not merely based on information, knowledge and scientific insights but also on political values, opinions and aspirations. This is dangerous territory for social scientists who want to abstain from making causal inferences between descriptive statements about what is happening in the world and prescriptive statements about what ought to happen. Nevertheless, we are convinced that a careful analytical mapping and comparison of relevant public governance paradigms and a research-based evaluation of their positive and negative effects will save us from illegitimate inferences and help to facilitate an informed political debate about the future development of the public sector.

While the study of public sector reform is an important and well-established part of administrative sciences, the study of administrative reform policy and shifting public governance paradigms is a relatively recent addition (see Christensen and Lægreid 2003; Barzelay and Gallego 2006; Hammerschmidt et al. 2016). For almost a century, the public sector was governed by ideas associated with Wilsonian and Weberian bureaucracy, which, to varying degrees, were combined with ideas about professional rule that were spurred by the post-war development of the welfare state that often delegated considerable power and influence on service delivery to strong professional groups of doctors, nurses, schoolteachers etc. In this period, change appeared to be limited and there was little to study in terms of administrative reform policy and shifting governance paradigms. As Kettl (2015) has shown, however, North American presidents have played a crucial role in driving change in the bureaucratic and liberal-democratic governance paradigm, sometimes accentuating themes and ideas that have been taken up by later public governance paradigms. If continuity prevailed over discontinuity in most of the twentieth century, the period since the early 1970s has been marked by disruption and change. The growing critique of public bureaucracy and professional rule has exploded the post-war consensus about the virtues of the continued expansion of a professional public bureaucracy. In response, we have seen the emergence of a handful of new governance paradigms, of which NPM has by far been the most influential despite mounting criticisms and numerous alternatives.

The emergence of the public governance ideas associated with NPM and the political and administrative controversies it has engendered have spurred the current revival of administrative reform policy. Whereas the development of the public administration was long considered a technical issue that was left for executive public managers and public law experts to solve, the form and function of public administration became subject to political contestation. As such, both US President Ronald Reagan and UK Prime Minister Margaret Thatcher campaigned against red-tape bureaucracy and in favour of 'less state and more market'. Reagan famously claimed that 'government is the problem, not the solution', and Thatcher wanted to 'roll back the welfare state'. These controversial political statements heralded the arrival of a new era of administration reform policy. Political leaders in other countries echoed the Anglophone political leaders' calls for de-regulation, marketization and the dismantling of public bureaucracy and introduced public sector reforms that were later described as a part of the NPM revolution. Since the countries on the European continent had administrative traditions that were very different from the ideas encapsulated by the NPM reform programme, the introduction of NPM-inspired reforms was accompanied by great scepticism and mounting complaints and criticisms. The immediate politicization of NPM served to keep the debate about administrative reform policy alive. The defenders and critics of NPM engaged in fierce disputes with each other while the advocates of new and alternative governance paradigms gradually came onto the stage and enhanced the ideational complexity by increasing the number of governance options and multiplying the arguments for and against different governance paradigms.

The debate on administrative reform policy started at the national level, with politicians suddenly taking a keen interest in transforming the public sector and executive managers pushing administrative reforms. It spread from country to country with the diffusion and adoption of NPM reforms. Gradually, the debate caught on at the international and supranational levels as new players such as the World Bank, the OECD, European Commission and to some extent also the UN started to produce a series of reports recommending different kinds of public sector reforms. The World Bank promoted norms about good governance that emphasized bureaucratic values such as transparency, impartiality and the rule of law. The OECD initially embraced and promoted NPM-associated reforms but became increasingly critical and more focused on spurring public innovation. In 2001, the European Commission issued a White Paper on Governance (EU, 2001), which focused on citizen involvement and public and private collaboration in and through networks and partnerships, and in 2009 the EU Committee of Regions published a White

Paper on Multi-level Governance (EU, 2009). Finally, the UN sustainable development goals recommended relevant and affected actors to be involved in bringing about global change through participation in networks and partnerships. In sum, international and supranational organizations seemed to play an important role as idea brokers for national public authorities in the field of public governance and administration.

In countries where local governments and regional authorities are of a considerable size and possess sufficient resources, capacities and self-confidence, they have also entered the discussion of administrative reform policy. Big-city mayors have occasionally taken the lead. At other times, the national associations of municipalities or regional authorities have contributed to the governance debate. Both local and regional governments are under pressure to deliver societal solutions and public services to the citizens in a situation characterized by scarce public resources. The elected politicians are in close proximity to the citizens they are serving, and they are often less ideological and more pragmatic than the national-level political leaders (Barber 2013). Together with the executive administrators, they struggle to make ends meet and are often open to experimentation as part of their pragmatic search for solutions that work in practice. As such, they are busy creating public sector reforms 'from below'. They often go their own ways and frequently inspire national-level political leaders to go in a new direction.

Researchers, consultancy firms, think-tanks and mass media have also contributed to the debate on administrative reform policy. Researchers have not only published a series of critical accounts on the recent public sectors reforms but also contributed positively to the development of administrative reform ideas. The publication of the Blacksburg Manifesto, which aimed to counter the growing 'bureaucrat bashing' and called for a 're-founding' of the normativity of public administration within a democratic state based on effective public participation, provides a famous example of a research-based intervention in administrative reform policy (Wamsley et al. 1990). More recently and in a different part of the world, a large group of Danish public administration scholars published a similar manifesto entitled 'An innovative public sector that enhances quality and joint responsibility' (Andersen et al. 2012). Currently, a large-scale research project at Utrecht University financed by the European Research Council aims to inspire public sector reform by identifying, analysing and drawing lessons from successful cases of public governance. Scores of public sector consultants have also aimed to identify new positive trends in public governance. Working on a more operational level, they aim to discover and describe solutions to specific governance problems and turn them into marketable products. While some consulting houses work closely together with researchers to learn about new theories and ideas, others take their cues from central government offices and the administrative cures that they are prescribing. Finally, mass media and a growing number of web-based newsletters and blogs have reported numerous policy and administration failures and given airtime to public sector commentators with different views and ideas about how to reform the public sector.

In sum, the political debate on public administration has attracted many different actors from multiple levels and circulated many conflicting ideas, views and assessments. It can therefore be difficult to obtain a clear sense of which way is up in the many debates. At the same time, the stakes in the debate are high since the choice of a particular type of governance or a particular administrative reform possibly has a profound impact on the ability of the public sector to deliver outputs and outcomes that are efficient, effective, robust, fair, democratic, sustainable, and so forth. This predicament explains why we have decided to heed the call for a systematic mapping, analysis and evaluation of the competing and co-existing public governance paradigms. We believe that this endeavour will provide a clearer understanding of the complex reform processes and institutional configurations in the public sector.

Depending on the individual reader's temperament, our book may be construed either as a scholarly contribution aiming to conceptualize and compare different governance paradigms, a guide for making well-informed decisions about public sector reform, or as yet another intervention in the ongoing political debate about administrative policy-making. Contrary to our intentions, if we have not succeeded in escaping the political debate that we want to inform (rather than contribute to), we hope that the political recommendation that can be gleaned from our exposition is that people in and around the public sector should make a pragmatic, context-sensitive choice of governance solutions while considering their complex environment and bearing in mind that the choice between competing governance paradigms has many trade-offs, and there is no one size that fits all. When it comes to the question of how to govern, organize and lead the public sector, there is no perfect and final solution, but rather only different and shifting combinations of imperfect – albeit perhaps adequate – governance solutions that match different public tasks, political ambitions and administrative cultures and contexts.

DEFINITION, CONTENT AND DEVELOPMENT OF PUBLIC GOVERNANCE PARADIGMS

As hinted above, public governance paradigms are defined as a relatively coherent and comprehensive set of norms and ideas about how to govern, organize and lead the public sector. The normative and ideational components of a governance regime may have different origins, but these are re-articulated and form part of a relative unified discourse. The eclectic, but relatively coherent governance paradigms tend to offer a critical diagnosis of the past and promise to provide solutions to the most pressing problems and challenges confronting the public sector in the future. The new solutions frequently recycle old ideas and practices, thereby contributing to the reinvention of the past. The old ideas are connected to new ones, however, giving rise to new practices with new functionalities. Public governance paradigms tend to be structured around a few core beliefs and assumptions that inform a larger set of loosely connected ideas and recommendations about how to govern and be governed, how to structure and organize the public sector, how it relates to wider society, and how leaders, managers and employees interact in the delivery of solutions and services to citizens and private stakeholders. As such, they provide an instance of 'third-order governance' that creates the normative, ideational and institutional conditions for the structure and processes of the overall system of public governance ('second-order governance'), which in turn conditions the daily interactions and operations through which concrete solutions, regulations and services are produced and delivered ('first-order governance') (see Kooiman 2003).

The third-order concept of public governance paradigms draws on Thomas Kuhn's famous idea of scientific revolutions that lead to the formation of new scientific paradigms that are gradually taken for granted by the scientists involved in 'normal science' (Kuhn 1962). Based on the spectacular transition from the old geocentric to the new heliocentric view of the universe, Kuhn perceives scientific paradigms as logically consistent theories that are tested rigorously in evidence-based ways. He also asserts that paradigmatic change will tend to be rare, exceptional and triggered by the continuous problematization of its basic assumptions.

As Margetts and Dunleavy (2013) rightly observe, these conditions do not apply in the social sciences and even less so in the non-academic spheres of life (e.g. public administration). Public governance paradigms are not logically consistent theories with a strong evidence base. They initially tend to consist of vaguely defined, loosely connected and normatively charged ideas. Depending on their political support and resonance with the administrative culture, they might gradually gain momentum and assume a more consistent form. Systematic evidence of their positive role and impact that goes beyond the sampling of isolated success stories tends to come much later. Moreover, changes in public governance paradigms tend to be more frequent and much faster than change in the more fundamental scientific paradigms. The heightened frequency of change is explained by the acceleration of global policy learning based on the exchange of best practices, the proliferation of think tanks and other idea brokers, and the steadily stronger interface between academia and public policy-making that has accelerated learning processes and boosted the circulation and selection of new ideas about what works in public administration and management.

Given these differences vis-à-vis Kuhn's theory of scientific paradigms, perhaps we should rather talk about 'quasi-paradigms' in public governance than paradigms in the Kuhnian sense of the term. However, we agree with Margetts and Dunleavy (2013) that public governance paradigms behave like ordinary paradigms in two important respects. First, they tend to have two levels, with an overall macro-level theory based on a few propositions that pull together and give direction to a wider range of supplementary concepts, detailed recommendations and preferred methods. Second, they develop in response to the problems of their predecessor, enter a period of relatively successful 'normal governance' and are problematized by the accumulation of problems to which they cannot provide an appropriate response. These resemblances to Kuhnian-type scientific paradigms serve to justify the notion of public governance paradigms.

Public governance paradigms give direction and meaning to specific governance reforms and the daily efforts to optimize the role and functioning of public administration in order to deliver solutions and services of high quality with the available means. However, we should not forget that the initial formulation of the governance paradigms is inspired by new developments in actual forms of public governance and administration. Thus, Weber (1947) got the idea for his famous bureaucracy model by studying the successful operation of the German postal system. Hood (1991) observed some new empirical reform tendencies in the public sectors in Australia, New Zealand and the UK, drew a ring around and named them 'New Public Management'. Pollitt and Bouckaert (2004) saw that some countries were not buying the whole NPM package, aiming instead to preserve classical Weberian values while making the public sector more efficient and user-friendly. This observation led them to coin the notion of the Neo-Weberian State. In much the same way, Dunleavy and his collaborators (2006a, b) and Osborne (2006, 2010) identified new trends in public governance that aimed to solve some of the problems created by NPM and denoted these trends Digital Era Governance and New Public Governance, respectively.

As such, the public governance paradigms are not invented out of thin air, but instead are inspired by actual trends and developments that are stylized and idealized in order to be able to provide a more generic account of the core governance principles and how they may offer a way forward for the public sector. When public governance paradigms have first been formulated and described in generic terms by academic researchers, they quickly attain their own life and provide a more or less coherent and comprehensive framework for thinking about and practising public governance. Supporters and advocates help fill in the blanks, and the number of specific recommendations grows while key ideas are adapted to new circumstances and new and compatible ideas are integrated. In sum, what begins as an ex-post rationalization of empirical trends that are subjected to academic scrutiny and systematization ends up being a result of a dialectical interplay between theory and practice.

The public governance paradigms discussed among researchers and practitioners are often reified and assumed to have an independent existence in reality. Frequently, they assume the character of an acting and wilful subject aiming to infuse the public sector with a particular set of norms and ideas. A particular government agency or think tank is sometimes seen as an incarnation of a particular governance paradigm that it promotes in any way possible. However, the only thing that exists in reality is a diverse set of governance ideas and administrative practices that, according to particular researchers, can be re-described as an integral part of particular governance paradigms. Hence, although the public governance paradigms provide different prescriptive models for how to govern, organize and lead the public sector, they are ideational constructions in the heads of the researchers and practitioners who subscribe to their core ideas. The constructed character of the public governance paradigms does not prevent them from having a real impact on administrative practices and the form and functioning of public organizations. When social and political actors in and around the public sector act, they tend to draw on relational systems of concepts and ideas and they shape the world of administrative practices based on these ideas and concepts. Their actions are subsequently legitimized with reference to the core beliefs of particular governance paradigms. Hence, what come to exist in reality are particular enactments of different governance regimes that over time are institutionalized and thus become relatively entrenched.

There is an interesting dynamic between norm and fact that feeds on the interface between academic scholars and public administration practitioners. Academics may aim to capture new empirical trends by describing new and important governance paradigms. The new norms and ideas about public governance are disseminated through white and grey literature, the graduation of new generations of public administration students and teaching in the growing number of mid-career management training programmes. Practitioners apply the new paradigmatic ideas about how to govern and be governed in their daily administrative practices, which are shaped and reshaped by new reform initiatives that also take their inspiration from the new governance paradigms. Researchers then conduct careful studies of what is going on in the public sector. While the studies tend to confirm the relevance of the public governance paradigms, they also detect deviations, conflicts and dilemmas; and perhaps even some new and emerging trends. This owes to the fact that the governance paradigms and the magic concepts they deploy do not come with easy-to-follow instructions. Rather, they are interpreted and translated in the course of the implementation process, where they tend to clash with ideas and practices associated with pre-existing governance paradigms leading to either reinventions or hybridization. As such, the object of study in the field of public administration is a moving target. The researchers will eventually come up with new ways of making sense of the dynamic changes in reality, which will in turn inform the practitioners' reflections and practices. A new dynamic and dialectical cycle begins.

Looking back at the post-war period, there is little doubt that the shifting governance paradigms have played a crucial role in prompting and guiding the development of the public sector. At first, the public sector was shaped in accordance with the principles of Weber's *bureaucracy model*, and this development created what researchers today refer to as Old Public Administration (OPA). Politics and administration were separated, a hierarchical chain of command ensured centralized control, a horizontal division of labour between different departments facilitated specialization, policies were created based on rational decision-making and implemented through rule-based governance, and public employees were hired based on their merits. The bureaucratic governance paradigm came to have different expressions in the European countries, where it is possible to identify different administrative traditions reflected in the different legal regimes in, for example, France, Germany and the UK (Andersen, Leisink and Vandenabeele 2017).

Some public bureaucracies developed a strong welfare sector in which professional groups with a specialized education have a large influence on service production. In countries with a high degree of devolution to local authorities and specialized public service organizations, a low level of centralized control based on rules and targets, a strong recognition of the need for professional discretion in public service delivery and a high degree of occupational closure, the power of welfare professionals became so strong that we can talk about *professional rule* (Noordegraaf 2016). Although professional rule is conditioned by the professionaliz-ation of the public sector, which is inherent to public bureaucracy, it introduces an autonomous power based on professional norms, values and theories that challenges the hierarchical chain of command. Profes-sional rule is based on horizontal collegiality, and the professional leaders are considered as *primus inter pares*. In some cases, the loyalty of the employees and their professional leaders will primarily be with their profession and their professional associations or trade unions rather than with the public sector as such.

In the 1970s and 1980s, there was growing criticism of public bureaucracy and the professional rule that it had nurtured in countries with strong, decentralized welfare states. Bureaucracy was criticized for its centralized steering and planning model and the rule-governed administration that creates unfortunate rigidities, as well as for the lack of competition and entrepreneurship that result in high-cost, poor-quality services. The autonomous, norm-based professional rule was criticized for leading to an upward drift in public expenditure, and the powerful welfare professions were accused of being self-serving, paternalistic and politically tone-deaf. The anti-bureaucratic backlash found academic support in public choice theory and principal–agent theory, and it did not take long before neo-liberal and neo-conservative politicians called for radical reforms of the public sector.

Reforms combining marketization with a new kind of managerialism were introduced under the umbrella term New Public Management (NPM), which also included a preference for contractualism, agentifi-cation and so forth. NPM was the name of the game in most countries in the Western Hemisphere throughout the 1980s, 1990s and 2000s. Many of the newly industrialized countries in South-East Asia also introduced NPM-inspired reforms that became a global reference point for public governance and administration. Despite its positive effects on budget discipline, result-orientation and user satisfaction, the criticisms of the broken promises and the unintended negative effects of marketization and managerialism soon picked up. Academics documented the failure to deliver on the promises of deregulation, innovation and cost-efficiency, as well as the negative impact on public service motivation, organizational fragmentation and core bureaucratic values such as fairness, equity and political accountability. Public employees complained that the strict enforcement of performance management distorts goal-attainment in the public sector, eliminates the room for professional discretion and takes precious time away from the production of core services. While central government offices continue to support the NPM paradigm, some countries have seen a growing popular mobilization against it. In some cases, the critique of NPM has led to a critique of public steering as such, and there are also examples of criticisms of NPM being merged with criticisms of globalization and neoliberalism, which when taken together are seen as the source of all evil. In most cases, however, the criticisms of NPM have spurred discussions about which parts should be abandoned or retained, which parts call for adjustment and reform, and which alternative governance paradigms the future may bring. In particular, four governance paradigms claim to remedy the problems with NPM and reinvigorate the public sector: the Neo-Weberian State, Digital Era Governance, Public Value Management and New Public Governance.

The Neo-Weberian State (NWS) paradigm has developed in countries that have been reluctant to implement NPM reforms (Pollitt and Bouckaert 2004) but may offer a bureaucratic corrective to NPM in other countries as well. The main concern is to return to classical bureaucratic values such as competence, fairness, equity, impartiality and political accountability. Here, the Neo-Weberian State paradigm draws on discussions from the late 1960s and early 1970s that are commonly referred to as New Public Administration (Marini 1971; Waldo 1971; Wamsley and Zald 1973). The position vis-à-vis NPM is somewhat ambivalent, as the marketization part is rejected whereas the strategic management part is welcomed. Finally, classical forms of bureaucracy are criticized for neglecting the needs and demands of the citizens. Hence, the paternalistic ethos that pervades public bureaucracy must be counteracted by a new responsiveness.

Its advocates depict Digital Era Governance (DEG) as a response to the crisis of NPM early in the new millennium and the fiscal crisis since 2008, which has emphasized the need to cut spending. The idea at the core of Digital Era Governance is to draw the full consequences of the digital revolution in information and communication technology for the development of public service delivery (Dunleavy et al. 2006a, b). Not merely a tool for enhancing administrative efficiency in the back office, digitalization may also help to reintegrate fragmented public and private service-delivery agencies, provide more holistic service to citizens and enhance democratic participation and public deliberation.

The Public Value Management (PVM) paradigm shares some of its core ideas with the Neo-Weberian State paradigm, but there is much greater emphasis on stakeholder involvement in public governance. The basic argument is that the public sector is not merely a parasite feeding off the value produced by the competitive and innovative private sector and validated by consumers in private markets. The public sector is unique in its production of tax-financed public value that is validated through political and democratic debate and processed by public bureaucracy. While the original contributions to Public Value Management (Moore 1995) place the responsibility for public value production with public managers engaged in strategic management combining the development and authorization of public value propositions with organizational capacity building, recent interpretations (Stoker 2006; Bryson et al. 2015) claim that the public value perspective opens up for the involvement of a plethora of public and private actors in collaborative governance taking place in networks and partnerships. Public Value Management thus lends itself to conflicting interpretations: its inherent managerialism points towards NPM while its potential support for network governance aligns it with New Public Governance.

New Public Governance (NPG) (Osborne 2006, 2010) claims that the reliance of the public sector on hierarchies and markets is problematic and that collaborative governance based on networks partnerships and the cultivation of an active and engaged citizenship is the only way to counteract organizational fragmentation, solve complex problems and mobilize resources and ideas capable of spurring public innovation. Its recommendation of horizontal forms of governance provides a radical departure from both the traditional forms of top-down government and the recent marketization of the public sector that replaces political rule with competition. Collaborative governance and the attempt to spur service innovation calls for leadership and management to be based more on trust-based facilitation and empowerment than on control-based performance management.

These four governance paradigms can all be seen as a reaction to the problems and challenges associated with NPM. At the risk of simplifying the rich and sophisticated arguments, the Neo-Weberian State can be said mainly to be a reaction to how NPM has undermined core public values. Digital Era Governance is a digitally enabled response to the need for continued efficiency gains and the need to ensure service quality for the citizenry through the integration of service and the adoption of a more holistic perspective. Public Value Management is a reaction to the failure of NPM to appreciate the unique character of the public sector, which consists of its contribution to public value production. New Public Governance represents a response to the growing fragmentation and pervasiveness of wicked problems that call for cross-cutting collaboration and public innovation. The triggering factors behind the emergence of the new governance paradigms are both functional (new problems require new solutions) and dynamic (unintended negative effects call for adjustments). Hence, public sector reforms can be seen both as planned and emerging, and they both represent continuity and discontinuity. While the new governance paradigms may introduce entirely new elements into the debate, they also react to excesses; rather like a pendulum that swings too far in one direction after which it swings back, albeit perhaps in a slightly different or new direction.

There are three important drivers in the development of public governance paradigms (Pollitt and Bouckaert 2004). The first is the societal and socio-technical development that both propels the formulation of new demands and provides new opportunities. Economic growth and decline, changing demographics, the growing service expectations of the affluent middle class, functional differentiation of society, new technologies and competitive pressures from economic globalization have each influenced the shifting conceptions of the role and functioning of the public sector. The second driver is the critique of the predominant governance paradigm and the organizational learning that it engenders. New and emerging public governance paradigms initially tend to produce gains and benefits. After a period of consolidation, their marginal return to scale slowly begins to decline and the unintended negative consequences become increasingly apparent. The accumulation of problems and criticisms triggers the search for new solutions. The third driver of change is the diffusion of new paradigmatic ideas about public governance across organizations, sectors and countries. Organizations may learn from their own experiments or from successful reforms in other organizations. Ideas from private sector governance may also find their way into the public sector. Most importantly, however, governments at different levels learn from the best in the class and copy governance designs from governments elsewhere. The new ideas circulating between organizations and governments and across sector boundaries may gradually congeal and assume the form of best practices that provide building blocks for the construction of new governance paradigms.

New paradigmatic ideas about public governance will only have an impact and become the new dominant trend if supported by political and administrative elites. While local-level public organizations and professional groups may exploit their relative autonomy to develop and test new paradigmatic governance practices, it is impossible without support from above to mainstream the new governance ideas and to realize their full potential. Hence, public administration politics is ultimately the result of elite decisions that are influenced by ideological and tactical concerns and often place considerable power in the hands of executive public managers who prefer stability and continuity rather than disruptive change, which creates uncertainty and the risk of failure. Despite the pivotal role of the political and administrative elites in driving public sector reform, we should be careful not to believe that central decision-makers are acting in accordance with a hidden masterplan. The intentions behind administrative reforms are not always clear, and compromises between the desirable and the possible are constantly being made (Pollitt and Bouckaert 2004). Considerable gaps often exist between the stated reform intentions and the reforms that are ultimately carried out, and the implementation of these reforms is an adaptive process that may result in administrative designs and governance solutions that nobody really wanted.

Finally, the development and implementation of a new governance paradigm does not mean that the old governance paradigms are eliminated and replaced with new ones. Drawing on the insights of historical institutionalism (Streeck and Thelen 2005),[1] we can safely say that the effect of the institutionalization of past political compromises means that new and old governance paradigms will co-exist, although in unstable and shifting relations of dominance. A new and fashionable governance paradigm may successfully relegate the existing governance paradigms to more marginal positions and will sometimes manage to transform their role and content to better match the new, predominant way of thinking and acting. The old paradigms will nevertheless continue to play a role and may delimit and obstruct the functioning of the new governance paradigm.

Not all new governance paradigms succeed in capturing the hearts and minds of the political and administrative elites, thereby constituting the new ideational horizon for designing public governance and adminis-tration. While new embryonic governance paradigms might appeal to particular groups of public and private actors and to particular parts of the public sector, they may continue to live in the shadow of other dominating governance paradigms. The new and emerging governance paradigms may fulfil a particular function by offering solutions to well-known problems but may lack active support from the political and

---

[1] While our overall argument about the competing and co-existing governance paradigms finds support in historical institutionalism and its keen eye for both the dynamic interaction between institutional structure and social and political agency and its emphasis on institutional inertia, this book is not based on a particular theory or theoretical framework. Theories are only invoked in order to shed light on the public governance paradigms that we aim to map and reconstruct.

administrative elites. They may supplement mainstream ideas for decades before losing their grip on the collective administrative imagination. Alternatively, they may suddenly become fashionable and guide public sector reforms. The fate of new governance paradigms is unpredictable; all we can do is to carefully map the ongoing transmutation of the norms and ideas about public governance and the actual ways that people are governed, processes are organized, society is regulated and services are provided.

THE PUBLIC GOVERNANCE DIAMOND

This book aims to analyse and evaluate no fewer than seven public governance paradigms in order to provide a solid foundation for discussing the need for public sector reform and understanding the current state and future development of public administration. In the presentation and analysis of each of the seven governance paradigms, we first describe its background before proceeding to account for its theoretical sources of inspiration and its main ideas and assumptions. Next, we examine the empirical evidence of its diffusion and impact. And finally, we discuss the arguments for and against its application in particular contexts and reflect on the governance dilemmas emerging from its usage.

In the analysis of the core ideas of a specific governance paradigm, we draw on the 'public governance diamond' we have developed to capture and compare different dimensions of the seven governance paradigms. Hence, we will place each of the paradigms on the five axes of the governance diamond, which enables us to visualize the variation on the key dimensions that we are interested in compared across the governance paradigms. They capture key aspects of how the governance of the public sector should be organized according to the governance paradigms.

The analytical dimensions that we measure from low to high along the five axes of the governance diamond are:

1. *Centralized control*: The degree of recommended centralized control in the vertical chain of command.
2. *Horizontal coordination*: The degree of recommended horizontal interagency coordination and collaboration.
3. *Use of value articulation*: The degree to which public governance should be based on the articulation of public values.
4. *Use of incentives*: The degree to which public governance should be based on conditional positive and negative incentives.

5. *Societal involvement*: The degree to which private for-profit or non-profit actors, including citizens, should be involved in public governance.

The first two dimensions focus on the vertical and horizontal structures in relation to governing processes in the public sector. The next two dimensions concern the preference for particular tools of governance, and the last dimension aims to capture the interface between the public sector and the surrounding society. The analytical dimensions aim to capture the institutional mechanisms through public governance that is produced and delivered rather than the political and democratic aspects of public governance.

The degree of centralized control considers where the key governance decisions are made. To what extent is the power to make key decisions about governance, regulation and service delivery concentrated at the top of the public sector? And to what extent is it devolved to lower levels and frontline organizations, managers and employees through deconcentration or decentralization? The continuum along the first axis goes from local, institutional and professional autonomy, via management by overall budgets and objectives, to centralized control with key governance decisions.

The degree of horizontal coordination aims to assess the relative importance of institutional specialization based on a strict separation of administrative departments and agencies vis-à-vis collaborative problem-solving across administrative agencies and silos. The continuum along the second axis goes from the strict separation of administrative silos, via knowledge sharing, negative coordination to avoid conflicts, gaps and overlaps and the occasional formation of an ad hoc task force, to holistic interagency collaboration and 'joined-up government' based on inter-organizational networking.

The use of value articulation concerns the active use of values in public governance. While all of the public governance paradigms are based on a particular set of norms and values aimed at capturing the content of good and desirable governance, they may not use norms and values actively as a tool of governance that endeavours to ensure that local agencies and public employees wholeheartedly pursue the goals they are supposed to pursue. In line with key academic contributions to leadership and management theory (Burns 1978; Bass and Riggio 2006), we define transformational leadership as behaviour that seeks to develop, share and sustain a common vision and to norms and values that may spur the production of desired outputs and outcomes. Influencing the normative perception of why, how and to what effect public agencies and employees should deal with particular public problems, challenges and tasks might provide a potent governance tool, but it is not recommended and deployed with equal strength and vigour by the different governance paradigms. Its prominence seems to depend on the underlying theory of social action. As such, it tends to be favoured by governance paradigms that assume that social actors are normatively integrated and basically do what they have been socialized to believe is appropriate to do in the situation in which they are placed (March and Olsen 1989, 1995). The continuum along the third axis goes from a relative absence of normative appeals, via occasional reminders of goals and purposes, to an active use of visions and values to influence public employee behaviour and the group and organization of which they are a part.

The use of incentives provides an alternative to the active use of norms and values as a governance tool. The reward and punishment of particular forms of behaviour is at the core of transactional leadership, and the use of 'sticks and carrots' as an alternative to 'sermons' reflects a reliance on a *homo economicus* model of social action that assumes that individuals aim to maximize their personal utility by seeking to receive as many rewards as possible while avoiding punishment. The alternative to such an extrinsic utility-maximizing motivation would be a more intrinsic task motivation or public-service motivation that is stimulated by the transformational form of leadership captured by the third axis. The continuum along the fourth axis, which measures the active use of transactional leadership, goes from the relative absence of incentives beyond the basic understanding that job security depends on a certain level of task compliance, via occasional use of praise and encouragement to create a positive working environment, to an active use of high-powered positive and negative incentives dependent on an individual or collective performance assessment.

Societal involvement is the last dimension in the public governance diamond. It captures the extent to which the different governance paradigms aim to involve private actors from civil society and the economy in public governance activities. If they are keen to involve private actors, the next question becomes who are these private actors (merely a small segment or a broad range of private actors?), and how deeply are they involved in public governance (are they merely endorsing or choosing between public services? Or do they play a role in shaping them?). The continuum along the fifth and final axis goes from the exclusion of external actors from the private sector beyond the role of citizens as voters and clients, via the inclusion of a few actors in clearly defined parts of public governance, to the full-scale involvement of relevant and affected actors in different phases of the governance process.

The five axes of the public governance diamond are shown in Figure 1.1. The figure also illustrates how a fictional public governance paradigm can be displayed graphically by connecting the dots on the five axes to form a diamond. The scale has the following categories: very low, low, low to medium, medium, medium to high, high and very high. We use these ascending categories to compare the seven governance paradigms. For example, when placing the paradigms on centralized control, the paradigm with the lowest degree of centralized control (New Public Governance) is categorized as 'very low' despite still having some centralized control. In other words, the categories are used relatively to compare the seven paradigms on each dimension of the public governance diamond.

The diamond will tend to expand when the values on the five dimensions (centralized control, horizontal collaboration, use of value articulation, use of incentives and societal involvement) increase. Since the dimensions measured along the five axes are forms of governance rather than governance objectives, the size of the diamond is less important. What is important is the shape and profile of the different

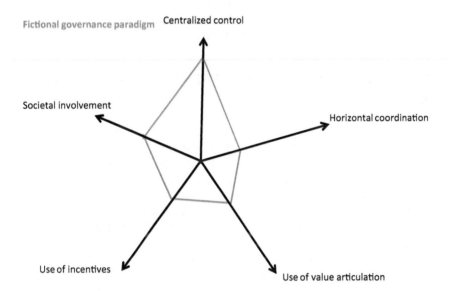

Figure 1.1   Public governance diamond with fictional example that illustrates its usage

governance diamonds that we will be analysing and how they either overlap or deviate from each other, reflecting their different assumptions, tools and strategies.

As the figure indicates, the five axes of the governance diamond go from low (close to the centre) to high (at the tip of the arrow). We have decided not to place any numerical values along the axes in order to avoid a false impression of the degree of precision that we can obtain when placing the seven governance paradigms along the five axes. In placing the governance paradigms on the five scales from low to high, we rely on our professional judgement, which is based on a mixture of analytical reasoning, academic studies and professional intuition. While we are quite confident about the relative ranking of the seven governance paradigms along each of the five dimensions, their precise location in the axes is less certain. What counts, however, is not so much where precisely we have placed the dots that are connected to form the various governance diamonds. The only thing that ultimately matters is the sequence of the dots (i.e. how they follow one after the other), thereby indicating their relative position on the axes when compared to each other on the particular dimension. As such, the governance diamonds that are constructed based on the different governance paradigms provide neither descriptive nor prescriptive measures for reality; rather, they constitute a heuristic device that enables the discussion of the similarities and differences between the different governance paradigms.

THE CONTENT, TARGET AUDIENCE AND PRACTICAL USES OF THIS BOOK

This book presents and discusses seven public governance paradigms, all of which have a certain relevance for understanding how the public sector is shaped and reshaped by countless administrative reforms, which ultimately determine the outputs and outcomes of public governance. The analysis and evaluation of the public governance paradigms draw on state-of-the-art research, and the chapters are structured in a manner that helps create overview and facilitates comparison. The chapters discussing each of the seven governance paradigms are followed by an overview chapter comparing the governance paradigms on the different dimensions and discussing whether there is a pattern or trend in their movement along the axes of the governance diamond. The book concludes with a chapter reflecting on how public leaders and managers can manoeuvre the complex terrain of competing and co-existing governance paradigms that call for a new type of situational leadership.

The target audience includes public leaders and managers, present and future generations of public employees, lay actors with a keen interest in the development of the public sector, and students and researchers who are curious about how the competing and co-existing governance paradigms compare on key dimensions. The book might supplement other scholarly texts in courses taught at institutions of higher education or be used in mid-career master programmes or leadership training initiatives.

Our hope is for the book to provide the reader with a deeper understanding of the main differences as well as the promises and pitfalls of the different governance paradigms that contribute to shaping the public sector. There is no perfect solution – only a series of context-dependent attempts at finding a satisfactory balance between different governance paradigms, and perhaps the opportunity to develop a contingency approach that brings different governance paradigms into play in different areas with different problems and tasks. Nevertheless, any reflection on the future governance of the public sector must begin with an understanding of the available options and trade-offs involved. We aim to take the first steps in providing such an understanding, thus enabling an informed and reasoned scholarly debate and policy choice.

2. Bureaucracy

BACKGROUND

Bureaucracy has many meanings. It is both an everyday word and an analytical concept. It combines the word 'bureau' (desk or office) with the word *kratos* (rule). In its simplest understanding, it is a system of government characterized by adherence to fixed rules and a hierarchy of authority (more detailed understandings presented below). Bureaucracy has a lengthy history. For example, the Chinese system of mandarins and Prussia under Bismarck have at least aspects of a bureaucratic governance paradigm. In China, beginning in the Qin dynasty (221–207 BC) and until the early twentieth century, mandarins were recruited based on merit through a rigorous imperial examination, a system underpinned by principles of Confucianism (Hood 1998: 76–82). While the hierarchical relations were certainly strong and top-down, the weight on formal rules is less certain. This is also the case with governance in Prussia under Bismarck (Darmstaedter 1948 [2017]). To paraphrase the subtitle of American political scientist James Q. Wilson's (1989) renowned book on bureaucracy, bureaucracy explains 'what governments do and why they do it'. Wilson (1989: 365) also states that incentives, culture and authority must go together to solve a given task.

Bureaucracy (together with professionalism) is one of the two classical governance paradigms, meaning that the time before bureaucracy was characterized by the absence of coherent organizing principles for effective management and leadership. Neither the transfer of positions in the public sector from farther to son (*patrimony*) nor the exchange of services for support (*political patronage*) were able to function in a complex, modern society. Originating especially in royal absolutism, patrimony lacked both legitimacy and the potential for recruiting persons with the necessary skills, while aspects of political patronage remain present in some countries (especially former British colonies). American ambassadors, for example, are typically political appointees, sometimes at least partially based on their monetary contributions to or work for the sitting president's election campaign (Andersen, Christensen and Pallesen 2008).

The predominance of special interests, clientelism and corruption was widespread in many countries until around 1900 (Knott and Miller 1987: 28; Christensen and Gregory 2008: 196), meaning that the search for universal, administrative principles dominated the discussion when bureaucracy was implemented as a governance paradigm. The idea was that these new governance principles could ensure the neutral and effective implementation of the laws and policies decided by elected politicians (Wilson 1887). US President Woodrow Wilson, a former political science professor, argued that a distinction should be drawn between politics and administration: politics would set the direction, whereas the purpose of the administration was to move in this direction in an efficient and effective manner. American political scientist Dwight Waldo (1948: 200) later argued that 'the means and measurements of efficiency ... were the same for all administrations: democracy, if it were to survive, [it] could not afford to ignore the lessons of central-ization, hierarchy and discipline'. Especially compared to the (lack of) governance in the preceding periods, these positions are understandable, because governance had previously been inefficient, illegitimate and arbitrary (Lane 1993). The argument is thus that the emergence and spread of bureaucracy as a public sector governance paradigm repre-sented a response to the specific historical context (Christensen and Gregory 2008: 195). This is similar to the emergence of more recent paradigms (e.g. New Public Management (NPM) as discussed in Chapter 4).

Country-specific factors contributed to how bureaucracy unfolded as a governance paradigm in individual countries. For example, Christensen and Gregory (2008: 195) argue that the interest of German rulers in increasing taxes to finance military expenses was important for the emergence of the merit bureaucracy in Germany. Otto von Bismarck, the first Chancellor of the German Empire (1871–90), provides a well-known example. Bismarck ruled with the help of a strong, well-trained bureau-cracy, and he relied on it when implementing the Health Insurance Act of 1883 and the Accident Insurance Act of 1884. To provide health insurance for German industrial labourers, a health service was estab-lished on the local level, and the individual local health bureaus were administered by a committee elected by the members of each bureau. Conversely, the administration of accident insurance was entrusted to the Organization of Employers in Occupational Corporations, establishing central, bureaucratic insurance offices (Darmstaedter 1948 [2017]; Hol-born 1969 [1982]: 291).

In the popular understanding, bureaucracy is often used to mean excessively complicated administrative procedures and rules and/or the many people in publicly funded positions who administer these rules. The famous Clinton–Gore report on reinventing government was entitled 'From Red Tape to Results' (Gore 1993). Still, large-scale public bureaucracies are a relatively recent phenomenon. Even the Scandinavian countries, which now have rather massive public sectors, had relatively few public employees until the late 1960s (Christensen and Pallesen 2008).

SOURCES OF INSPIRATION, THEORETICAL POSITIONS AND EXEMPLARY COUNTRIES

Norwegian political scientist Johan P. Olsen (2006) argues that we should separate the analytical meaning of bureaucracy from the polemical context. We follow this approach and use the concept analytically. Max Weber (1919 [2015]: 76) argued that the modern bureaucracy in both public and private organizations 'is based on the general principle of precisely defined and organized across-the-board competencies of the various offices. These competencies are underpinned by rules, laws, or administrative regulations'. The first aspect is a rigid division of labour that clearly identifies regular tasks and duties in the hierarchy. The second aspect is regulations describing firmly established chains of command and the duties and capacity to coerce others to comply. The third aspect is that people are hired according to their particular, certified qualifications that support the regular and continuous execution of the assigned duties. According to Weber (1919 [2015]), the main principles of bureaucracy are:

1. Specialized roles
2. Merit-based recruitment
3. Uniform principles of placement, promotion and transfer in an administrative system
4. Careerism with a systematic salary structure
5. Hierarchy, responsibility and accountability
6. Subjection of official conduct to strict rules of discipline and control
7. Supremacy of abstract rules
8. Impersonal authority
9. Political neutrality

Weber (1919 [2015]) was very aware of both the merits (e.g. effectiveness regarding better output) and potential problems (inflexible, neglect of creativity and little sense of belonging for the employees). In our treatment of the concepts, we focus on bureaucracy as an organizational setting with hierarchical structure and a high level of formalization; that is, ruled-based governance with clear relationships between each supervisor and their subordinates. In the public sector, these rule-bound, hierarchical relations can be within the administration, between administrators and citizens, between politicians and the administration and between citizens and politicians. We focus primarily on relations between supervisors and their employees (hierarchical relations within the public administration).

Down through the hierarchy, the bureaucratic logic suggests that commands and rules are followed, because they are given by officeholders as trustees of an impersonal rational-legal order, where administrative tasks are seen as technical. The division of labour is specialized and functional when bureaucratic governance is predominant. The staff consists of full-time, salaried employees with lifelong employment with strong emphasis on formal education, merit and tenure. The normative basis is the belief in a legitimate, rational-legal political order and the right of the elected politicians to define and enforce their decisions through administrators with the requisite skills (Olsen 2006: 2–3). The key task for administrators at all levels is to identify logically correct solutions by interpreting rules and facts or applying expert knowledge (Olsen 2006: 3). Compare this to British Professor Christopher Pollitt's (2016b: 14) list of 'distinctive issues for public managers', which consisted of: 'managing in a socio-political system, working with public pressure and protest, a sense of accountability, understanding public behaviour, the management of rationing, the management of influence, assessing multi-dimensional performance, and understanding a wider responsibility to a changing society'. The list of managerial issues has certainly expanded.

As already mentioned, the American academic tradition originally viewed bureaucracy as something positive (Wilson 1887; Waldo 1948). Nevertheless, the most pronounced *bureaucrat bashing* has since taken place in the USA, and several American presidents, including Reagan, saw the weakening of bureaucracy as an important goal unto itself. This may explain the passionate defences of bureaucracy in the same country, as discussed in *The Oxford Handbook of American Bureaucracy* (Durant 2012). Examples include Goodsell's work (2004, 2015) and the so-called Blacksburg Manifesto, wherein several American academics formulated a defence for bureaucracy as a governance paradigm (Wamsley et al. 1990). European researchers have since contributed to the same agenda, including Paul du Gay's books *In Praise of Bureaucracy* (2000) and *The Values of Bureaucracy* (2005). Rosser (2018) has traced Max Weber's influence on the European public administration, arguing that administrative law remains an important source of conflict resolution between the state and society and that NPM-inspired reforms have led to more administrative rules and, hence, to more bureaucratic paperwork (see also Jakobsen and Mortensen 2016). More generally, he notes that certain characteristics of Weberian bureaucracy seem to be a prerequisite for the success of NPM-inspired administrative reforms.

Swedish political scientist Lennart Lundquist (1998) and Norwegian Johan P. Olsen (2006) have promoted the notion of a public sector ethos, arguing that bureaucratic impartiality is immensely important. Their argument is that public employees (i.e. the bureaucrats) should be the guardians of public values, defending the ethics of bureaucracy, and that civil servants display a sense of administrative statesmanship (du Gay 2009b, 2017). At the same time, there has been a discussion of the feasibility of the ideal typical bureaucracy model in practice, and Thomas Hammond and Paul Thomas (1989) argue that a neutral hierarchy is impossible, because all of the organizing principles will affect the prioritization of different considerations.

MAIN GOVERNANCE IDEA: GOALS AND MEANS

We argue that rules and hierarchy are the defining characteristic of bureaucracy as a governance paradigm (see also Lane 1993; Jakobsen 2009) and that the other factors follow from these aspects. Bureaucracy shares an emphasis on the importance of formal education with professionalism, as discussed in the next chapter. The main goal of bureaucracy is the neutral implementation of political goals decided by democratically elected politicians. Neutrality means that bureaucrats should not pay attention (or at least pay equal attention) to specific values in the surrounding society and that they should leave their own personal value judgement at home, considering only the rules and facts in front of them. 'Creating a capable bureaucracy with loyalists' (Ha and Kang 2011: 78) can for example be a viable strategy to achieve economic development in late-industrializing countries. Values such as legality and loyalty towards the system have high priority within the organizations. Economic incentives are not used (except for the career incentive embedded in the base salary and how salaries increase up the hierarchy). This is meant to increase loyalty, prevent corruption and ultimately to enhance legitimacy. Hierarchical loyalty is so important that managers and employees can be expected to focus their attention upwards in the hierarchy, ultimately towards the politicians. Combined with the importance of stability and playing by the rules, this can make bureaucracy rigid and less prone to innovation. This was the basis of the criticism of bureaucracy in moving from the 'old public administration' to NPM (Dunleavy and Hood 1994).

Linked to rules and hierarchy, other important aspects of bureaucracy are specialization, merit recruitment and formalization. The need to specialize can be seen as both an antecedent and a consequence of the hierarchy. The combination of a more complex society and larger (public) organizations is a well-known argument for a functional hierarchy with specialization, and hierarchy can be seen as necessary to ensure work is coordinated with other functions (Lazear and Gibbs 2015). The specialization in skills and tasks makes it unlikely that employees will take into account the perspectives of employees in other functions (Lazear and Gibbs 2015: 128–9). This is linked to the merit principle. Weber (1919, 1947) believed that expert training should form the basis of admission to specialist positions in the hierarchy. This is different from the principle in professional rule discussed in the next chapter, because bureaucracy as a governance paradigm links training and thus merit to tasks in the positions in the hierarchy, not to a given occupation and the connected knowledge and norms. Finally, formalization concerns the character of both rules and hierarchical structures in the sense that both are explicit, structured and typically written.

Figure 2.1 shows our classification of bureaucracy along the five dimensions discussed in Chapter 1. The degree of centralized control in the vertical chain of command is very high. Both formal rules and hierarchical structures increase the centralization, and the normative idea behind bureaucracy (the belief in a legitimate, rational-legal political order and the right of the elected politician to define and enforce their decisions through administrators) strengthens the degree of central control in this governance paradigm.

The degree of horizontal interagency coordination and collaboration is low. This is a consequence of the functional specialization and vertical logic of command inherent in the bureaucratic governance paradigm. While there is still coordination, it is hierarchical rather than horizontal.

The degree to which public governance is based on the articulation of public values is medium to low. On the one hand, some values are important. As mentioned, loyalty and neutrality are thus integral parts of the governance logic for bureaucracy. On the other hand, values are not actively used by managers to give direction. Public values are often taken for granted in the bureaucratic governance paradigm and implicitly expected to be internalized among employees as part of a culture emphasizing appropriate bureaucratic conduct.

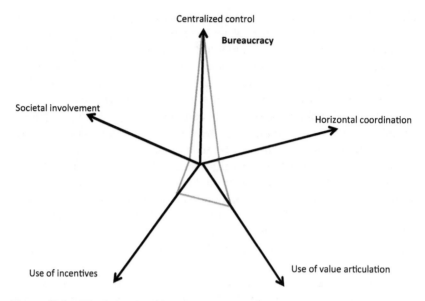

Figure 2.1   The bureaucratic governance diamond

Concerning the use of incentives in governance, the bureaucratic paradigm suggests that all employees and leaders should receive a full-time
salary from which they can live, and this constitutes (although to a low
degree) a contingent incentive, as it can be lost if the employees and
leaders fail to perform. Still, the paradigm does not recommend
performance-related pay, and the emphasis on lifelong careers means that
the contingency of the fixed pay is small. Much of the feedback that the
individual employee receives in this paradigm stems from collegial
supervision and recognition, which can also function as an informal
incentive. Still, the degree to which public governance is based on
conditional positive and negative incentives is low for bureaucracy.

Finally, societal involvement is very low. In the bureaucratic governance
paradigm, neither private for-profit nor non-profit actors are involved. The
ideal is for outputs and outcomes to be generated in and through the formal
chain of command in public organizations; in other words, there is little
room for non-state actors in bureaucratic governance.

EMPIRICAL RESULTS

It is difficult to test the effects of bureaucracy, because it is seldom totally
absent in public (and private) organizations. Still, variations in the

aforementioned elements of bureaucracy allow us to gain some insight into its effects. Dahlström et al. (2012), for example, show how merit-based recruitment reduces corruption, and Rothstein and Teorell's studies (2008) remind us that we should not forget the benefits of neutral knowledge-based implementation. Andrews (2010) makes a critical assessment of the bureaucratic paradigm that concerns the organizational structure. Analysing the degree of centralization, formalization and specialization, he reviewed the most important findings in the literature. As regards centralization, the results suggest that the effect depends on the context. In some cases (e.g. municipalities in Wales), there is no association, but there is a positive correlation between centralization and productivity for American human service organizations. Another general finding is that it makes a great difference which performance criteria are analysed. While Andrews (2010: 101–2) finds both positive and negative effects in his discussion of the studies of formalization, most studies suggest that formalization affects productivity positively. Still, similar positive results are found for leadership autonomy (e.g. Nielsen 2013), and although it is not the exact opposite compared to formalization and centralization, it still suggests that formalization and centralization have both pros and cons. Finally, Andrews (2010: 103) finds that there is no consistent association between specialization and performance.

Another study of relevance for the effects of bureaucratization is Cho et al.'s (2013) investigation of the 103 participating countries in the Quality of Government Surveys in 2008 and 2010. Specifically, they analyse the effect of merit-based recruitment, internal promotion, career stability and competitive salaries to public employees. In addition to the survey questions, the authors include data from the World Bank, ICRG and Freedom House to measure the public service quality and level of democracy. The conclusion is that the investigated version of bureaucracy is most positively associated with performance in countries where democracy is less developed. This suggests that bureaucracy as a governance paradigm results in numerous benefits when first introduced (compared to what came before), whereas in modern societies, which already have elaborate bureaucratic structures combined with elements from the other governance paradigms, bureaucracy produces less added value. In this context, additional rules and more hierarchical structures can be counterproductive, suggesting an A-formed relationship between the level of bureaucracy and goal attainment in public organizations.

Before elaborating on the critique of bureaucracy (which argues that there are too many rules and too little decentralized discretion), we should also note that bureaucracy was a significant improvement in many countries in terms of effectiveness compared to the situation prior to its implementation. We still benefit from many of these improvements, often without noticing them. No governance paradigm is without problems, however, and the next section discusses the most important drawback of bureaucratic organization.

DEBATE AND DILEMMAS

The disadvantages of excessive rules are discussed in the so-called *red tape* literature (Bozeman and Feeney 2011; Kaufmann 1997 [2015]). Red tape can be understood as either the actual existence of burdensome and unnecessary rules or (for perceived red tape) the subjective understanding that such rules exist. The latter understanding is far easier to handle analytically, as it is difficult to determine whether all agents see a given rules as necessary. As Kaufmann (1997 [2015]: 1) famously pointed out, 'one person's red tape may be another person's treasured safeguard'. While teachers might think that the rules regulating a student's right to complain over grades are unnecessary and burdensome, students probably see them as securing a necessary right (see also Jakobsen and Mortensen (2014: 16) for further discussion of this point). Different stakeholders can thus experience the same rule very differently, and there are different pictures of the extent to which rules limit the actors' degrees of freedom. The experienced number of rules also varies significantly (e.g. Baldwin 1990).

Rules can be objectively measured (e.g. Jakobsen and Mortensen 2014), and such accounts tend to indicate that the number of rules increases over time (Melchiorsen 2012; van Witteloostuijn and De Jong 2009). In a study of rules at Stanford University, March et al. (2000) show that attention to existing and potential rules is a frequent response to problems. Rules can be created, modified or eliminated due to events in the outside environment (e.g. new government regulations) or to events within the organization (e.g. alterations in internal government structures). Changes introduced in one part of a rule system can create adjustments in other parts, including the same rule later in time. As Jakobsen and Mortensen (2014) show, rules often develop to become both broader (regulating more aspects) and deeper (more specific for a given aspect). Regardless of the number of rules, governments around the world seem to want to reduce their number. Since 1983, all Danish governments, for example, have attempted some type of de-bureaucratization (Ejersbo and Greve 2014), and many American presidents have had anti-bureaucracy agendas (e.g.

Wamsley et al. 1990). Cutting red tape is an essential feature in most public management reform (Hood 1998: 4–5; Pollitt and Bouckaert 2017: 9).

One of the reasons that citizens sometimes experience rules (and the public sector in general) as unnecessarily burdensome and negative might be coping behaviour among the public employees who have direct contact with citizens. These 'street-level bureaucrats' (Lipsky 1980) exercise a lot of power and do not only follow rules or hierarchical directions. According to the street-level literature, limited resources, continuous negotiations linked to meeting targets, and the relations with (non-voluntary) clients make the street-level bureaucrats use different types of coping behaviours (Lipsky 1980). Coping, for example, includes routinizing and controlling clients, and such behaviours can make the citizens believe that public organizations are full of red tape. Coping behaviours either rationalize, automate or reduce the demand of the bureaucrat's service/activity (Nielsen 2006: 865). Street-level bureaucrats use them to make their jobs psychologically easier to manage as a response to job stress and to avoid confrontations with work failures (Lipsky 1980: 141, 144). The street-level perspective is a critique of the bureaucracy governance paradigm in several respects. The high level of centralization is indirectly criticized, given that street-level bureaucrats are seen as relatively powerful, because many decisions in policy implementation are taken by the street-level bureaucrats (Lipsky 1980). This also questions the merit-based neutral implementation of rules and hierarchical orders in the bureaucratic governance paradigm, because Lipsky's (1980) arguments imply that street-level bureaucrats are primarily interested in a manageable workload (see also Nielsen 2006: 865). Finally, the clients and their demands play a much bigger role in the street-level literature compared to classical bureaucracy theory.

Another debate connects the critique of bureaucracy to the complexity in the environment. Thomson (1967: 4-5) thus argued that the bureaucracy literature employs rational, closed-system assumptions focusing on staffing and structure as means of handling clients with efficiency as the ultimate criterion. Thomson (1967 [2003]: 5–6) described three potential holes through which empirical reality might penetrate this logic: Policy-makers can alter the goals, bureaucrats can be more complicated than the model describes (as illustrated by the street-level perspective above), and the clientele might be a factor that cannot be nullified by depersonalizing and categorizing clients. Thomson's (1967 [2003]: 6) core argument is that when a system contains more variables than we can comprehend at one time, or when some of the variables are subject to influences we cannot control or predict, we must use an open system logic. The organization is then seen as a set of interdependent parts that make up a whole, contributing something and receiving something from the whole, which in turn is interdependent with some larger environment. This external environment can be more or less stable and more or less homogeneous (Thomson 1967 [2003]: 70–73). This constitutes a simple four-cell typology that implies that the closed system approach of bureaucracy as a governance paradigm is most problematic for heterogeneous and shifting environments and least problematic for homogeneous and stable environments (with homogeneous-shifting and heterogeneous-stable environments in between).

Especially if a heterogeneous-shifting environment is combined with many non-routine problems within the organization, it becomes a relevant question whether there are good and viable alternatives to rules and hierarchy (Yeboah-Assiamah et al. 2016: 391). Can public sectors in a modern society function without hierarchical structures, high levels of specialization and rule-bound regulation? Olsen (2006) responds that bureaucracy is still needed as a governance paradigm focused on formalization, functional specialization, hierarchy, standardization, rationality and impartiality. His point is, however, that bureaucracy can fit better or worse with different tasks in the public sector and that it can still be too much, thereby becoming pathological. Rules might therefore lose their function and meaning and become 'rules for the sake of rules'. Still, as discussed in connection to the red tape concept, rules can be perceived as meaningless (and a waste of time) by some actors, while others see them as necessary to ensure justice. Du Gay (2005) ties bureaucracy closer to the role of civil servants as the guardians of the state and examines how administrative statesmanship is conducted. Diefenbach and Sillince (2011) argue that hierarchy persists despite organizational changes towards flatter and postmodern organizations. They present a differentiated understanding of hierarchy as either formal or informal, finding that hierarchy is much more widespread than often thought. They argue that 'postmodern, representative democratic and network organizations are much less "alternative" and "hierarchy-free" than their labels and common understanding may suggest' (ibid.: 1515). They argue that the persistence of hierarchy in different types of organizations can be explained by different dynamic relationships between formal and informal hierarchy. Specifically, they find that informal hierarchy facilitates formal hierarchy in professional organizations, while the formal is instrumental to the informal in representative, democratic organizations. In hybrid organizations, they find that the informal complements the formal; and in network organizations, the 'informal sneaks its way in as an unobtrusive phenomenon' (ibid.: 1531). While bureaucracy (through the hierarchy) aims at transparency and disregards clientelistic mechanisms, this can sometimes make the networks invisible and framed by personal, intersubjective connections. This creates a potential for tensions when managers aim at infusing hierarchies with networks, cross-sectional teams and matrixes in order to increase their flexibility.

The advantages and disadvantages of bureaucracy plausibly depend on what the decision-makers want from the public sector. What is high performance and when can a public organization be deemed successful? If they want stability and loyal implementation, bureaucracy has several advantages. If they want innovation, the disadvantages are more numerous. Bommert (2010) thus argues that bureaucratic ways of innovating do not yield the quantity and quality of innovations necessary to solve emergent and persistent policy challenges. The argument is that it is a problem if the locus of innovation is determined by the formal boundaries of a bureaucratic organization and if the role of the actors is defined by formal rules and hierarchical structures rather than by the match between innovation assets and the problem. Bureaucracy weakens the innovation cycle and restricts it to a limited number of participants within the government. The lack of integration of other actors (e.g. private sector, citizens, and voluntary organizations) is due to the low score on the society involvement dimension in Figure 2.1. Ignoring these innovation resources can reduce the quantity and quality of ideas generated, selected, implemented and diffused, and the closed nature of public sector innovation can reduce transparency, trust and the commitment to take up innovations (Bommert 2010: 21; see also De Jong 2016). Nevertheless, 'good governance' is more than innovation. When codes of conduct spell out how states or countries should be governed, they all include traditional bureaucratic characteristics such as the rule of law, neutrality, impartiality and legality (Jørgensen and Sørensen 2012). This suggests that bureaucracy may be supplemented with new governance paradigms, but it is hardly supplanted.

A related point is that there are few public organizations in modern societies without fulltime (professional) employees to secure the implementation of political decisions. This suggests that representative democracy and at least some level of bureaucracy are tied together, suggesting that bureaucracy constitutes an important mechanism for deciding who gets what. Still, the literature about privatization and contracting out argues that fewer citizens today meet a government bureaucrat in the delivery of public service; they are often more likely to be served by an employee of a private contractor (Kettl 2002; Amirkhanyan and Lambright 2018). The tendency towards contracting out and outsourcing is currently being countered by renewed calls to 'bring back the bureaucrats' (DiIulio 2014), the argument being that bureaucrats will perform more efficiently than a diverse set of private contractors (see also Byrkjeflot and Engelstad 2018 for a recent review of bureaucracies in selected European countries). Yeboah-Assiamah et al. (2016) argue that it is not useful to let the literature be a battlefield between bureaucracy, NPM and post-NPM governance paradigms. They see the new governance paradigms as corrections or additions to bureaucracy without replacing it completely. This proposition will be discussed further after the following chapters have described and evaluated the other governance paradigms.

3.   Professional rule

BACKGROUND

Professional rule as a governance paradigm developed in response to the growing specialization of knowledge. While medieval and early modern societies only recognized three knowledge-based professions (clergymen rooted in theology, doctors in medicine and judges in the study of the law), other occupations, such as accountants, dentists, teachers and engineers, gained professional status parallel to bureaucracy developing as a governance paradigm. The increasing power of these occupations meant a corresponding increase in autonomy (Knott and Miller 1987: 55), and knowledge and occupational norms became key mechanisms in professional rule. In the 1930s, professionals such as engineers were generally believed to know 'the one best way' (Knott and Miller 1987: 56). This valuation of professional knowledge became the foundation for professional rule as a governance paradigm. As such, professional rule involves an understanding of steering and leadership whereby well-educated professions are assumed to possess the best knowledge and can therefore be trusted to govern themselves based on their professional norms and highly specialized knowledge.

In the public sector, employees with highly specialized knowledge are responsible for delivering the lion's share of public services. According to the sociology of professions, this means that expertise plays a unique role in public governance (Brint 1993: 3; Scott 2008: 221). This chapter describes the traditional forms of professional rule together with newer tendencies that have had an impact on professionalism, partly in response to NPM-inspired reforms (see Chapter 4), and questioned the entrenched role of professionals in public services (Clarke and Newman 1997; Exworthy and Halford 1999). On the one hand, due to strong intra-occupational norms and a strong collective influence on policy-making, we must examine the professions as collective actors. On the other hand, many important decisions are placed in the hands of the individual professional, which renders the analysis of professions as collective actors insufficient. The study of professional rule as a governance paradigm is therefore concerned with both professions and professionals. The traditional sociology of professions (Parsons 1951; Freidson 1970a, b; Johnson 1972; Parkin 1979) primarily analysed the internal workings of professional groups, highlighting the governance of professions, but paid little attention to the attempt to govern professionals or to the importance of professionals for governing the public sector. Fortunately, this is not the case for more recent contributions (e.g. Noordegraaf 2011a; Schott et al. 2016, 2018).

SOURCES OF INSPIRATION, THEORETICAL POSITIONS AND EXEMPLARY COUNTRIES

The concept of 'profession' is defined differently in different parts of the literature (Freidson 1994; Evetts 2003). The original functionalist approach in the sociology of professions focuses on professional traits, which are achieved collectively; that is, the possession of a body of expert knowledge, specialized education and a code of ethics. Elements from this approach are still used, especially in combination with an economic perspective on professionalism (Burau and Andersen 2014). The argument is that if the production of a service calls for special expertise, the usual information asymmetry in principal–agent relationships is exacerbated by a knowledge asymmetry, since persons outside the profession have insufficient knowledge about how an agent (the professional) should do a job (Sharma 1997). If the knowledge is theoretical and therefore less transferable, the information asymmetry is even stronger (Roberts and Dietrich 1999: 985), and persons outside the profession might not even be able to evaluate the outcome. In this strand of literature, the existence of professional standards is an important element for understanding professionalism (Moe 1987: 261; Miller 2000: 320). The argument is that politicians face a serious dilemma in relation to public services that demand specialized, theoretical knowledge. The politicians (or their generalist managers) cannot control the service production, but voters still hold them responsible for its availability and quality. This dilemma urges the politicians to strike a deal with the public sector professionals according to which the latter commit themselves to upholding high service standards in exchange for higher autonomy and status together with pecuniary rewards (Day and Klein 1987: 19; Watson 1980 [2003]: 192). Professional status can be defined as the general public's recognition of an occupation's specialized, theoretical knowledge and professional norms (Burau and Andersen 2014). The basic logic is that the decision-makers (who do not have the necessary theoretical, specialized knowledge) delegate governance to the professions, which govern the professionals through norms sanctioned by the relevant professional occupation.

Seen from this perspective, norms and standards are only expected to be followed if there are sanctions at the level of the individual professional. Given that professional status is a collective asset, the argument is that professions organize and sanction non-compliance with professional norms and standards, because they have a collective interest in the power that lies in having high professional autonomy and status. Despite information asymmetry, an occupation cannot maintain its professional status in the long run if shirking and sloppy practices are widespread among individual professionals. Here, the key governance mechanism is the professional norms that prescribe particular professional behaviours. Only if these norms are sanctioned can the individuals in each profession succeed in their joint effort to uphold their professional status. Being a collective good for all professionals within the same occupation, requires coordination. The profession must maintain its status by 'boasting' careful and competitive selection procedures, training and credentials and by establishing protocols, defining best practices and creating ethics codes that limit agent discretion (Shapiro 2005: 275). Hence, the key aspect of professional rule is that the profession formulates and sanctions professional norms; that is, normative prescriptions that are commonly known and used by the members of an occupation and that clearly specify which actions are required, prohibited or permitted in a particular situation (Burau and Andersen 2014; Tonon 2008: 286).

One of the important distinctions in the sociology of professions is between the aforementioned functionalist schools and the neo-Weberian approach (not to be confused with the Neo-Weberian State discussed in Chapter 5; the only commonality is the inspiration from Max Weber). The functionalist approach assumes that the professions have a beneficial societal effect in terms of maintaining high service standards (functional logic), while the neo-Weberian sociology of professions focuses on the efforts of the professions to maintain power and act strategically in relation to other occupations (instrumental logic). A key difference between these two perspectives is their basic assumptions regarding the professionals. While the functionalist school sees knowledge and norms as important and real assets, neo-Weberian scholars argue that this is merely a smokescreen for the professionals' efforts to obtain power, wealth and status (Johnson 1972). As mentioned above, the functionalist approach focuses on professional traits such as specialized, theoretical knowledge and professional norms. However, it also focuses on the internal organization of the profession, the use of competitive formal education as entrance criterion for being part of the profession, the strong element of research-based education separated from practical learning, the high degree of work autonomy, the strong norms about service orientation towards clients, and the profession's jurisdiction over certain tasks (Kragh Jespersen 2005: 65). The jurisdiction is the domain where a given profession has a monopoly on service provision.

Some authors combine insights from the functionalist school and the neo-Weberian approach. Inspired by the functionalists, Roberts and Dietrich (1999) argue that the information asymmetry in relation to political and administrative leaders based on specialized theoretical and methodological knowledge constitutes the economic basis of a given profession. The profession is necessary (and therefore has a function) because the relevant knowledge is not transferable; heart surgeons cannot be supplanted by laypeople without medical training, and engineers are required to build a bridge. The necessity of knowledge and skill combined with barriers to information transfer means that society needs the professions to guarantee that individual professionals perform adequately. This can also be seen as a solution to a principal–agent problem. Based on its collective knowledge, if a profession functions as a guarantee for good practice, then 'ignorant principals can trust the agents to behave in appropriate ways' (Roberts and Dietrich 1999: 986). There is a dark side to this solution, since 'the more effectively a principal–agent problem is resolved by effective professional regulation, the more entrenched will be professional activity, and therefore monopoly power' (ibid.: 987). Inspired by the neo-Weberian approach, Roberts and Dietrich (1999) do not assume that the altruism of professionals safe-guards the interests of the general public. Accordingly, they argue that it is problematic that the solution to the principal–agent problem, caused by non-transferable knowledge, constitutes the economic rationale for the formation of professional organizations that enhance the economic bargaining power of professionals.

Roberts and Dietrich (1999) urge us to study the institutionalization processes that are necessary for professionals to emerge as an occupation with high professional status. The sociological basis of professional institutions is their power to succeed in obtaining the collective (and individual) goals of the profession through collective action. This question concerns the ability of the occupation to gain social recognition as a profession. Here, factors such as gender composition and the organization of the occupation in a professional association become relevant (ibid.). The sociological basis can also be seen as the level of professional status; that is, the degree of recognition of the occupation's specialized, theoretical knowledge and professional norms.

The better the economic and sociological basis of relevant professions in a given field, the more important will professional rule be as a governance paradigm. The core profession combines economic and sociological assets, thereby providing the highest level of power to the profession. One example could be medical doctors. Some professions have specialized knowledge without having (yet) achieved a sociological basis for their power. Roberts and Dietrich (1999: 990) mention nurses in some countries, arguing that the professional status of nursing is often questioned even though it displays the necessary characteristics of an 'economic profession' (information asymmetry between patient and nurse, a tacit and non-observable knowledge base and need for access to this knowledge base to practise nursing). In contrast, they mention that accounting is readily accepted as a profession even though certain routinized areas (e.g. auditing) do not meet the requirements of an economic profession.

The next question is how the professionals in different occupations attain and maintain autonomy over their work, and perhaps even dominate the division of labour with other groups. How do employees become professionals who are part of different professions? Especially the institutionalist sociology of professions argues that professions are dynamic entities that take shape through specific, institutionally conditioned struggles for power (Burau 2005). Burrage et al. (1990) introduce an actor-based framework for studying professions, and suggest that we look at the key actors who have a stake in the governance of a given profession. More specifically, the authors identify the state, organized users and the practising and university-based parts of a profession as the key actors. While the university-based part of a profession primarily develops the specialized, theoretical knowledge, the practising part translates knowledge into norms and sanctions them. This is negotiated with the (organized) users, because a profession cannot maintain legitimacy if the users are generally dissatisfied, and with the state, which often pays most of the costs of the professionalized service provision, at least in universal welfare states. Burau et al. (2004) focus more on the organization of work and analyse individual professional groups as part of a given field of work. Here, the organization of work also includes the relationship between professionals from different occupations. Who does what in a hospital ward could be one of the key questions in this approach. This highlights the relations among professional groups in the context of delivering given services. Using an open definition of professions, the institutionalist sociology of professions focuses on the interplay between actors who have a stake in governance or as contingent on the specific organization of work.

In terms of exemplary countries, there is a marked difference between the role of professional rule in the Anglo-Saxon countries and in Central and Northern Europe. The simplified version is that professions are more independent in the Anglo-Saxon countries because the individual professionals are more private practitioners than government employees. They typically own the means of production (e.g. the clinic in which a general practitioner works), which gives them more autonomy. This seems to be due to the more passive role that states have played in the professionalization process in these countries. State intervention has primarily been restricted to the granting of legally based privileges, such as credentials and monopolies of practice. In Central Europe, countries have tended to have a higher level of 'stateness' (Heidenheimer 1989). Here, the states have often directly employed and regulated the professions, meaning that the state in continental countries such as France, Italy and Germany almost created the professional groups and professional jurisdictions. Abbott (1988: 161), for example, argues that: 'The French state not only organizes professions and structures their jurisdictions, it also displays an endless ability to create professional work.' This means that the state has extensive control over the professions and that professional rule as a governance paradigm is less dominant than bureaucracy. The Nordic countries have far more decentralized public sectors, and the professions have played an important role for many years in the service provision of municipalities and regions. Moreover, they are not as state-dominated as in central Europe (Christensen and Pallesen 2008). Accordingly, professional rule has historically played an important role in these countries.

Even within this group of Nordic countries, there is considerable variation that bears witness to the complex mechanisms behind the formation of professional rule. Danish medical doctors, for example, have succeeded in maintaining general practitioners as a liberal profession without state ownership (but with public funding), whereas some GPs have become public employees in Norway. This means that the relative professional status of medical doctors and other health professionals differs in the two countries. For example, physiotherapists enjoy relatively higher professional status in Norway, including the right to prescribe medicine – which is not the case in Denmark (Andersen 2014). More generally, the relationship between different professions is an important element in professional rule, and the literature uses the concept 'exclusion' to describe one profession's strategic attempts to keep another profession out (of their jurisdiction), whereas usurpation is a profession's attempts to force its way into another profession's jurisdiction. The literature refers to a profession using both strategies simultaneously as 'dual closure' (Murphy 1986).

MAIN GOVERNANCE IDEA: GOALS AND MEANS

The rationale behind professional rule is that the information asymmetry for some tasks is so severe that the laity (person outside the profession) cannot be part of governance or can only participate in governance activities to a very limited extent. The argument is that, given that professionalism is an exclusive identity, developed through qualifications, training and socialization, only professionals can understand certain services (McGivern et al. 2015). Political and administrative leaders therefore delegate decision-making power (autonomy as discussed below) to the relevant profession(s) and professionals. In return, the professions promise to uphold good practice through professional norms. In the classical form, professional rule means that one occupational group has the monopoly on providing certain services (i.e. their jurisdiction). The pure form is rare, and (as discussed further below) bureaucracy and NPM have limited the power of the professionals in most parts of the public sector (Byrkjeflot 2011: 68–70).

Professional autonomy is a key concept. The professions tend to have a high degree of control over their own affairs. Professions are autonomous if, within the occupational domain, they can make independent judgments about their work. Individual professionals belong to a particular professional group, meaning that they have the freedom to exercise their professional judgement with accountability only towards their professional peers. Still, Hoogland and Jochemsen (2000) remind us that while professional autonomy can be regarded as the opportunity of professionals to serve their own interests, the profession must restrict the individual professionals. Their 'professional autonomy can only be maintained if members of the profession subject their activities and decisions to a critical evaluation by other members of the profession and by patients and if they continue to critically reflect on the values that regulate [the relevant professional practice]' (ibid.: 457). The concept of autonomy thus embraces not only judgement, but also self-interest and the profession's continuous critical self-evaluation process. The main governance idea in professional rule is thus that professional norms function as the mechanism allowing the profession to govern the professionals (enabling the public to trust both profession and professionals).

Our classification of professional rule on the five dimensions of the governance diamond discussed in Chapter 1 is presented in Figure 3.1. The degree of centralized control in the vertical chain of command is low to medium. While some centralized control exists, it is primarily within the profession. As a whole, the profession enjoys considerable autonomy

Public governance paradigms

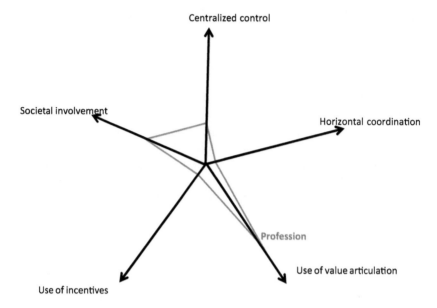

Figure 3.1   The professionalized rule governance diamond

when going about its service-related tasks. Still, when professional rule
and bureaucracy are integrated, as is the case in many countries,
professionals within the central state administration control the individual
professionals in decentralized welfare institutions through procedures
combining professionalism (e.g. a patient protection committee in the
state with members from the relevant professions) and formal rules (e.g.
laws, budgets, administrative decrees).

The degree of horizontal coordination is very low. This is a consequence of the specialization of knowledge and skills in different professions. Coordination between occupations with different professional
norms and different bodies of specialized, theoretical knowledge is
notoriously difficult. They simply speak different languages and each of
them thinks that their norms and values should prevail, which renders
attempts at horizontal coordination difficult.

The degree to which public governance is based on the articulation of
public values is medium to high. Professional norms represent a specific
type of values, and they are the key governance mechanism in professional rule. The individual professionals are governed by professional
norms and values, because they find them desirable and/or because they
fear disapproval from the rest of the profession if they fail to comply
with the norms. Still, the values are often tacit and implicit, and they are

less active in governance than in a situation in which organizational strategies are heavily imbued by values and where leaders actively articulate values as part of their leadership behaviour.

Professional rule relies very little on incentives, which are often seen as contrasting with the professional norms. Nevertheless, a collective incentive remains relevant for this governance paradigm. Inherent to the logic of the professionalism contract is the (often tacit) agreement that the profession guarantees good quality in return for a relatively high level of autonomy and remuneration. The degree to which public governance is based on conditional positive and negative incentives is very low for professional rule, because the incentive is on such an aggregate level.

Finally, the only private for-profit or non-profit actors involved in governance are the profession and notably the organized profession (professional associations, which are also often unions). The score on this dimension is medium. On the one hand, the individual professional providers of public services can be private practitioners or public employees, but the professional associations are non-profit, societal organizations that often play a crucial role in the governance of public services. On the other hand, the other societal actors (e.g. private firms and users) have very limited influence, because they do not speak the professional language; they are not privy to the professional norms, knowledge and expertise. Professional rule as a governance paradigm only trusts professionals in the relevant jurisdiction.

EMPIRICAL RESULTS

One way to investigate the validity of the main governance idea in professional rule (i.e. that intra-organizational norms regulate behaviour) is to see whether the professionals follow the norms when they are encouraged to deviate from them by using incentives. Especially for general practitioners, this has been a theme in the supplier-induced demand literature. In short, professional norms dictate that medical services should not depend on the fee or the demand situation, but rather on strictly medical criteria defined by the professional norms among GPs. When we consider this claim empirically, the evidence is mixed. Krasnik et al. (1990) find that a change in the remuneration systems for GPs had a very substantial effect on their activity, suggesting that incentives are more important than professional norms. Iversen and Lurås (2000) arrive at more mixed findings, arguing that economic motives are primarily important when professional opinions differ. Andersen and Serritzlew (2012) follow this idea and investigate two types of professional services where the professional norms are firm for one service and almost non-existent for the other. As expected, economic incentives matter much more for the supply of the latter service type (talk-based therapy). Generally, there is some support to the claim that professional norms regulate behaviour. Importantly, there may not be professional norms for all types of professional behaviour, and other factors can also be important for professionals. This bears evidence to the fact that professional rule is rarely the only relevant governance paradigm, even for a very strong profession such as general practitioners of medicine. The next step is therefore to examine empirically the combination of professionalism and other logics.

Some of the most interesting recent contributions address the combination of identity and motivation of professions. Schott et al. (2018) study the basis of the decisions made by public service professionals. They find that the decision-making of the professionals (veterinary inspectors) is influenced by how they interpret their professional role, whereas their public service motivation (PSM) does not seem to matter. PSM is the individual orientation to do good for others and society by delivering services, and Andersen and Pedersen (2012) find that individuals belonging to occupations with higher or lower levels of professionalism do not have different overall levels of PSM. Professionalism is negatively related to the dimension of public service motivation called 'compassion' (based on an affective logic), but positively related to the dimension called 'attraction to policy-making' (based on an instrumental logic). Both associations are weak, and the dimension commitment to the public interest and professionalism are unrelated. This highlights how professionalism primarily concerns the norms and identities linked to the collective group (the profession) rather than the motivation structure of the individuals. It also emphasizes professional role identities as one of the foundations for the key mechanisms in professional rule (specialized, theoretical knowledge and professional norms). Still, professional rule is normally combined with other governance paradigms in modern societies, and Schott et al. (2016) find that professionals experience conflicts as less stressful when they accept organizational factors (e.g. the organizational goals) or when they are able to enact a more integrated set of professional/organizational work principles. Their research suggests that modern professionals face conflicting situations due to clashes between multifaceted professional, organizational and societal factors, but that these conflicts can be handled.

In line with this, Noordegraaf (2011a, b) argues that professionals must deal with organizational issues. Specifically, he focuses on the connections between professional and organizational logics arising in the course of professional education. Traditionally, many professionals were educated and prepared for rendering services and securing quality irrespective of the organizational surroundings. Noordegraaf (2011b) argues that contemporary service production environments force professional associations to 'remake' professionals so that professional behaviours become more attuned to organizational logics. He finds that new connections between professionalism and organizations are established, but primarily at the level of general guidelines. This means, for example, that medical students are still not equipped for organizational matters despite their performance of an increasing amount of administrative tasks and duties. In another contribution, Noordegraaf (2011a) argues that the enhanced organizational role of professionals necessitates the formation of new linkages between occupational and organizational domains. He finds that professional norms are often at odds with managerial and organizational control principles, generating numerous dualisms. Instead of either returning to professionalism (to protect occupational spaces and 'rescue' professional work) or move beyond professionalism in order to restrict autonomies and discipline professional work, Noordegraaf (2011a) calls for new forms of organized professionalism; for example, professionals must develop new work preferences and face new cases, which are difficult to categorize and call for well-organized, multi-professional acts. These realities are only slowly incorporated into professional practices, and Noordegraaf (2011a) recommends that professionals take organizing and managing more seriously and develop organizational capacities and connective organizational standards. This suggests that leadership is a relevant part of professionalism, because leaders can coordinate it and give direction to the efforts.

While leadership is almost absent in the classical empirical literature on professional rule, recent contributions do emphasize the possible importance of leadership among professionals, especially if the leader is able to combine professional and managerial logics. McGivern et al. (2015) examine how and why professionals develop and use hybrid roles, how identity work is part of this, and how professionals draw on professional and managerial institutional logics as part of their identity work. This research differentiates between 'incidental hybrids' that represent and protect traditional institutionalized forms of professionalism while temporarily imbedded in hybrid roles, and 'willing hybrids' that are hybridized professional–managerial identities developed during formative identity work or, later on, in reaction to potential professional identity violations. McGivern et al. find that 'willing hybrids' use and integrate professionalism and managerialism, creating more legitimate hybrid professionalism in their managerial context. Importantly, they also find that these 'willing hybrids' align professionalism with their personal identity and become able to lead other professionals. Further along these lines, Andersen et al. (2018) discuss how leaders with a professional background can contribute to developing a shared understanding of professional quality among professionals and ultimately to higher levels of professional quality. Their results suggest that a key mechanism is agreement between rank-and-file professionals and their (hybrid) leaders about the most important performance criteria. Here, a key question becomes whether the leaders are part of the same profession as the professionals they are leading. Few empirical studies of hybrid leaders address this question, but a recent article by Grøn et al. (2019) suggests that leadership and occupational identities can co-exist and that a strong occupational identity is not a problem for the ability to exert active leadership unless it is stronger than the leadership identity.

The combined focus on professionalism and leadership shows that professional rule co-exists with other managerial and leadership principles and has done so for many years. More than a decade ago, Noordegraaf (2007) thus argued that classical professions were weakened and that we were transitioning from pure to hybrid professionalism in domains such as healthcare and social work. In line with this, several of the recent empirical contributions investigate the interplay between professionalism and one of the other governance paradigms discussed in this book. For example, Ackroyd et al. (2007) analyse three services in the UK, each dominated by organized professions: healthcare, housing and social services. They find significant variation in the effectiveness of NPM reforms and argue that these outcomes have been inversely proportional to the efforts expended on introducing NPM practices. The most radical changes were in housing, where successive UK governments focused the least attention. In contrast, management restructuring was less effective in health and social services despite greater resources being devoted to it. Ackroyd et al. (2007) argue that this is due to the professional values and institutions against which reforms were directed, which suggests that professional rule remains an important governance paradigm. The next section addresses how the relationship between NPM and professional rule has been discussed in the debate about the governance of professionals.

A key question is whether professionals actually follow norms and whether such norm-guided behaviour leads to better results. Examples from Denmark illustrate that the glass is both half full and half empty. Andersen, Heinesen and Pedersen (2014) thus find that students obtain higher grades when taught by a professionally certified teacher, but the difference is not very substantial. In a study of general practitioners,

Andersen and Serritzlew (2012) find that this highly professionalized group of service providers only follow professional norms if such norms are firm, and that economic incentives otherwise have a substantial impact on their behaviour. Similarly, Andersen and Blegvad (2003) demonstrate that dentists treat children differently (depending on the economic incentives) unless the professional norms are very firm. These results suggest that professional norms and financial incentives are both important and that professionalism can have an 'economic basis' in terms of increasing effectiveness – but that other mechanisms are also highly relevant.

DEBATE AND DILEMMAS

Professional rule and bureaucracy have co-existed in many countries, and it can be discussed whether professional rule is a separate governance paradigm. Mintzberg (1992, 2009) for example presents an organizational configurations framework, describing six organizational configurations, including 'professional bureaucracy'. This configuration uses standardization of skills as its prime coordinating mechanism and it is relatively decentralized (both vertically and horizontally) to provide autonomy to professionals. The idea is that highly trained professionals provide the services (ordered by the politicians through the hierarchy) to clients. There are few managers, and the core value is professional quality. Examples include universities, hospitals and large law firms. Even when the bureaucratic governance paradigm is dominant, many organizations provide complex services through highly trained professionals, and this broadens individual and occupational discretion. This makes the street-level bureaucracy discussion mentioned in Chapter 2 relevant for a combination of bureaucracy and professional rule, although the assumptions behind street-level theory (Lipsky 1980) differ significantly from the assumptions behind professional rule. Most importantly, street-level bureaucrats are primarily interested in a manageable workload (Nielsen 2006: 865), while professional rule implies that professionals are primarily interested in following professional rules. When the governance paradigms are combined, there might be more discretion for street-level bureaucrats to use the coping behaviours described in Chapter 2. It can be very problematic for professional rule if the individual professionals use their discretion to benefit themselves, for example through coping mechanisms, because it delegitimizes the governance paradigm.

Even in contexts where professional rule dominates, there are typically several aspects of bureaucracy, although the levels of the hierarchy with professionals (for example the schools) and the levels with bureaucrats (for example the municipal school administration) are relatively detached. In that way, Mintzberg's contribution can be seen as a critique of this book's separation of bureaucracy and professional rule. Mintzberg's work also reminds us that professionals in bureaucracies often act in accordance with their own style and are flexible in the delivery of content even within the constraints of the state- and district-mandated curriculum. They also tend to identify more with their professions than with the organization (see also Lunenburg 2012). How the governance paradigms interact and compete is discussed in more detail later, but a key point here is that there are strong (empirical and theoretical) links between bureaucracy and professional rule.

NPM was a critique of both paradigms as discussed in Chapter 4. It challenged professional autonomy, for example by introducing standards and measures of performance and by increasing competition and discipline in the use of resources (Hood 1991: 5). This means that many other actors (than professions and professionals) now have a say in professionalized services. The positioning of these other actors, both internally and relative to professional actors, largely depends on the macro-institutional set-up (as discussed in greater detail in Chapter 10). The emerging cross-country comparative literature on the effects of NPM (e.g. Flynn 2000) thus points to the important role played by macro institutions in shaping the new governance arrangements. At the same time, the introduction of market mechanisms has strengthened some of the incentives in the individual remuneration systems. While the introduction of NPM has challenged the traditional logic of governing based on expert authority, bringing incentives to the fore, NPM reforms have also occurred widely across different European countries, which highlights the need to understand the relationship between professional and public actors in different macro-institutional set-ups. Krejsler (2005: 350–54), for example, argues that we must discuss professional rule in light of the NPM practices in the public sector. As presented in Figure 3.1 (compared to Figure 4.1 in the next chapter), professional rule scores very low on incentives, whereas NPM scores very high. In that regard, these governance paradigms are contrasts.

Although professional rule appears to co-exist with NPM-inspired market- and incentive-based governance, professional associations often play an active role in seeking to prevent privatization, contracting out and the use of performance management that may contradict the professional norms that the professions aim to maintain. Hence, in countries like France, Germany and Denmark, where professional associations are strong and part of the corporatist arrangements that influence public sector reforms, there have been strong protests against incentive-driven governance, and NPM reforms seem to have had less influence on public governance than in the Anglophone countries.

It is also relevant to discuss the relationship between bureaucracy and professional rule. Byrkjeflot (2011: 153) argues that these two governance paradigms should not be understood as contrasts, as the early sociology of professions did (as discussed by Freidson 2001). These early contributions focused on how bureaucracy limits professional autonomy, for example through centralized control and rules. Later contributions have discussed the *regulative bargain* between political and administrative leaders, on one hand, and the profession on the other. Medical doctors in particular have had considerable power over the field through such bargains. Byrkjeflot (2011: 153–4), however, argues that NPM has threatened the partnership between top leaders in ministries and agencies and the professions (as suggested above and discussed further in the next chapter). It is highly relevant to note that this debate between professional autonomy, bureaucracy and NPM continues in many countries (see, e.g. Ejler 2017).

As indicated above in the discussion between the functionalist approach and the neo-Weberians, there is an ongoing discussion about whether the professional occupations actually possess specialized, theoretical knowledge and uphold the norms – or if they merely pretend to do so. Professional status concerns the public perception of these two aspects, while the professionalism concept captures the more objective degrees of knowledge and norm firmness and sanctioning. If the knowledge and norms are 'real', the argument is that professional rule will mean better decisions and better practice. If not, it is only a question of the professions exerting power over the rest of society, exploiting their privileged position to obtain money, power and status.

Another question is whether strong professions can bias the resource allocation so that resources are allocated to their area rather than to other parts of the public sector, where the net utility for society would be higher. It is very difficult to determine whether this is the case, also because different stakeholders have different priorities. Still, it is relevant to consider whether the tendency of professions to promote their own services distorts the public sector if some professions are much stronger than others (and stronger than politicians and generalist leaders).

This makes it relevant to ask whether persons who do not belong to a given professionalized occupation be leaders for members of the occupation? Can they tell the professionals what to do without having the professions' specialized, theoretical knowledge and without knowing the intra-occupational norms? On the one hand, generalist leaders from outside the profession may be unable to provide specific feedback or a vision that the professionals find motivating (Andersen et al. 2018). On the other hand, a public sector with many different services and professions must find a way to coordinate and prioritize between the professional silos. One answer could be the development of the above-mentioned hybrid leaders. These hybrid leaders are professionals engaged in managing professional work, professional colleagues, and other staff roles, framed by both professionalism and managerial logics (McGivern et al. 2015). Given the aforementioned differences between incidental and willing hybrid leaders (in terms of using and integrating profession-alism and managerialism and actually exerting leadership), an important new question concerns how we motivate professionals to become willing hybrid leaders. Another question is whether the knowledge element in professionalism is so strong that it is not possible to become a hybrid leader from the opposite starting point. Can a generalist acquire the professional knowledge and norms that allow them to succeed in leading professionals? Given how there are many examples where this happens, the question may be under what circumstances this combination of professional rule and the managerialist component of NPM (see Chapter 4) can work.

There are other pros and cons in relation to the knowledge element of professional rule; that is, the claim that professionals alone can under-stand and provide certain services. Most importantly, public-service users are equally, or perhaps even more, important as stakeholders than the political and administrative leaders discussed above. Will professional rule prevent or promote the users' interests? And who has the right to define their interests? Will the professional autonomy preserve the integrity of the two-party professional–client relationship? Or, to use the terminology of Le Grand (2010), will the professionals behave as 'paternalistic knights'? Knights are individuals oriented to do good for others and society, hence, as defined by Perry and Hondeghem (2008), they have a high public service motivation (PSM). As mentioned, professionals do not have a monopoly on PSM, but the combination of knowledge and PSM can make them more paternalistic than individuals from occupations with lower degrees of professionalism. Paternalistic knights think that they know best what 'doing good' is about and will therefore not listen to or act upon the voices of users (or politicians) unless they happen to coincide with their own views (Le Grand 2010: 65). The professionals might sometimes actually 'know best' (if we believe that their knowledge and norms are real), but it is probably relatively seldom that the service-user perspective is not also relevant. In a democratic society, the politicians' perspective is almost per definition relevant. Additionally, today, many public services involve more than one profession, and if the different professionals all think that they know best, professional rule can become a very inefficient type of governance. It can also hinder innovation. The political vision for services to senior citizens, for example, has changed from being eldercare to becoming help to self-help. This has been a difficult transition for the professions where the professional knowledge and norms have focused on care, not least for nurses. In many countries, the professionals have redefined their roles and norms. This exemplifies how governance paradigms such as professional rule evolve over time, but the core remains a combination of specialized, theoretical knowledge and professional norms.

4. New Public Management

BACKGROUND

When Christopher Hood coined the term 'New Public Management' (NPM) in his famous 1991 article on 'A public management for all seasons?', he could not possibly have foreseen the impact that this new concept would have for decades to come. NPM became the catchphrase for numerous reforms emerging in the late 1970s, which swept through most of the Western world from the early 1980s onwards and continues to this day to play a major role in most countries. There are other concepts aiming to diagnose public sector illnesses and make recommendations for how to modernize public administration, including the notion of New Public Administration (New PA) (Marini 1971; Waldo 1971; Wamsley and Zald 1973), but the NPM concept is different. In fact, it was quite the opposite of the New PA, which was an intellectual recommendation for reviving the classical public sector values associated with bureaucracy and professional rule. As proficiently captured by Aucoin (1990), the rise of NPM indicated that the pendulum was indeed swinging in the opposite direction.

As a reform programme, NPM aims to import tools, instruments and technologies perceived to work well in the private sector into the public sector. Amongst the most prominent imports was the introduction of business-like management styles that underscored that the ambition was not only to reform public administration – as in New PA – but to rethink public leadership and management. The introduction of private sector management techniques was motivated by the comparison between the allegedly dynamic, efficient, effective and service-minded private sector with the static, inefficient, ineffective and unresponsive public sector. The NPM cure for the problems of the public sector was to emulate the private sector by introducing private sector management styles and enhancing the reliance on market mechanisms in public governance.

Because NPM strongly praised private sector solutions and was promoted by neo-conservative political leaders such as Ronald Reagan in the USA and Margaret Thatcher in the UK, both of whom aimed to roll back the welfare state, it immediately became politically disputed and subject to intense criticism from scientists, professional associations and public commentators. In the years following World War II, many Western democracies were preoccupied with building up welfare states, often supported by social democratic or Christian democratic parties. While these endeavours can be seen as part of a mega-reform cycle lasting from the 1940s until the 1980s, the advancement of NPM reforms instigated a new mega-reform cycle changing the direction of the pendulum based on neo-liberalist ideology. It was a global reform wave (Borins 1998) aimed at radically transforming the public sector (Kettl 1997). No wonder it became disputed. Furthermore, as Pollitt and Bouckaert remark (2011: 5–6), whereas public management reform in the 1950s and 1960s was seen to be of a national, technical and/or legal character, it was now seen to be of a political, economic and international character. Public management reform was no longer a dull matter of organizational and procedural changes; it became subject to intense public interest and political contestation.

There are both political and economic reasons for the embrace of NPM reforms. The economic stagflation crises in the 1970s had been difficult to handle using the classic combination of Keynesian economic policy and welfare state programmes, and the inability to tackle the economic crisis left many with the impression that the public sector was both ineffective and unaffordable. The public sector was increasingly equated with increasing public expenditure, high taxes, poor service and bureaucratic regulation. To paraphrase Ronald Reagan, government is the problem, not the solution. The political demand for radical reforms was growing.

The Trilateral Commission (Crozier et al. 1975) claimed that the large public sectors in the Western world were 'overloaded' with problems and demands and that society and the economy were becoming more and more 'ungovernable'. The solution to both of these problems was to shift the responsibilities for the production of welfare solutions from the public to the private sector, thereby increasing the reliance on self-regulating markets and communities.

SOURCE OF INSPIRATION, THEORETICAL POSITIONS AND EXEMPLARY COUNTRIES

There were numerous important wake-up calls in the 1970s aimed at arousing public and political interest in public sector reform. Some came from left-wing intellectuals associated with the Frankfurt School (e.g. Habermas), while others were from conservative think tanks and neoliberal philosophers (e.g. Nozick). Both camps criticized the consequences of public bureaucracy, which Weber himself had described as an 'iron cage'. While these critical voices destabilized the post-war consensus about the stabilizing impact of the expansion of large-scale welfare bureaucracies, the economic problems and ongoing globalization of the economy created the strongest impetus for public sector reform.

Most researchers agree that the intellectual source of inspiration for NPM is to be found in neoclassical economics (e.g. public choice and principal–agent theory). Neoclassical public choice theories can be identified with: (1) the ideas of laissez faire economics, i.e. letting loose the forces of the free market and enhancing competition to achieve greater efficiency; (2) the critique of ossified state bureaucracy for creating market-distorting regulations and service monopolies; and (3) the idea of limiting the role of the state in order to individualize societal risks and boost private entrepreneurship. Key proponents of neoliberal economics were Friedman, Stigler, Buchannan and other North American scholars associated with the Chicago School. Principal–agent theory focusses on the information asymmetry between the principals and hired agents. The principals lack important knowledge about the actual competences and performance of the agents and the cost of local service production, while the rational, self-interested agents may exploit this knowledge deficit to indulge in opportunistic action that involves being overpaid, slacking and shirking, and creating an economic buffer that enhances local job security. The cure for this problem is competition supplemented with performance measurement linked to conditional incentives.

The way in which and the extent to which the NPM concept has been adopted and implemented varies considerably with the context, from country to country and over time in each setting. It is a matter of politics and of circumstance precisely how the paradigms are adopted. NPM spread much more rapidly in Anglo-Saxon countries such as Great Britain, New Zealand and the USA, than in Mediterranean countries such as Spain, Italy and Greece. While the former may be termed first movers and forerunners the latter may be termed late followers, whereas the Scandinavian countries and the Netherlands may be termed reluctant followers. Canada may be seen as a special case, being reluctant and part of the Anglo-Saxon hemisphere on the one hand and succeeding in making public management reorganization and substantial budget cuts on the other. The translation and the editing of NPM reforms reflect national and local political (and ideological) preferences and drivers. So, in countries like Denmark, Finland, Norway, Sweden, the Netherlands and Germany the managerial elements were adopted more readily than the elements concerning competition and markets. Again, some of the Anglo-Saxon countries, notably Great Britain, New Zealand and the USA (under Reagan) have witnessed a more radical use of privatization, tendering and built in quasi-markets than we have seen elsewhere, while the US reforms under Clinton had an organizational and a managerial focus.

While the most comprehensive application of NPM was presumably found in Great Britain under Margaret Thatcher (Gruening 2001), the first attempts to reform the public sector based on the combination of marketization and performance management were found in New Zealand (Kettl 2005). The history of NPM in New Zealand illustrates the theoretical source of inspiration, as it is closely linked to a number of young economists who had returned to New Zealand after finishing their education in the USA, where they were heavily influenced by neo-classical economics. They were granted considerable administrative authority by the Labour government to initiate wide-sweeping NPM reforms, which were facilitated by a relatively centralized state.

The new reform recipe spread rapidly throughout the OECD countries (OECD 1995), with powerful actors such as the OECD, the World Bank and national ministries of finance as the primary political, ideological and managerial drivers. While the British experience had a significant but varied impact on the countries in continental Europe (e.g. with Finland being a keen follower and France being more resistant), the Americans developed their own version of NPM, both under Reagan and Clinton, Vice President Al Gore making it his mission to modernize the public sector (Gore 1993). In the USA, NPM was primarily a management reform aimed at boosting the entrepreneurial spirit of executive managers by separating steering from rowing (Osborne and Gaebler 1992). In this respect, NPM was combined with an old American tradition stemming back to at least Woodrow Wilson (1887), who (as mentioned in Chapter 2) advocated the separation of politics and administration (remember that in the USA, the top layers of the administration are politically appointed and therefore heavily involved in politics). While Wilson (1887: 201) argued in favour of traditional bureaucratic values, such as dutifulness, the key mechanisms in NPM to make administration more efficient were incentives, leadership and the creation of a business-like culture, as discussed in detail below.

MAIN GOVERNANCE IDEA: GOALS AND MEANS

Upon his return to England after a couple of years in New Zealand, Hood (1991: 3) identified four administrative megatrends, namely: (1) attempts to slow down or reverse government growth in terms of overt public spending and staffing; (2) a shift towards privatization and quasi-privatization and away from core government institutions; (3) the development of automation, particularly through the introduction of information technology; and (4) the development of a more international agenda focusing on general issues of public management (Hood 1991: 3). He found that NPM, though ill-defined, offered a convenient shorthand for a handful of broadly similar administrative doctrines dominating the reform agenda in a number of OECD countries. There were seven such doctrinal components of NPM found in various combinations in many OECD countries (see Box 4.1).

BOX 4.1 HOOD'S LIST OF DOCTRINAL COMPONENTS OF NEW PUBLIC MANAGEMENT

- 'Hands-on professional management' in the public sector (accountability/clear assignment of responsibility).
- Explicit standards and measures of performance (clear statement of goals and a 'hard' look at objectives).
- Greater emphasis on output controls (stressing results rather than procedures).
- Shift to disaggregation of units in the public sector (manageable units and separation of provision from production).
- Shift to greater competition in the public sector (rivalry to lower costs and better standards).
- Stress on private sector styles of management practice (use 'proven' private sector management tools).
- Stress on greater discipline and parsimony in resource use (check resource demands and 'do more with less').

NPM can be boiled down in many ways. Dunleavy et al. (2006a, b) state that the main components are disaggregation, competition and the use of incentives, while Ferlie et al. (1996) distinguish between four core features of NPM: the efficiency drive, the attempt to downsize and decentralize the public sector, the search for excellence via the identification of best practice, and public service orientation aimed at enhancing user satisfaction. For analytical reasons and in accordance with the theoretical roots of NPM (Aucoin 1990; Hood 1991; Gruening 2001), we distinguish between two principally different aspects of NPM: (1) marketization recommended by economic theory; and (2) managerialism rooted in management theory. The marketization aspect of NPM is the most theoretically and paradigmatically coherent, while the new managerialism tends to follow the current management fad (see Box 4.2). Classical theories of organization, management and leadership claim to be generic. Their insights therefore apply equally to public and private organizations, despite possible sector differences, and they are applicable around the world, despite historical, national and cultural differences. These assumptions explain the NPM claims to universality.

BOX 4.2 ELEMENTS WHICH ARE PART OF THE TWO PRINCIPAL ASPECTS OF NPM

Marketization based on economic theory	Managerialism based on management theory
Competition and incentives (make the managers manage) Privatization Tendering and contracting out Public–private partnerships Quasi public–private firms Gathering of external funding and taking a salary and or payment for a service product User choice of (public or private) provider Bonus salary systems (use of incentives to motivate managers and employees alike) Pay for performance and other systems for the allocation of public funding based on vouchers and performance Contracts	Flexibility, accountability and decentralization of authority (let managers manage) Corporate-like organization (with top-management teams) Strategic management Strategic communication Personnel management (HRM) Service management Entrepreneurial management Quality management (e.g. auditing, evaluation, MBO, TQM, Lean) Team management Budgetary and economy control systems (e.g. ABC, Balanced scorecard, accrual accounting) Performance management based on goal and framework steering and continuous measuring and benchmarking of results Digitalization and robotization

---

The marketization of the public sector encourages the decentralization of public authority and the establishment of competing units that will facilitate initiatives and dynamics from below, whereas new managerialism aims for the removal of (unnecessary) bureaucracy and red tape to improve flexibility and make room for entrepreneurial leadership and management. These two elements may play well together, as when competition for contracts and customers, and pay for performance, force public service organizations to strengthen their capacity for strategic management in order to improve their performance and stay in business (hence, the call to let managers manage and make managers manage). The two constitutive elements of NPM also give rise to inherent contradictions and paradoxes, such as the demand for both centralization (as in corporatization and performance management) and decentralization (as in marketization and the devolution of public authority to local agencies). There also seems to be tension between the hard economic incentives and soft HRM encouragements in relation to employee motivation. In sum, the marketization–managerialism marriage in NPM is both rational and conflictual.

The distinction between marketization and managerialism is by no means clear-cut. Hence, there are elements of NPM, such as the use of incentives, that are both part of marketization and managerialism. Both performance management and budgetary control systems have an affinity for economic thinking in so far as it is assumed that control and the conditional use of positive and negative incentives can reduce opportunistic behaviour in the principal and agent relations between managers and employees, or between central and decentral agencies. Likewise, the use of economic bonus salary systems in both executive leadership contracts and in relation to street-level employees are managerial tools, because they can be used actively by managers to achieve particular goals. However, since they are so clearly anchored in an economic logic of seeing humans as self-interested opportunity seekers driven by external incentives, it seems natural to view them as a part of the marketization logic. Yet another example of the confusion about how to categorize key elements of NPM is provided by the Service Management concept (Normann 2001). Service Management is both a management system aimed at refocussing public service organizations by placing service excellence at the centre and it is an economic strategy for ensuring user and customer satisfaction, thereby securing the market position of the public service organization in an environment characterized by fierce competition.

NPM has been criticized for being steeped in mistrust towards public employees and having an obsession with control and punishment. This criticism arises from public choice and principal–agent theory both assuming that people are driven by a rational and self-interested utility maximization and can therefore neither be trusted to deliver what they are supposed to deliver nor to serve the community by producing public value. People are selfish and must be controlled by elaborate auditing systems and disciplined by the incentives inherent to competitive markets and performance management.

The NPM governance paradigm is distinctly different from the two previous paradigms discussed in the book. There is a clear preference for governance based on market competition rather than bureaucratic government, and the ambition to limit the autonomy of public employees is strong. The distinctiveness of the NPM paradigm is clearly discernible from how it is marked out in the governance diamond. There is a certain ambiguity when placing NPM along the five axes, however, since it depends on how weight is given to marketization and managerialism, which sometimes contradict each other on key dimensions.

This ambiguity is evident on the first axis in Figure 4.1, where we try to pinpoint the degree of centralized control in the vertical chain of command. The economic aspect of NPM scores very low on this dimension, because it recommends the decentralization of authority to organizational units that compete for contracts and customers. In contrast, the managerial part of NPM scores medium to high. On the one hand, it subjects the decentral institutions to centralized control based on performance management that combines strategic goal-setting and budget frames with a strict measuring of key performance indicators. On the other hand, the managerial version of NPM recommends giving public managers leeway to make decentral decisions in accordance with the centrally defined goals. After all, one of the decisive elements of NPM as a paradigmatic programme was to 'let the leaders lead' and to grant them autonomy to compete both with other agencies within the public sector and in cases of tendering, i.e. with private contenders. Weighing the economic and managerial aspects of NPM against each other, we conclude that the level of centralized control in NPM is low.

Ambiguity also pervades NPM in relation to the second axis: the degree of horizontal coordination. The economic part of NPM prescribes the separation of and competition between decentral organizational units rather than cross-boundary coordination and collaboration (i.e. low on horizontal coordination). In contrast, the managerial part of NPM – partly in response to the growing fragmentation following in the wake of the first years of 'agentification' – recommends the formation of cross-cutting matrix structures, task forces and project teams aimed at integrating different forms of expertise (i.e. a high degree of horizontal coordination). The 'silo problem', which is deepened by the introduction of goal and framework steering combined with executive wage bonuses, is counteracted by the formation of small groups of chief executives and larger groups of strategic managers who aim to facilitate coordination and concerted action (joined-up government; see Bogdanor 2005). In sum, while NPM reforms can increase compartmentalization and create more specialized (single-task) public and private organizations, leading to fragmentation, there is also a growing concern with promoting cross-sectoral and inter-agency collaboration. We arrive at a medium-to-low grade for NPM on this axis.

The third axis concerns the degree to which public governance is based on the articulation of (public) values. Here, there is no disagreement between the two core aspects of NPM. NPM believes that the public sector should be run like a private firm and therefore pay less attention to classical public values (e.g. rule of law, equity). Motivation is not secured, primarily, by appealing to values, but rather by external incentives. However, whereas transactional leadership based on positive and negative inducements dominated NPM in the early years, there has been growing interest in the exercise of transformational leadership (Burns 1978) by visionary and charismatic leaders and managers who invoke references to both the public purpose and moral foundation of their leadership. Nevertheless, we end up categorizing NPM as very low on the use of value articulation.

The ambiguity of NPM reappears in relation to the fourth axis regarding the degree to which public governance is based on conditional positive and negative incentives. This time, the ambiguity has a different form, since both of the core aspects of NPM argue in favour of the use of incentives, but they have different kinds of incentives in mind. While the economic logic of NPM has a strong belief in hard (pecuniary) incentives, its managerial logic has a strong belief in the value of non-pecuniary incentives based on feedback and encouragement to employees (the Human Resource Management part of NPM). We categorize NPM as very high on the use of incentives.

Finally, NPM has a distinct profile on the fifth axis regarding the degree to which societal actors, including citizens, are involved in public governance, but again the two parts of NPM have a different say. The economic aspect of NPM strongly urges decision-makers to contract out public service provision to private firms or even privatize the service production. The managerial part of NPM welcomes strategic cooperation with private firms as a part of a more general strategic management practice. Citizens are involved either through their free 'consumer choice' or through participation in user satisfaction surveys (Hirschman 1970). Still, the involvement of societal actors in NPM is very specific, both in terms of what types of actors are involved and in the form of their involvement. Professional associations, citizens beyond users and civil society in a broader sense are not invited. NPM ends up scoring medium to high on this axis.

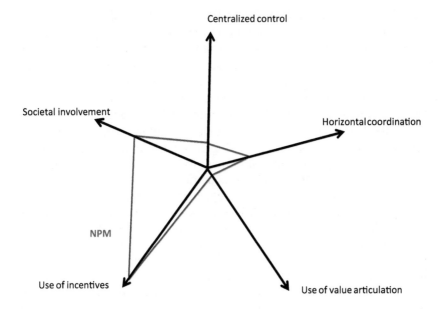

Figure 4.1   The NPM governance diamond

EMPIRICAL RESULTS

NPM has been implemented in many different ways. Moreover, NPM has been promoted not only by right-wing neo-liberalist governments, but also by social democratic governments in the UK, New Zealand and the Scandinavian countries that have supported NPM reforms. So although being a child of neoliberalism, NPM became the conventional wisdom of the time, in accordance with, if not even the conceptualization of, what German philosopher Friedrich Hegel calls *Zeitgeist*; that is, a dominant set of ideas that presents itself as a necessity against which it is difficult to argue. Indeed, this is precisely the idea of a paradigm, namely that it is taken for granted by many different people at a particular point in time.

The hegemony of neoliberalism has been analysed by Campbell and Pedersen (2006), who claim that neoliberalist economic thinking is the dominant politico-economic ideology of our time (at least in the Western world) and that NPM is the tool for modernizing the public sector in accordance with this politico-economic doctrine.

In the Scandinavian countries, NPM reforms have been launched by consecutive left- and right-wing governments since the early 1980s, but never in the radical way that we find in Anglo-Saxon countries (e.g. Australia, Canada, New Zealand, the UK and the USA). Among the Scandinavian countries, the scepticism towards NPM was perhaps greatest in Norway. Overall, it appears as though the Scandinavian countries have once again chosen a third way between capitalism and socialism, at least in the sense that NPM reforms are seen to be less ideological and more sceptical, reluctant, experimental and pragmatic in orientation (Klausen and Ståhlberg 1998). In countries such as France, Germany and the Netherlands, we find a similar reluctant attitude with less dramatic reform initiatives. However, the timing of NPM reforms and the presence of leaders and laggards makes it difficult to make categorical conclusions about the fate of NPM in different countries.

The NPM reforms have been implemented top-down by executive managers in alliance with dedicated political leaders, which might explain why the managerial component focussing on devolution and performance management has prevailed over the marketization component (Kettl 2005). The managerial component allowed the executive public leaders to enhance their control over the public sector without taking direct responsibility for the decentralized service production, while the marketization component shrunk their kingdom and carried an imminent risk of public scandals when private contractors did not perform well or went bankrupt. Consequently, privatization was a key element in the policy of the Reagan administration but lost momentum under Clinton and Gore, and it was the managerial aspect that came to the fore supported by the idea of creating a government that worked better and cost less (Gore 1993). Osborne and Gaebler's *Reinventing Government* (1992) became renowned for stating and framing this key point in the US NPM reforms. Many of their points (Box 4.3) are the

---

BOX 4.3   THE NPM PRINCIPLES ACCORDING TO
OSBORNE AND GAEBLER (1992)

1. Catalytic government: steering rather than rowing.
2. Community-owned government: empowering rather than serving.
3. Competitive government: injecting competition into service delivery.
4. Mission-driven government: transforming rule-driven organizations.
5. Results-oriented government: funding outcomes, not inputs.
6. Customer driven government: meeting the needs of the customer (not bureaucracy).
7. Enterprising government: earning rather than spending.
8. Anticipatory government: prevention rather than cure.
9. Decentralized government: from hierarchy to participation and teamwork.
10. Market-oriented government: leveraging change through the market.

same as the principles mentioned by Hood and others, and the general idea of cutting public expenditure by enhancing efficiency is more or less identical with key aspects of Hood's definition of NPM (compare Hood's point 7 with Osborne and Gaebler's points 5 and 7).

Osborne and Gaebler both mention the economic and managerial components of NPM; nevertheless, the general idea is that the key to better public performance lies in leadership and management. Public leaders and managers must step up and assume responsibility for developing the public sector. We need charismatic, visionary and entre-preneurial leaders capable of improving the public service delivery systems. At the operational level, the new managerialism boils down to performance management that combines well-known management tech-niques from the private sector, such as management by objectives, total quality management and balanced scoreboard. Strategic management might be the managerial tool that comes closest to capturing the management ideas of NPM because it is intentionally deliberate, forward-looking and all-encompassing. This becomes clear in Osborne and Plastrik's book *Banishing Bureaucracy* (1998), in which they argue that the necessary changes in the public sector stem from an active and determinate use of strategies aimed at creating clarity of purpose, drawing out the consequences for performance, putting the customer in the driver's seat, shifting control away from the top and the centre, and creating an entrepreneurial culture.

Once again, we find the market-based demand-side orientation (putting the customer in the driver's seat). It should be clear, however, that the marketization logic is downplayed vis-à-vis the managerial logic, because the emphasis is on the implementation of NPM reforms through mana-gerial initiatives based on strategic thinking and action. We have seen this strategic management perspective many times before, not least in the recipes and recommendations found in mainstream management litera-ture such as the theories of organizational change (Kotter 1996) and learning organizations (Senge 1990). What is new about NPM is the explicit focus on the public sector and the clear adherence to NPM-reform thinking.

While there is little doubt regarding the impact of NPM on decades of public sector reforms in the Western world and beyond, the impact of NPM on actual public sector performance is far more disputable. As noted above, NPM has been critically 'evaluated' from the beginning, and even if most of these 'evaluations' are based on single case studies and anecdotal evidence, they are all very sceptical about the actual impact.

Since New Zealand was both a first mover and a radical implementer of NPM, its experiences have been thoroughly scrutinized. However, the results defy easy summarization. Reports about efficiency gains have typically been oversold (Goldfinch 1998). Furthermore, both the reforms and the effects have changed over time, leading to different and contradictory results (Norman and Gregory 2003; Chapman and Duncan 2007). British studies also seem to point in different directions. Boyne and Gould-Williams (2003) reached the conclusion that NPM reforms of UK education, healthcare and housing in the 1980s and 1990s had raised efficiency and improved responsiveness to service users, but reduced equity.

The systematic reviews aiming to evaluate the recent public sector reforms are typically balancing the pros and cons and tend to conclude that the effects are difficult to interpret with certainty (Pollitt and Bouckaert 2003; Dunleavy and Carrera 2013; Christensen and Lægreid 2016). In the social sciences, causes and effects are neither linear nor straightforward. For example, the percentage of public sector spending relative to the GDP may have fallen within a given period without necessarily having anything to do with the impact of NPM reforms. There are many other factors to take into account, such as the general economic development, other policy reforms and managerial initiatives that might influence the dependent variables.

Among the most recent systematic evaluations, we find Andrews (2011), Christensen and Lægreid (2001, 2011), Pollitt and Bouckaert (2011), Dunleavy and Carrera (2013) and Hood and Dixon (2015a, b).

Andrews (2011) has provided a systematic review based on 18 studies of public sector efficiency and concluded that there may be some improvement in technical efficiency due to agentification, performance management, enhanced competition and public–private partnerships. However, little is known about allocative and distributive efficiency. Even if Andrews is aware of the scarcity of the empirical evidence, he is relatively sceptical about the positive effects of NPM, ultimately concluding:

> What little is known about the effects of NPM on efficiency therefore suggests that policy-makers should think twice before embarking on extensive reform programmes to enhance the cost-effectiveness of the public sector. (2011: 294)

Christensen and Lægreid (2011) conclude that after several decades of NPM, we know surprisingly little about its impact. The most important lesson from comparative research on the effects of NPM is that they are context-dependent and difficult to generalize. What may work well in one context may be dysfunctional in another depending on both local circumstances and how the reforms are implemented. What is good from an economic perspective may be detrimental from a managerial, let alone from a motivational perspective. There are also countries in which NPM reforms have officially been launched but never implemented in practice. This lack of implementation is found in several countries in southern Europe (Kickert 2011).

According to Pollitt and Bouckaert (2011), there is no straightforward 'yes' or 'no' to the question of whether NPM has been successful. Assessing the results of administrative reforms is notoriously difficult. Hence, it comes as no surprise that there are few systematic studies of the actual effects of NPM. The most important of these effects might be the heightened awareness of the importance of public management and leadership, the shift in what we talk about and how we understand problems facing the public sector, how we look upon change and the need for better strategic leadership.

The Hood and Dixon evaluation of some 30 years of NPM in the UK is rather depressing. Not only have consecutive governments failed to provide adequate data allowing the consistent measurement of the results, the results are highly disappointing. Thorough time-series analyses show that NPM has achieved the exact opposite of what it originally promised. Instead of a public sector that works better and costs less, the results of three decades of NPM reforms:

> fit within a range between government costing about the same (but not less) and working about as well (but not better), to a darker picture of government costing substantially more and working decidedly worse. (Hood and Dixon 2015a: 19)

Their argument is that the running costs have gone up when controlled for inflation, while complaints and legal challenges have soared. Obviously, it is difficult to know whether this is a consequence of NPM or if other societal developments have caused at least some of the changes. For now, the evidence regarding the consequences of NPM can be said to be mixed.

DEBATE AND DILEMMAS

Those arguing in favour of NPM reforms are typically either: (1) elected politicians with a neoliberalist ideology or a strong preference for a public sector that is more cost-efficient, effective and user-oriented; or (2) public managers loyal to these politicians and their policies or eager to enhance bureaucratic control over the performance of lower-level agencies and their employees.

Those arguing against NPM reforms are typically either: (1) those who are politically and ideologically against the combination of marketization and managerialism; (2) employees who have experienced the negative effects of NPM reforms; or (3) those who have done research on the impact of NPM (e.g. the above-mentioned critics). Both the public debate and workplace-level discussions tend to be marked by clashes between the professional culture and values of the employees and the managerial practices of the administrative leadership (Raelin 1983; Exworthy and Halford 1999; Golden et al. 2000). Such clashes between the equally legitimate demand for professional discretion and autonomy and the managerial concern for increasing cost-efficiency are transformed into managerial dilemmas when managers have to decide and explain what is to be done.

Hood's initial article on NPM (1991) raises important and grave criticism of NPM that remains relevant and widely discussed (Pollitt and Bouckaert 2011; Christensen and Lægreid 2016; Hood and Dixon 2016). This is so, despite the fact that the theoretical roots of NPM not only include public choice and principal–agent theory, but also mainstream organic, classical rational and neoclassical public administration theories (Gruening 2001). Furthermore, the critical questions raised towards NPM not only have a continued relevance, they are also universal. Paradoxically, the critique of NPM is universal and therefore valid even if NPM can be and has been applied in many different ways.

As Hood and (many) others have noticed, NPM is obviously not one thing, but a number of more or less coherent reform elements that are implemented in numerous ways over time and in different settings. Given the predominance of NPM as a guide for public sector reform and the political attention it has received, it is understandable that hardly any aspect of NPM has avoided criticism. While this leaves us with an overly negative image of NMP, we should bear in mind that the hypothetical and counterfactual question of what might have happened had there been no NPM reforms is seldom raised. As such, while NPM may have failed to achieve its stated objectives, the absence of reforms may have been much worse. While speculative and debatable, such questions are worth reflecting upon.

There will always be unforeseen negative consequences of legislation, policies and modernization programmes. Hence, it is hardly surprising that NPM has been accused of producing the opposite of the intended effects, thereby giving rise to increasing bureaucracy, decreasing efficiency and the demotivation of public employees (Moynihan 2008; Bellé and Ongaro 2014; Hood and Dixon 2015a). This is certainly true regarding centralization and bureaucratization. The idea of running the public sector like a business based on top-down management, monitoring all activities of decentral public agencies thoroughly and correcting failures by issuing new rules, and regulating quasi-markets in order to prevent market failures, corruption and scandals has contributed to strengthening bureaucracy and centralized control. In addition, the mandatory reporting activities associated with performance management tend to steal an increasing amount of time and resources from the daily operations and risks, undermining public employee motivation if they perceive performance management as an unproductive, unjustified and ultimately meaningless activity motivated by the lack of trust in the dedication and skills of public employees.

Since the criticism of NPM is so ubiquitous and all-encompassing, it is difficult to decide where to start and stop. Let us therefore conclude our discussion with a critical examination of the claim that NPM provides a universal and generic form of governance. This discussion questions the idea that NPM provides 'a public management for all seasons' (Hood 1991).

There are at least three ways of problematizing the NPM claim to being a universal and generic form of governance and alternatively embracing the contingency and context-dependency of specific forms of governance. First, NPM represents a direct attack on the very idea of the specificity of the public sector vis-à-vis the private sector. Second, NPM ignores national and cultural context and heritage. Third, NPM constitutes a threat to the whole idea of having a welfare state and to particular national manifestations of the idea of a welfare state. Let us consider each of these three arguments in turn.

The first problem is that the NPM claim to universality challenges the distinctiveness of the public sector. Many prominent researchers have argued that the public sector is different from the private sector and that 'public management is unique and uniquely difficult' (Lynn 1996: 137). These arguments have long historical roots and have been repeated endlessly (e.g. Appleby 1945; Wamsley and Zald 1973; Rainey et al. 1976; Lynn 1981; Heffron 1989). For example, Allison famously asserted that 'public and private management are fundamentally alike in all unimportant respects' (1980: 510). A similar argument about the distinctiveness of the public sector is the claim that public managers are haunted by wicked problems (Rittel and Webber 1973) that render the transfer of linear management techniques from the private sector a dubious enterprise. It also makes the idea of privatization a utopian mirage, since it is not possible to earn a profit from dealing with hard-to-solve problems that are difficult to handle because they have no clear definition, conflicting objectives and no known solution, and are intertwined with other problems in complex webs. Furthermore, Moore (1995) makes clear that the public sector produces public rather than private value (see Chapter 7). It does not seek to meet the demand of customers in private markets and produce a profit for private shareholders. Instead, it engages in tax-financed activities supporting people in need who cannot take care of themselves and in activities that are justified simply because they are just and correct from a political point of view. Such activities may be simply regarded as expenses with no economic pay-off. Finally, Perry and Wise (1990) have insisted that public employees are not merely motivated by concerns for individual utility maximization, often choosing to work in the public sector because they want to do good for others and society (see also Andersen, Heinesen and Pedersen 2014). Moral obligations are no strangers to employees working for the common good and with citizens in need. In sum, the public sector is different from the private sector, which undermines the fundamental idea of NPM that the public sector should be run like a private business.

The second problem is that the NPM claim to universality challenges what we know from history, anthropology, political sociology and organization theory about the specificity of regions, countries and cultures. The idea that NPM provides a universal governance model that can be exported to all countries and will develop the same benefits in terms of low-cost and high-quality services everywhere goes against the argument about path-dependent historical developments. We have not reached 'the end of history' (Fukuyama 1992) in which only the triumphant neoliberal model is left standing. Today, hardly any historian, anthropologist and/or sociologist would agree that what works well in one country, sector or organization will necessarily fit with and work well in another context. Research in state- and nation-building have strong arguments against these geo-centralist views, instead emphasizing national and historical dependencies and specificity (see Tilly 1975; Fukuyama 2004). Similar arguments appear in French historiography (Braudel 1982), organizational analyses (Powell and DiMaggio 1991) and sociological and historical institutionalism (Hall and Taylor 1996). As Olsen observes (1991), contemporary modernization programmes such as NPM are often based on simplifying and instrumental views on organizational decision-making and change rather than seeing how programmes and initiatives are affected by the properties of already-existing institutions. Perhaps the strongest warning against the idea of NPM as the one best way is found in theories on organization and culture in which national cultures are seen as very different in important respects such as power distance, risk aversion, individualism and masculinity (Hofstede 1980). Taking these differences seriously means that public governance reforms are always conditioned by rather unique historical, cultural and organizational traditions that prevent the easy transfer of new formats. In short, the generic and universal approach to governance, organization and leadership, management and leadership has been abandoned long ago in favour of a contingency approach (Blake and Mouton 1969; Pfeffer and Salancik 1978; Scott 1981; Hatch 1997). On this background, it is indeed paradoxical that NPM tries to reclaim the long lost universalistic and generic approach.

The third and final problem is that NPM – far from being a set of generic and universalistic reform guidelines – appears to offer a neo-liberal challenge to the very idea of the modern welfare state and its different national manifestations. NPM is frequently 'sold' as a way of trimming and consolidating the welfare state in times of economic crisis, but the preference for private solutions, the recasting of citizens as customers and the neoliberal insistence on the individualization of societal risks is the very opposite of the welfare state. NPM may co-exist with the liberal, residual and market-based welfare model in the Anglo-Saxon countries and some versions of the performance-based social insurance model found in some European countries. However, NPM is the antidote to the universalistic welfare state model found in the Scandinavian countries. It can be disputed whether there is a distinctive Scandinavian welfare state model, but most observers agree that the welfare systems in Denmark, Norway and Sweden share a number of common characteristics (Erikson et al. 1987; Hansen et al. 1993; Kuhnle 2000). These common traits include a consensus-oriented political culture, a strong commitment to social and regional redistribution, universal rights of all citizens to welfare provision free of charge in areas such as education, health and social security, and a large tax-financed public sector with a high degree of devolution. On the background of these common traits, NPM was strongly criticized in all three countries, the Norwegian scholars in particular having been very critical and highly sceptical (Olsen 1991; Olsen and Peters 1996; Klausen and Ståhlberg 1998; Christensen and Lægreid 2001). In an early evaluation and reflection on administrative reforms, renowned Norwegian political scientist Johan P. Olsen (1986) identified three contemporary and competing reform ideologies: the red (social democratic values), the green (environmental consciousness) and the blue (liberal values). While the heyday of red reform ideas was over and the green reform ideas were needed to secure future survival, the blue (NPM) reform ideas are depicted as a useful correction as regards public spending, but also as a potential threat to the very idea of the welfare state.

The reception of NPM in the Scandinavian countries varied across political parties, but many politicians and most public managers and researchers have been strongly against the core NPM ideas. The critique of NPM was often informed by the differences in beliefs and values that separate NPM from the Scandinavian welfare state (see Box 4.4).

BOX 4.4　IDEAL-TYPE DIFFERENCES BETWEEN THE BELIEFS AND VALUES OF NPM AND THE SCANDINAVIAN WELFARE STATE

Scandinavian welfare state beliefs, values and recommendations	NPM beliefs, values and recommendations
• Social democratic orientation • Universalistic coverage free of charge • Collectivistic and solidaristic values • Large public sector • Many public employees • Public service production • Cooperation • Political and governmental rule	• Liberalistic orientation • Private insurance and pay for services • Individualistic values • Diminished public sector • Many private employees • Private service production • Competition • Markets and invisible hands rule

---

Despite the critical reception of NPM in Scandinavia, it has had considerable impact. As such, NPM seems to have been supported by economic pressures on the welfare state and perhaps also by a *Zeitgeist* that has fostered a willingness to make concessions both in relation to the classical forms of bureaucracy and professional rule and in relation to the welfare state. In sum, while NPM does not provide universal instructions for reform, it seems to have had a considerable impact and to a certain extent has even become institutionalized in countries that provide a hostile environment.

As a governance paradigm, NPM has provided new answers to the alleged problem of public bureaucracy and professional rule. Many have seen NPM as the remedy for the problems tormenting Western societies and their public sectors in the 1970s and 1980s. It has spread beyond the Western Hemisphere. Nevertheless, it does not constitute a generic and universal modernization programme that is easily adopted in all regions, countries and organizations. In the first quarter of the twenty-first century, NPM continues to be a dominant governance paradigm despite its inherent contradictions and the political and institutional barriers to its implementation. In the last decade, however, criticism of the status, political impact and unintended negative consequences has become stronger and stronger. Today, the widespread criticisms of NPM call for new remedies. And that is where the next governance paradigms come in.

5. Neo-Weberian State

BACKGROUND

The Neo-Weberian State (NWS) was developed by Christopher Pollitt and Geert Bouckaert as a governance paradigm in their book, *Public Management Reform* (fourth edition, 2017), originally published in 2000. In their own words, it is 'a vision of a modernized, efficient, citizen-friendly state apparatus' (2017: 122). The conceptualization of the NWS emerged after Pollitt and Bouckaert had described and analysed public management reforms in 12 countries and the European Commission. They had observed how some states did not follow the prescriptions in New Public Management (NPM) and that they had not engaged fully in the type of networks described by New Public Governance (NPG). Instead, these countries (mainly those in northern Europe) still had a strong state presence in public service delivery that relied on well-trusted bureaucratic means (the 'Weberian state' part). Simultaneously, they were keen to provide more efficient and user-oriented service delivery (the 'neo' part). It was also noted that the state was often just as capable as the private sector in driving change. This observation related to the elected politicians at the level of central government having a more prominent position than merely overseeing market-based service production. For want of a better alternative, Pollitt and Bouckaert coined their empirical observation 'the Neo-Weberian State' model in an effort to clearly distance it from both NPM and NPG.

NWS is therefore a label that can be used to describe the approach to public management reform taken by states that have neither gone down the radical NPM route nor have become fully enthralled with public policy networks and the co-creation features of NPG. All of the Nordic countries have strong welfare states, and it was therefore hardly surprising that the Nordics are among the key NWS exemplars. The states that are most associated with NPM prescriptions were the Anglophone states (e.g. the UK, USA and the Antipodes), whereas states such as France, Germany, Netherlands, Sweden and Finland epitomized the continued reliance on an active state in shaping the public sector specifically and the wider society generally. Pollitt and Bouckaert (2017: 19) suggested that NWS was conceived as 'an attempt to modernize traditional bureaucracy by making it more professional, efficient and citizen-friendly'. The characterization of the Nordic countries as robust welfare states that did not wholeheartedly buy into NPM is also found in the work of Nordic researchers (see, e.g., Christensen and Lægreid 2011, 2016; Greve et al. 2016).

NWS sees the fragmentation caused by NPM as a key problem. NPM has split the public sector into various smaller organizations and agencies, many of which are furnished with performance contracts, and it has contracted out or privatized public services to a host of private providers. The resulting fragmentation has caused great coordination problems for the public sector. In their empirical observations of European reform trends, Pollitt and Bouckaert noted a different development whereby public sector organizations were merged and grew bigger and more powerful, and where performance management was used to create more coherent performance management systems across many organizations. At the same time, the public sector became highly digitalized, which enabled a stronger user orientation as many services were made available online so that people no longer had to go to a bureaucratic office in their local town hall to receive a particular service. They could instead interact with the public sector from their mobile phone or from a personal computer at home. The focus is therefore on a modernized bureaucracy that serves citizens using digital government tools and makes room for an efficient, service-minded state.

NWS recognizes that both the networks and co-creation processes associated with NPG and the digital tools and developments associated with Digital Era Governance (DEG) are often the driving forces behind public management reforms, but it does not believe that these forces have more power than the state's rediscovered strength in NWS and the continued dominance empirically of NPM in many countries. Pollitt has reiterated his argument about how NPM remains the megatrend to which other governance paradigms must relate, and he boldly claims that NPM is the long-term dominant trend that no other paradigm has yet to surpass (Pollitt 2016a: 435–6).

On this background, the NWS concept plays an important role in providing an exception to the rule. Hence, it shows how some states have not undergone a radical NPM phase or have aimed to swing the pendulum back from the market to the state as the main governance mechanism.

SOURCES OF INSPIRATION, THEORETICAL POSITIONS AND EXEMPLARY COUNTRIES

The international debate on NWS has been based on Pollitt and Bouckaert's use of the term, as they introduced it. Early discussion of the term can be found in Laurence Lynn's (2008) paper on what makes a state 'neo-Weberian'. Here, Lynn also reflects on the specific European origins of the term and on its limited relevance in the North American context, where the system of government does not encompass a strong, centralized state in the traditional European sense.

According to many international indexes, the northern European states that Pollitt and Bouckaert associate with NWS have been able to maintain an effective and efficient public sector that caters to citizens' needs and secures a high level of trust and transparency (see below for a more elaborate discussion). As noted by Christensen and Lægreid (2017) and Greve and colleagues (2016), the Nordic states are usually at the top of most rankings of the least corrupt states in the world, and the Nordic citizens have a higher degree of trust in the state and their politicians than do people in other Western countries.

Characteristic of countries with a strong welfare state tradition is that politicians, research communities and public managers will often pay tribute to the basic ideas of free healthcare for all and free access to education, eldercare, childcare and specialized social services. The manner in which public service delivery is institutionally interwoven with the universalistic welfare state has meant that there has always been a scepticism towards NPM and its market-based solutions, and this scepticism persists to this day. Prominent politicians in some of the Nordic countries, including Social Democrats Stefan Löfven in Sweden and Mette Frederiksen in Denmark, have therefore declared NPM 'dead'. While this may be an overstatement, it reflects a strong urge to defend welfare state values and practices and a sharp criticism of pure market-based solutions in those NWS-type countries.

MAIN GOVERNANCE IDEA: GOALS AND MEANS

This section begins with the main characteristics of NWS in one of the recent works of Pollitt and Bouckaert (2017: 121). In an attempt to explicate the notion of NWS, they divide the concept into its two constitutive parts:

'Weberian' elements:

- Reaffirmation of the role of the state as the main facilitator of solutions to new problems
- Reaffirmation of the role of representative democracies
- Reaffirmation of the role of administrative law
- Preservation of the idea of a public service with a distinctive status, culture and, to some extent, terms and conditions

'Neo' elements:

- From internal orientation to external orientation towards meeting citizens' needs
- Supplementation of the role of representative democracy with a range of devices for consultation and the direct representation of citizen's views
- Greater orientation to the achievement of results and a shift from ex-ante to ex-post control
- A professionalization of public service emphasizing the professional manager oriented towards the citizens

After having spelled out the core features of the NWS paradigm, Pollitt and Bouckaert describe how they initially conceived of NWS merely as a descriptive tool; they did not perceive it to be a concept unto itself. Many read it as a normative vision for public sector reform, however, and they are not themselves opposed to that line of thinking (Pollitt and Bouckaert 2017: 122). Consequently, the descriptive term of NWS has ascended to the status of a governance paradigm.

Pollitt and Bouckaert elaborate on how they see the need for improved public service that the state can help facilitate. After initially acknowledging that some critics might see their reference to core Weberian elements as a sign of 'being stuck in the past', they argue that a fresh look at public bureaucracy is needed – which is precisely what NWS offers. As such, they claim that Weberian bureaucracy, far from being demolished, is becoming modernized:

> Yet, looked at from the *outside*, what is striking – in comparison with the core NPM states – is how far the underlying assumption of a positive state, a distinctive public service, and a particular legal order survived as the foundations beneath the various national packages of modernizing reforms. What was going on, it seems, was the modernization of the Weberian tradition, not its outright rejection: a process of addition, not demolition (even

if some of the additions fitted on the foundations quite awkwardly). (Pollitt and Bouckaert 2017: 123)

The typical example of an NWS is a European state-centric welfare state that cares for its citizens, upholds the rule of law, and adheres to classical public sector values. Pollitt and Bouckaert mention both a 'northern variant' of the NWS that includes the Netherlands and the Nordic countries (although they only describe Sweden and Finland), and a central European variant that includes France and Germany. As stated below, many of these countries might be described in a rather rosy light that make them appear as Neo-Weberian States.

NWS promotes both a centralized and active state with professional bureaucratic responsibility in the classical Weberian sense and a stronger focus on performance management and improved service delivery. The NWS embrace of strategic management is compatible with the managerial aspect of NPM but less compatible with the marketization aspect.

Pollitt and Bouckaert draw on a wide variety of theories and approaches in order to arrive at their NWS model, including theories on representative democracy and participatory democracy, administrative law, theories on professionalization and civil service ethics, theories on performance management, theories on service delivery, and theories on citizen involvement and co-production. It is a tall order to include all of these theories (and many more) in a comprehensive concept of NWS. Obviously, the different analytical approaches do not all share the same theoretical foundations.

Pollitt and Bouckaert's overriding objective seems to be the realization of the vision of a modernized, efficient and citizen-friendly state that combines the classical features of both the administrative state and the welfare state with the more recent focus on performance management, professional public management and attention to citizen needs.

The concrete tools involve a range of 'devices' to involve citizens. The credo seems to be democratic dialogue, education and the mid-career training of public personnel as well as an extended performance management system. The NWS faith in government and professional public managers could also be combined with Mark Moore's notion of Public Value Management (PVM). In his original book, Moore (1995) wrote about how public managers are 'explorers' searching for the unexploited use of public value opportunities. In his later work, Moore (2013) has been interested in how to keep score of what kind of public value professional public managers have been creating. From here it is only a small step to the NWS recommendations regarding how public managers use performance management to produce value for the citizenry.

The classification of NWS is shown in Figure 5.1.

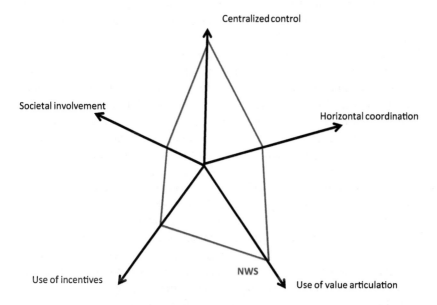

Figure 5.1   The NWS governance diamond

NWS scores high on the degree of centralized control and signals a return to centralized state rule. The governance paradigm recommends that central government initiates and implements top-down public management reforms. The argument is that centralized control can ensure uniform (and equal) welfare standards for all citizens across sectors and jurisdictions and renders it possible to exploit increasing returns to scale through joint service provision.

NWS scores medium on the degree of horizontal interagency coordination. Compared to PVM, DEG and NPG, it emphasizes vertical coordination rather than horizontal coordination. Consistent with the classical Weberian bureaucracy model, added value from specialization is prioritized relatively higher than holistic service provision and problem-solving. However, NWS recognizes the silo problem inherent to classical bureaucracy and tries to handle it through organizational mergers and amalgamations. Compared to NPM, there are lower barriers to horizontal coordination in terms of separate managerial responsibilities, separate budgets and intra-organizational competition. NWS has little explicit discussion of coordination between professional groups, but its embrace of NPM's managerialism leads it to recommend that hybrid managers emphasize their generalist leadership tasks over their professional background. In addition, it is seen as advantageous that hybrid managers are responsible for managing and coordinating multiple service institutions, since such distance provides overview and instils managerial integrity, protecting them from professional favouritism.

NWS scores high on the degree of value articulation. Reference to classical bureaucratic values is actively used to govern public agencies and employees. Representative democracy, rule of law and impartiality serve as a yardstick for good governance. NWS wants public managers to be the traditional guardians of the public interests, responsible translators of political goals, and oriented towards the needs of citizens. Although the balance between these three roles is secured through value articulation, it scores lower than PVM because NWS neither expects nor wants public managers to actively create and promote new public values.

NWS scores medium to high on the use of incentives in governance. Unlike professional rule, classical bureaucracy, NPM and PVM, NWS does not see the active use of incentives as contrasting with value articulation. Some types of incentives, such as encouraging goal attainment, praising high effort and promoting skilled employees, are thus seen as useful in terms of upholding the value foundation of the public sector. Compared to NPM, NWS prefers strategic management based on a combination of value articulation and non-pecuniary incentives to market mechanisms and pecuniary incentives. Along the lines of the Weberian bureaucratic ethos, career incentives are considered important, while NWS does not recommend competition and contingent rewards. The whole bureaucracy should serve the legitimate political rulers and obey the rule of law as a unified corps.

NWS scores low on the degree of societal involvement. Although NWS aims to be responsive towards the demands and needs of citizens, it does not promote the active involvement of societal actors outside the public sector in public governance. Co-creation and co-production are not in focus. Even though NWS praises 'friendly' and 'efficient' attitudes towards citizens, the full commitment and focus on getting citizens more actively engaged in public service production is less evident. While professional rule and NPM specifically recommend the involvement of professional associations and private contractors, NWS is only concerned with giving citizens opportunity to express their needs, wants and evaluations of public services.

EMPIRICAL RESULTS: EVIDENCE OF SPREAD AND PERFORMANCE

Christensen and Lægreid (2011, 2016), Hammerschmidt et al. (2016) and Pollitt and Bouckaert all document important developments in public management reforms throughout Europe. With an appendix presenting specific country profiles, Pollitt and Bouckaert show how France, Germany, the Netherlands, Sweden and Finland have developed their respective public management reforms and how the core features of these states resemble the NWS model of a modern, efficient and citizen-friendly state apparatus. Other descriptions of states that are characterized as NWS but are not in the Pollitt and Bouckaert book can be found elsewhere, including contributions on Denmark as a 'neo-Weberian state in a digital era' (Ejersbo and Greve 2016b).

Many indexes and reports have recently attempted to assess the quality of governance in different states. Bo Rothstein initiated the Quality of Government Institute, which measures quality in a number of countries. Compiled by the World Bank, the Worldwide Governance Indicators measure governance quality based on a huge number of different investigations and reports. The Sustainable Governance Indicators, developed by the Bertelsmann Foundation, use a variety of measures to assess how states are governed. The OECD Governance at a Glance reports provide an impressive number of indicators of good governance. There is also the OECD Better Life Index, which measures a variety of different healthy living measures for governments. Even though all of these indexes have emerged in recent years, Fukuyama (2013) has famously argued that we need an even better measurement of good governance. Fukuyama (2013: 350) defines governance as 'government's ability to make and enforce rules, and to deliver services, regardless of whether that government is democratic or not'.

Many of these indexes support the conclusions that NWS researchers have reached about how public management reforms have been implemented by central government agencies in countries sceptical to NPM and the kind of desirable results these reforms have produced. In 2018, the Transparency International Corruption Perceptions Index placed the Nordic countries high on the list of non-corrupt countries. Denmark came out on top as the least corrupt country in the world, followed by New Zealand, Finland, Singapore, Sweden, Switzerland, Norway, Netherlands, Canada and Luxembourg. It might be interesting to note that the NWS countries here find themselves together with a country like New Zealand, which is often referred to as being dominated by NPM.

The OECD (2018) Better Life Index is also interesting. Norway topped the 'life satisfaction' category, followed by Denmark, Switzerland, Iceland, Finland, Netherlands, Canada, New Zealand, Sweden and Australia. In the 'work–life balance' category, the Netherlands ranked first, followed by Denmark, France, Spain, Belgium, Norway, Sweden, Germany, Russia and Ireland. There are eleven categories in the OECD *Better Life Index*.

The Bertelsmann Foundation Sustainable Governance Indicators measure the key categories of policy performance, democracy and governance (with sub-categories) (Bertelsmann Stiftung 2019). In the 2018 survey, Sweden came out on top of the 'quality of democracy' category, followed by Finland, Norway, Denmark, Germany, Switzerland, New Zealand, Estonia, Ireland and Lithuania. The 'governance' category includes a sub-category called 'executive capacity', which consists of strategic capacity, inter-ministerial coordination, evidence-based instruments, societal consultation, policy communication, implementation, adaptability and a sub-category entitled 'executive accountability', which consists of citizens' participation competence, legislative actors' resources, media, parties and interest associations. Sweden ranked first in this 'Governance' category, followed by Denmark, Norway, Finland, New Zealand, Luxembourg, Canada, Germany, the UK and Australia. As can be seen, many of the same countries, many with NWS-features, occupy the top positions in the various indexes measuring good governance.

The large-scale COCOPS research project (Coordination for Cohesion in the Public Sector of the Future), supported by the EU's FP7 research programme, aimed at tracking the transformation of the public sectors in Europe. One of the sub-projects focused on public management reform developments. A European-wide survey including 19 states drew responses from 7077 professional public managers in central government. From this examination of public management reform developments, at least two publications are relevant to the assessment of NWS. Hammerschmidt et al.'s (2016) *Public Administration Reforms in Europe: The View from the Top* picks up the mantle from Pollitt and Bouckaert's seminal work. Hammerschmidt and his colleagues analyse how a variety of primarily NPM-related governance tools have been implemented in European states. They note how the focus has increased over the years on outcomes and transparency across European states, while cut-back management has also become prevalent in a number of countries (e.g. the Netherlands, Ireland and the UK) since the 2007 financial crisis. While some states (e.g. Estonia, the Netherlands, Norway) remain under the influence of NPM and especially the attempt to strengthen performance management, other states (e.g. Austria, France, Germany, Spain, Hungary) are characterized by a more legalistic approach to public administration that tends to move them away from NPM and towards NWS.

Nordic Administrative Reforms (Greve et al. 2016) is a book based on the same COCOPS survey but focussing specifically on the five Nordic countries. Here, the conclusion is that Nordic public administrations are characterized by being pragmatic and responsible modernizers, where the focus is less on market competition and more on implementing performance management systems and emphasizing citizen involvement (especially Sweden and Norway). The Nordic states have enhanced their focus on performance management while still retaining their adherence to classical Weberian notions of representative democracy, administrative law and transparency. Taken together, the COCOPS examination of the Nordic states appears to reinforce the NWS model based on the analysis of national reform initiatives. This might also relate to the fact that the COCOPS survey focused on central government and not on the decentralized welfare states in the local governments. The aspects of citizen participation and possibly market-based governance could have come out rather differently, because the local municipalities, which are responsible for most of the service delivery to the citizens, enjoy considerable autonomy and might oppose implementing the public sector reforms recommended by central government.

Judging the wider reform implications in the European states in the COCOPS survey, Andrews et al. (2016) painted a picture of NWS simultaneously losing ground and maintaining its strength:

Broadly speaking, the findings presented in this book [*Public Administrations Reforms in Europe: The View from the Top*, Hammerschmid et al. 2016] suggest that multiple administrative reforms did indeed occur across Europe between 2008–2013, but they were largely of the Neo-Weberian/NPG form, especially reforms centered on improvements in transparency, collaboration and e-government [note: the COCOPS survey did not discuss DEG as a separate model] … Likewise, the survey respondents point towards the introduction of multiple management instruments, especially performance appraisal, strategic planning and management by objectives, which have become a kind of standard practice in European central governments. As expected, we see clear country differences between management 'champions' such as the UK, Estonia, Norway and the Netherlands, and more legalistic and traditional public administrations such as in Austria, France, Germany and Spain. These findings suggest that in many respects the Weberian state may now be in decline due to the dominance of newer reform ideas. On the other hand, many results of the survey suggest that its main ideas are still deeply embedded in several European countries. (Andrews et al. 2016: 274)

The COCOPS survey found some differences between the experiences in the southern and northern parts of Europe in terms of the implementation and results of the reforms. While the NPM reforms certainly have made their headway into the public sector in Europe, many of the classical Weberian elements as well as the Neo-Weberian features, such as strategic planning and centralized management by objectives, are key features in the contemporary public sector. So while the COCOPS survey is one of the most comprehensive data sets thus far, work remains to be done to determine the outcome of reforms.

In 2018, the European Commission prepared another comprehensive examination of the state of the art of public sector administrations in the EU28. The synthesis report came out in March 2018 and is entitled *A Comparative Overview of Public Administration Characteristics and Performance in EU28*. In an overall assessment of the public administration capacity and performance of the EU member states, Denmark comes out on top followed by Finland, Sweden, the Netherlands, the UK, Estonia, Austria, Ireland, Luxembourg and Germany (European Commission 2018: 58, graph 40). Hence, the four top countries all qualify as NWS countries. The report also concludes that 'the overall state system, history and current politics' play a key role in shaping particular reforms (European Commission, 2018: 57). Central bureaucratic state agencies therefore seem to remain in control in relation to public sector reform.

DEBATE AND DILEMMAS

How can the arrival of the NWS public governance paradigm be explained? There is currently a general shift towards 'the return of the state' in the debate on public management reform. Calls for a return of the state are a common feature in both the literature on public administration and, more specifically, the literature on state theory. In the late 1960s and early 1970s, North American public administration researchers published *The Blacksburg Manifesto*, which was supposed to herald a New Public Administration focusing on the legitimacy of professional public managers. Political scientist Theda Skocpol and her colleagues (Evans et al. 1985) famously argued to 'bring the state back in' in the 1980s, Bob Jessop and colleagues aimed at 'putting states in their place' in the 1990s (e.g. Jessop 1990), and John Campbell and John Hall (2015) have reported on *The World of States* in their recent book. Public management scholar Brinton Milward and his colleagues (2016) recently published an article asking 'Is public management neglecting the state?' The latest addition comes from Fukuyama (2013: 347), who asserts in an essay entitled 'What is Governance?' in the journal *Governance* that 'the state, that is the functioning of executive branches and their bureaucracies, has received relatively little attention in contemporary political science'. While this claim might be contested by public administration scholars and state theorists, it bears witness to the growing interest in the role of the state in public governance and, thus, to ideas informing NWS.

One of the criticisms of the ideas associated with NWS is grounded in Weber's theory of bureaucracy. In the research on Weber's model of bureaucracy, there is an established strand of research on Neo-Weberian State Theory focussing on the impact of Weber's notion of bureaucracy for modern state thinking (du Gay 2009a), but it does not aim to present a model for public sector reform (Byrkjeflot et al. 2018). From this perspective, NWS appears to present a superficial characterization of a bureaucratic governance model that fails to do justice to Weber's complex thinking and argumentation as well as failing to appreciate the role of administrative statesmanship in shaping public governance and administration (du Gay 2000, 2005). It could also be added that the positive evaluation of bureaucracy in NWS overlooks Weber's critical description of bureaucracy as an 'iron cage'.

Another criticism is that many states have now been influenced by both the marketization and managerialism ascribed to NPM while simultaneously introducing the elements of network governance and co-creation associated with NPG, meaning that few states can be characterized as 'pure NWS' states (Byrkjeflot et al. 2018).

A third criticism is that NWS has become too much of a middle-of-the-road-argument, attempting to position itself as a pragmatic alternative to the NPM markets and managerialism and the NPG networks and co-creation processes. In a rather eclectic gesture, it tries to build parts of both governance paradigms into the NWS framework in order to produce the image of a more effective and friendlier state.

Instead of leaving all of the ground to NPM and its exclusive focus on markets and managers, the NWS concept seemed to arrive at a particularly interesting time, when the popularity of NPM was fading, and where there was a variety of (mostly confused) calls for a post-NPM development. Perhaps it was inevitable that someone should come up with an alternative concept that reformulated the role of the state in the new millennium. The NWS paradigm has provided such a reformulation.

A recurring critique about NWS as a public governance paradigm is how the lack of theoretical precision renders application in concrete analysis difficult. The state is analysed as possessing a sophisticated and well-developed performance management system that satisfies politicians because it makes them govern with greater precision while also enabling a cadre of professional public managers with measurement tools and review reports to monitor the attempt to provide services customized to the needs of individual citizens. The question then becomes whether performance management will make way for a subsequent contracting out of services to private providers who are accustomed to operating based on specific performance indicators, albeit more difficult to govern and hold to account. Alternatively, the development of a coherent and responsible performance management system may allow politicians to carry out their constitutional duty of being far-sighted policymakers who enable professional public managers to implement the higher purposes of the state. As such, we may ask whether performance management can be a feature of both NPM and NWS. To a point, it seems as though both NPM and NWS build on well-developed performance systems. This may be a problem for analytical rigour, since we cannot really distinguish between the two governance paradigms on this point.

The recent debate on the role of the state spurred by NWS has led to a new and interesting focus on 'state-crafting'. Pollitt (2016b) noted the tendency to lose sight of 'the big picture' in public management reforms because administrative and scholarly attention has become focused on the micro-issues within public sector organizations and their relation to the end-users. Pollitt called attention to external megatrends (fiscal austerity, technological change, climate change) as something of which public management reform scholars should be aware, but also noted the difficulties in studying these external megatrends and their consequences for public sector organizations (Pollitt 2016b: 134).

The relevance of megatrends and the need for a new or altered role for the state has possibly been promoted most forcefully within the public administration research community by Alasdair Roberts (2017). Roberts claims that the public administration scholarly community should revisit the active role of the state and that external megatrends and the increasingly globalized world mean that public administration should once again focus on macro-questions as a supplement to the internal organizational issues in individual public sector organizations. Roberts calls for more 'state-crafting' studies and even started a website of that name. In one of his recent books, Roberts (2017) analyses *Four Crises of American Democracy*, arguing that democracies are periodically under threat but that states and the democratic citizenry seem to pull through and survive every time. Although public management reform efforts might initially be slow and existing institutions make the introduction of new governance paradigms difficult, it is nevertheless possible when necessary. Hence, Roberts (2017: 185) contends that 'change, not stasis, is the reality of American government'.

In a more recent book, Roberts (2018) asks whether government can do anything right. He answers in the affirmative and puts faith in the role of government and its capacity to see the big picture. Roberts thus tries to remind the research community and administrative practitioners about the basic strategic functions of government.

Roberts further outlines the office holders' responsibilities for developing the state:

> The job of holding a state together is especially difficult because the conditions of governance are constantly changing. Leaders craft a certain strategy for advancing the national interest and develop a level of confidence about their mastery of the world around them. But then the world is unexpectedly altered. We have already noted some of the dimensions of changeability: demography, technology, patterns of commerce and finance, the structure of international politics and climate. When conditions change, governance strategies have to be reconsidered and laws and institutions amended. (Roberts 2018: 103)

Roberts has aimed to draw out the practical consequences of his argument. After his long stint as editor of the journal *Governance*, he is now launching a new teaching course entitled 'Strategies for governing' and has been lecturing on state-crafting and governing strategies. He makes frequent media appearances in which he advocates for a macro-oriented view of public administration and public management reform. In a similar vein, Paul 't Hart and an international group of colleagues have embarked on a new research agenda for 'successful public governance' and launched a book series on that topic.

Among the scholars who can relate to the new macroscopic state-crafting agenda is Donald F. Kettl, who has written several books analysing the various trends in public management reform and the role of government herein. In one his most recent books, Kettl (2016: 182) argues that governments face various scenarios for the future of governing: weakened government, muscle-bound government, empowered government and leveraged government. Among the common denominators across these possible futures is the need to rely on data and evidence and the need to invest in competence and capacity for government action. This conclusion is very much in line with Pollitt and Bouckaert's approach to public management reform and their emphasis on NWS.

That we all live in turbulent times dominated by mega-change has become part of the conventional wisdom in public administration literature (West 2016; Ansell et al. 2017), and there is also agreement that institutions, professional public managers and politicians need to adapt government institutions and practices to these changes. One of the key questions for the next couple of years is how state institutions can change and how well they can be adapted. NWS offers one way to conceptualize and discuss the role of the state in the current reform period.

This chapter has analysed the concept of the Neo-Weberian State model as a public governance paradigm. The NWS concept began with Pollitt and Bouckaert's introduction of the term in their book entitled *Public Management Reform*, which examined public administration reform in a comparative perspective. The concept describes how modern bureaucracies aim to reform themselves by emphasizing the role of professional public managers, the need for efficient governance, and the provision of citizen-friendly service delivery. It was first meant to characterize the lukewarm reception of NPM in north-western European democracies with stable, well-managed bureaucracies and comprehensive public welfare systems, but it has since developed into a positive vision for the modernization of bureaucratic state systems. NWS has both 'Weberian' and 'neo' elements that, when combined, present an alternative to NPM, albeit with certain overlaps. There has been considerable debate as to whether the term 'Weberian' is appropriate or if it signals a past era, but NWS combines Weberian values and ideas with a new emphasis on performance management and efficient service delivery to citizens. The idea of focusing more on the role of the state in contrast to NPM and its market-based governance has been taken up by a number of other researchers. Among the researchers focussing on the state's role are Tom Christensen and Per Lægreid on the continuing relevance of welfare states; Francis Fukuyama on what factors constitute governance; Donald F. Kettl on the role of the state in a situation where networks exist; and Alasdair Roberts, who is currently exploring the concept of 'strategies for governing' and a return to a macro-perspective on public administration.

6.   Digital Era Governance

BACKGROUND

Digital Era Governance (DEG) is a new governance paradigm that focuses on how digital solutions and technologies are transforming public governance in a profound and systematic manner. It explores how digitalization changes the way the public sector works and how bureaucracy relates to citizens. Instead of treating digitalization as just another variable in the big public sector equation, DEG claims that digital solutions will change the public sector in much the same way they have changed other areas, such as private business and social life, including the mass media, retail industry, the communications industry and social media.

DEG was launched as a public governance paradigm by Patrick Dunleavy and Helen Margetts. It focuses on the increasing importance of the digitalization of public services and draws our attention to the profound dynamics of reform and change that are triggered by digitalization. Three key publications were paramount in establishing DEG as a public governance paradigm: the co-authored book *Digital Era Governance* (Dunleavy et al. 2006a), and an accompanying journal article with the catchy title 'New Public Management is Dead – Long Live Digital Era Governance' (Dunleavy et al. 2006b) and an article revising the governance paradigm in lieu of new empirical developments entitled 'The Second Wave of Digital Era Governance: A Quasi-Paradigm for Government on the Web' (Margetts and Dunleavy 2013). In relation to the latter publication's normative recommendation that governments should step up their interest and engagement in the digitalization of public services, the intriguing question becomes whether digitalization is a means to accomplish new goals or a goal unto itself.

The empirical background of the emergence of DEG is the astonishing technological development that the world has witnessed in recent decades wherein new digital solutions have been introduced at an unprecedented pace. Technological change and the digitalization of public and private life constitute one of the mega-changes that authors such as Darrell West (2016) from the Brookings Institution and many more with him have conjured up in recent years. Some observers also talk about digitalization as the 'fourth industrial revolution' (Schwab 2017), and the word 'disruption' seems to be on everybody's lips, two decades into the new millennium. The impressive technological development that we are witnessing springs in many ways from inventions in the private sector, although the public sector is also regarded as a facilitator and incubator of technological development due to its massive investments in research and development. A well-known observation in recent years has been that the US government is behind many technological innovations, including those supporting the iPhone and GPS systems, which private companies ultimately exploit commercially (Mazzucato 2013). In reality, the push for technological change is often produced by a partnership or a mix of actors from the public and private sectors, as anyone who has read the story about the birth of the internet will appreciate (Hafner and Lyon 1996).

Digital solutions have obviously been a feature in public administration for a long time, often under the guise of 'e-government' or 'ICT in government'. This literature is well-known in the public administration community, and there has always been a specialized group of researchers following digital developments (Danziger and Andersen 2002; Homburg 2008; Henriksen and Rukonova 2011; Barbosa et al. 2013; Lips 2019). For several decades, digitalization has been seen as an integral part of public management reform developments (Pollitt and Bouckaert 2017).

The novel elements in Dunleavy and Margetts' approach is the argument that digitalization will fundamentally change how the public sector operates. Hence, Dunleavy and Margetts foreshadowed the current talk of 'disruption' when they first described the radical changes resulting from digitalization.

The conceptualization of DEG as a governance paradigm was a two-step process. The first step was taken with the publication of *Digital Era Governance* (Dunleavy et al. 2006a), which was based on detailed studies of the digitalization of public services in seven countries. Dunleavy, Margetts and their associates identified three core elements of DEG:

1. 'Reintegration', meaning that public sector operations will become reintegrated through digital solutions after years of organizational fragmentation under NPM.
2. 'Needs-based holism', meaning that it will now become possible to design service delivery around citizens' individual needs to a much greater degree than previously. Because of all of the available and

retrievable data, services can be designed and communicated with much more precision to suit the needs of individual citizens.

3. 'Digitalization', meaning that services that were previously analogue will now become digital, and new digital services will become available due to the new digital opportunities. Service solutions can also be adapted in real time.

The second step in the development of DEG was when Dunleavy and Margetts presented their revised version in 2013. When the DEG concept was first presented, social media and big data had not yet been developed in the same way as they existed eight years later. Dunleavy and Margetts therefore had to create an updated version of DEG that took notice of all of the recent developments in the digitalization of public services. In the 'second wave of DEG', the focus of DEG's 'reintegration' dimension was on the use of big data through the establishment of giant data warehouses and on load-shedding, where governments outsourced the development and operation of public ICT systems to large, private ICT companies. An example from Denmark was the outsourcing of routine administrative tasks from 98 local governments to one single contractor – *Udbetaling Danmark*, a private entity on contract with the Danish state – which processes all of the social benefits payments for the entire country.

Social media has changed how people communicate with each other in their private lives, but it has also affected how public sector organizations communicate with citizens. The contact between public sector organizations and citizens has largely become digitalized, and sending an old-fashioned letter or trying to reach a public sector organization by phone has become difficult in some instances. As anyone who has watched Ken Loach's movie, *I, Daniel Blake*, can attest, digital challenges confront ordinary citizens. Loach's movie tells the story of an elderly, unemployed man, who tries to get in contact with the social services but is constantly told that he needs to communicate via the internet. The advent of big data also facilitated the mash-up of data, and citizens and companies can utilize data to make their own apps. The main point made by Dunleavy and Margetts is that digitalization has irrevocably changed how public services are delivered and that a special governance paradigm – DEG – is required to fully grasp the changes.

Because Dunleavy and Margetts presented DEG in stark contrast to NPM, the impact on the academic community was possibly stronger than if the concept had been launched in isolation. People were craving alternatives to NPM, and Dunleavy and Margetts presented their alternative argument in favour of digital governance in a rather forceful manner. At the beginning of their 2013 article, Dunleavy and Margetts clearly marked their distance from NPM:

> The erstwhile quasi-paradigm of NPM marginalized technological change in favour of managerialist emphasis on organizational arrangements and strong corporate leadership. NPM stressed a trinity of macro-themes: disaggregation (chunking up government hierarchies into smaller organizations), competition (especially with private sector contractors but also in internal quasi-markets within government), and incentivatization (built on pecuniary motivations instead of professionalism) ... However, NPM always prioritized managerialist elements and assigned little intellectual significance to digital developments. (Margetts and Dunleavy 2013: 2)

Clearly, NPM is seen as the problem that DEG can help remedy.

SOURCES OF INSPIRATION, THEORETICAL POSITIONS AND EXEMPLARY COUNTRIES

As a concept, DEG has dominated much of the recent writings on digitalization in the academic community. Computers, digitalization and technological change have been with us for some time, and academics have often commented on the problems and challenges associated with living in an age of disruptive change. A useful illustration of this is found in Donald Schön's (1973) far-sighted book from the 1970s, *Beyond the Stable State*:

> The most powerful of the new technologies have been 'meta' technologies. Their effect has been to facilitate the processes of technological innovation and diffusion and thereby to increase the society's leverage on technological change itself ... The invention of the organization of invention, first brought to visibility in the laboratory of Thomas Edison, has come into good currency with the spread of the large-scale industrial and government research laboratory. The technology of the computer carries with it potentials for the management of technological innovation and diffusion which have only begun to be tapped. (Schön 1973: 26)

These are wise words indeed about how computer technology would eventually go on to change the world. Since Schön was preoccupied with organizational theory, he also reflected on what the new technologies would do for intra-organizational communications:

> In this sense, too, electronic technology stimulates new forms of organization based on the networks and grids of electronic devices, characterized by complex matrices of relationships rather than by simple lines of authority, and

by the fact that information is available simultaneously at the crucial nodes of decision. (Schön 1973: 27)

One of the key developments in digitalization has been the emergence of so-called 'big data'. In their book entitled *Big Data*, Viktor Mayer-Schönberger and Kenneth Cuckier (2013) describe how the production and distribution of huge amounts of data will profoundly transform how society, including the public sector, will operate.

Big data means that large-scale data collection and processing are available to organizations. It is essentially about doing things on a larger scale and providing new insights by identifying emerging patterns in big data sets. The most astonishing proposition that has been advanced is that the focus on theory-building and causation before data collection and data analysis appears to be unnecessary: Just look at the data and ask what it shows rather than why it shows it (Mayer-Schönberger and Cuckier 2013: 6–7).

Flyverbom and Madsen (2015) distinguish between the production, structuring, distribution and visualization of data. The debate on the diffusion, practice and consequences of using big data is raging in many academic disciplines (Constantiou and Kallinikos 2015; Flyverbom et al. 2017; Mergel et al. 2017). There are now also specialized journals devoted to big data, including *Big Data & Society*.

The advent of big data has been a game-changer for government. Until recently, government has been the primary collector and organizer of data based on pre-designed formats that citizens and companies are required to fill out. In the era of big data, data is simply being produced and stored without regard for particular pre-designed government formats. Governments also find that they rely on search tools such as Google and use social media platforms like Facebook and Twitter when communicating with citizens and society. This means that governments are no longer sovereign in terms of deciding what kind of information should be collected for public purposes and how it should be structured and ordered.

Another major driver of digital change is the rise of social media, which Dunleavy and Margetts examined in their 2013 contribution and which has since exerted a major influence on how governments communicate and relate to citizens and social and political actors in civil society. Mergel and Bretschneider (2013) were some of the first in the field of public administration to study how governments adapted to the use of social media in their daily practice and their strategic communications with citizens and other actors. Recent studies have investigated the use of social media by governments in general and by public managers in particular (Mergel 2016; Wukich and Mergel 2016). Social media policy is often handled at the level of the individual organization, meaning that the general impression of how governments use social media in their day-to-day operations can be very confusing from an external perspective. Presidents, prime ministers and elected politicians in general have obviously become highly adept in using social media, often as their primary means of communication (US President Donald Trump's infamous Twitter account offers a case in point).

That which there seems to be less evidence for – but a huge appetite for more knowledge about – is how public organizations use social media in their everyday bureaucratic routines and how the relationship between citizens and government changes when citizens circumvent the formal channels of communication and take to filing requests or complaints regarding public services via Facebook. There can be little doubt that communication via social media will become a major topic for future studies in public administration, as it is transforming the arena and tone of public debate and public–private interaction.

As with the general development in the previous studies of 'e-government' and 'ICT in government', DEG draws on different well-known theoretical components from political science, public administration, public policy, organization studies and so forth. Notwithstanding, with DEG there has been an attempt to advance an improved and dedicated theoretical framework for studying the digitalization of public governance. From a governance paradigm perspective, the main argument is that digitalization is not a peripheral component that is optional for governments to either incorporate or reject; rather, it has become a core strategy, and perhaps even a vehicle for public administration reforms, and therefore requires in-depth scrutiny by both scholars and policymakers. Digitalization is therefore argued to be unstoppable, as digital public services are constantly proliferating and new technological advances are made at a constant rate by global companies such as Google, Microsoft and Facebook. There is no way for governments to opt out of the digital development or to ignore new initiatives from the big tech companies. The strategic use of digital technologies to develop and improve the public sector, and thus DEG as a governance paradigm, is here to stay and will only grow more important in the future.

The list of leading countries that have adopted digital governance includes a large number of OECD countries. There is now an abundance of ranking lists and league tables demonstrating how governments have coped with and introduced digital governance and showing which states are leaders and laggards. The states usually referred to as leaders in digital service provision include the Nordics (Denmark, Sweden, Norway, Iceland, Finland), Australia, Estonia, the Netherlands, New Zealand, the UK and the USA.

One highly reliable ranking is the Digital Economy and Society Index published by the EU. This composite index measures a number of digital services in both the public and private sectors. It shows how Denmark leads the way together with Sweden, Finland, the Netherlands and Luxembourg. The index measures connectivity, human capital, internet service use, the integration of digital technology and digital public services. The European Commission (2017) recently published a paper in connection with the celebration of its 50-year anniversary in which it sketched out the road for states wanting to improve their digital services:

> Complete the Digital Single Market, invest in data economy infrastructure, invest in connectivity, step up the digitalization of industry, support start-ups to scale up, implement education reform and reskilling to enable people to adapt to change, ensure high levels of data protection and cyber security to promote trust and to protect assets, launch common European digital projects which cannot be implemented by individual countries on their own.

The UN presented their *E-Government Survey 2018* in July 2018 (United Nations 2018). The report examines several areas of digitalization: mobilizing e-government to build resilient societies, e-government initiatives for leaving no one behind, e-resilience through e-government, global and regional development in e-government, improving cities' resilience and sustainability through e-government, and government platforms and artificial intelligence. The UN reports demonstrate how the digitalization of public governance has become a global agenda and is not merely a North American and European phenomenon. As such, the UN ranking of states in 2018 shows that the 'leading countries in e-government development' were Denmark followed by Australia, South Korea, the UK and Sweden (United Nations 2018: 89).

The European Commission (2018) has published a report entitled *A Comparative Overview of Public Administration Characteristics in EU28*, which focuses on seven indicators of digitalization in government. The leading countries here are Austria, Estonia, Denmark, Finland, the Netherlands and Sweden (European Commission 2018: 48).

In summary, digitalization has become a pervasive feature of a modern public administration, and there is a group of states that is consistently being viewed as front-runner countries in designing and implementing new digital solutions and services for citizens.

MAIN GOVERNANCE IDEA: GOALS AND MEANS

The main idea of DEG as a governance paradigm is that digitalization is the driving force behind changes in public governance and administration and has the capacity to both enhance coherence and produce better public outcomes. As mentioned above, Dunleavy and Margetts identified three key elements in DEG, which define it in terms of a governance paradigm for the public sector:

- Reintegration
- Needs-based holism
- Digital changes

In the first wave of DEG, *reintegration* involved 'creating new central government processes to do things once instead of many times' and 'squeezing process costs and using shared services to drive out NPM's duplicate organizational hierarchies'. *Needs-based holism* involved the 'end-to-end redesign of services from a client perspective', and the creation of 'agile and resilient government structures that can respond in real time to problems instead of catching up on them after long time lags'. *Digital changes* meant 'the adaption of the public sector to *completely* embrace and embed electronic delivery at the heart of the government business model, wherever possible' and included the ambition to 'digitalize interactions with citizens and businesses'.

In the second wave from 2006 and until 2013, *reintegration* includes the 'use of big data', 'central government disengagement and load-shedding', 'single tax and benefits systems (using real-time data)', and 'reintegrative outsourcing'. *Needs-based holism* includes 'integrated-service stops at central/federal level', 'co-production of services', 'social security systems moving online' and 'citizen online testimonials/evaluations substituting central regulation'. *Digital changes* include the creation of 'government clouds', 'free storage/comprehensive data retention' and 'freeing public information for reuse, mash-ups etc. (open data initiatives)'.

Reintegration provides possibilities for new centralized and holistic solutions across the public sector by introducing a particular ICT system, such as a personal identification programme like the Danish 'NEM-ID' system, which allows citizens to log on to government services using a single log-on. The Danish single log-on solution is also available to many private sector services, including home banking. Likewise, there are many shared service solutions in operation in different public service areas. *Needs-based holism* often allows citizens to tailor their own service profile and lets the government provide an even more precise type of service delivery because the government has access to data in real time and pulls together data from a broad range of public agencies. *Digital changes* continue to develop in the public and private sectors, and they are changing how citizens interact with government. In healthcare, many hospitals are using new coherent digital platforms that promise improved efficiency and allow for new forms of data exchange between ICT systems.

New opportunities open up as governments no longer depend on semi-annual or quarterly auditing reports to be able to respond to a problem, as they can now access real-time data to address current challenges. Employment policy is likely to be one of the most digitalized policy areas, where most of the processing of employment data and the communications with job-seekers occur through digital channels. Some countries, such as Denmark, have personal identification numbers for their citizens, which enable cross-sector and inter-agency data integration with a high level of data security.

Figure 6.1 presents the classification of DEG in the governance diamond. As indicated above, the many uses of digitalization make it difficult to classify DEG on the five axes. Digitalization can be both a means and an end unto itself, and DEG as a governance paradigm primarily draws on principles linked to digitalization as an end unto itself. The problem with the categorization arises if, for example, centralization promotes digitalization under some circumstances and hinders it in other contexts.

DEG scores medium to high on the degree of centralized control. On the one hand, digital solutions are seen as a key driver for promoting and monitoring the implementation of centralized decisions and service standards from the top down. They create transparency and enable constant feedback to central decision-makers. DEG calls for the re-integration of services to allow for more centralized digital solutions to be implemented. Conversely, DEG also supports decentralized, inter-agency data sharing, and centralization is not a goal unto itself, as is the case in classical bureaucracy and NWS.

DEG scores high on the degree of horizontal coordination. Digital solutions enable public agencies to pull information from many different organizational units together to draw a holistic picture of a citizen's needs. They also provide a tool for the coordination of service provision between agencies if the digital channel is not blocked by data regulations. Still, in comparison, NPG more actively promotes the formation of networks for horizontal coordination based on both knowledge sharing and joint action.

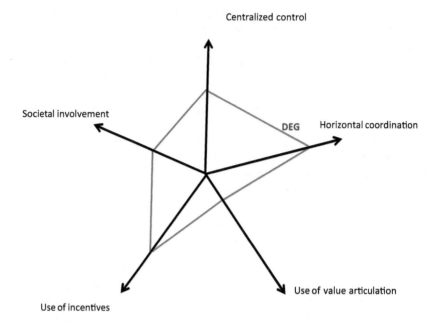

Figure 6.1   The DEG governance diamond

DEG scores low on the use of value articulation. It is based on values of efficiency, effectiveness and transparency, but it does not use values as a primary driver in the governance paradigm and therefore scores low on the third axis. Still, compared to NPM, value articulation as a governance mechanism is not in contrast with DEG's main governance principles. Digitalization is therefore increasingly accompanied by articulated data ethics.[1]

DEG scores medium to high on the degree of use of incentives. It recommends using classical governing and regulation measures to instruct citizens, public employees and all types of organizations to use all of the available digital tools (hence, the expression 'digitalization by default'), but an elaborate use of incentives is neither a part of the governance paradigm nor seen in organizations with strong emphasis on DEG.

DEG scores low to medium on the degree of societal involvement. Again, DEG is ambiguous. On the one hand, it can be truly encompassing and involving of citizens as they can interact digitally and through

---

[1]   See the EU's General Data Protection Regulation, https://gdpr.eu.

social media with politicians and bureaucrats. DEG is forging links to different economic and societal sectors and reaches out to many citizens. Conversely, digital involvement is often a thin form of participation compared to face-to-face interaction in collaborative networks (Nabatchi and Leighninger 2015).

EMPIRICAL RESULTS

The empirical results of DEG are primarily related to the documentation reported above, which demonstrates the pervasive use of digital services in the public sector throughout most of the world. Compared to ten (or more) years ago, a wide range of public services is now delivered online or is supported by digital solutions (as documented in the UN report from 2018 and the websites of individual countries). Digitalization is seen in public services in healthcare, police operations, transport solutions, social security and many other types of services. There is little doubt that digital services have become an essential element in government operations and in the daily lives of millions of citizens worldwide. It is therefore relevant to examine a number of countries to see how digitalization has changed how their public sector operates.

Academic studies of DEG and the digitalization of public services generally seem to have moved beyond the wider descriptions of how the process by which states uptake digital services is progressing. These studies now include different sub-topics and empirical evaluations of how highly specialized digital solutions are implemented. As such, there is a growing literature on how governments use big data and large public data systems and what this usage means for our lives as citizens. There is also a growing literature on the nature of social media in the field of public administration and on how new disruptive technologies, such as Block-chain, Artificial Intelligence and the use of robotics, are changing how work is carried out by public sector employees. There are also new studies on the nature of digital solutions in big public management reforms, such as the Affordable Care Act in the USA, where the crucial website crashed but was mended by hi-tech wizards who proceeded to develop other digitalized government solutions (Eggers 2016). Finally, there is an important literature on cybersecurity and the need for data protection in lieu of discussions on the dark side of the internet (see more below).

The role of social media has been explored recently in the book *Political Turbulence: How Social Media Shape Collective Action* by Margetts et al. (2017). Here, they explore how the mobilization of different causes via social media is unpredictable, unstable and unsustainable, and they demonstrate how the new and merging forms of political pluralism are more chaotic and turbulent. Mergel (2017) has argued that social media data, if properly harvested by researchers, can lead to new insights into how public sector organizations relate to their environment. Having studied social media practices in the USA, he concluded that public sector organizations using social media need to ensure strategic alignment with key points in their overall strategy and secure routinization of social media practices in order to enhance efficiency and impact (Mergel 2016).

Clarke and Margetts (2014) discuss the role of big data and examine how it may bring citizens and governments closer together. Here, they argue that since governments have loads of data about citizens, big data might offer a way of improving the relationships between public managers and citizens. Poel et al. (2018) have investigated what happened to the great expectations for big data in public policymaking and asked whether any real progress has been achieved. They conclude that it is still early days and that big data does not seem be used much in implementation and evaluation processes, but more in foresight, agenda-setting and interim performance monitoring. Big data relevant to public sector organizations is seen as a combination of administrative data collected the usual way and large-scale data sets created by multiple sensors and computer networks and by individuals as they use the internet.

There has been considerable growth in the studies on DEG and digitalization, and the field has seen the formation of new journals and new institutes dedicated to the study of digitalization, such as Oxford University's Oxford Internet Institute.[2] The institute's research areas provide a good indication of how widespread the research on digitalization has become: digital economies, information geography and inequality, digital politics and government, education, digital life and wellbeing, ethics and philosophy of information, digital knowledge and culture, information governance and technology and social data science.

DEBATE AND DILEMMAS

There are several ongoing debates concerning the impact of DEG. First, there is a debate about the latest development in digital services regarding the 'dark side' of digitalization, including the fear of the loss of privacy, the dominance of big multinational tech companies and the

---

[2] https://www.oii.ox.ac.uk.

threat of cyberattacks. Second, there is debate between scholars from the other governance paradigms about how DEG fits into the overall picture. Let us consider these two debates in turn.

Since the Snowden revelations regarding the surveillance programmes and techniques used by the National Security Agency in the USA, the debate about the added value of digital communications and services has raged on. Snowden showed the world what the surveillance techniques that use information from the internet and the public sector are doing to the lives of ordinary citizens, other states and private businesses. His revelations triggered an uproar around the world. As it turns out, the free exchange of information between all kinds of actors, including private citizens, not only led to an information-rich society where news and updates were shared among many users, it also enabled state agencies in the field of national security to look into a great amount of detailed and sensitive information about how citizens go about their daily lives, thus undermining the civil right to privacy.

The big multinational tech companies have also been the target of increasing criticism. Once hailed as cool places to work and the champions of the new information society, big tech companies are increasingly being portrayed as ever more dominant market actors that shun competition, evade tax payments and possess personal information about citizens that they exploit commercially to the fullest. Public regulators are trying to keep up with the big tech companies, and the European Commission (not least European Commissioner Margrethe Vestager) has been very active in trying to regulate and break up the big tech companies and force them to pay taxes. In July 2018, a record fine of USD 5 billion was issued to Google because the European Commission thinks Google is distorting competition in the smartphone market.

The cybersecurity issue has also risen to the top of the agenda for states and businesses as the threat of cyberattacks and cyberwarfare has become increasingly real. Especially the alleged 'troll factories', based out of states such as Russia, seem to cause deep concern among many NATO members. Private citizens can also be hit by the consequences of breaches in cybersecurity, including exposure to identity theft. The EU has a strategy for improving cybersecurity, and individual states are developing their own cybersecurity strategies, as the attacks only seem to be getting worse. In Denmark, for example, the government published a Danish Cyber and Information Strategy in 2018 (Danish Government 2018).

For the public sector, this all means that new negative challenges must be addressed, which tends to take us beyond the initial optimism that accompanied the first decades of digital services to citizens. Politicians and public managers alike spend considerable time and energy on how to use digital services to improve public services, but they also worry about and prepare for what can go wrong in the future and how the digital infrastructure can be secured and protected against known and unknown threats.

While we have presented DEG as an independent public governance paradigm, there is disagreement on this point among scholars supporting different governance paradigms. Margetts and Dunleavy (2013) claim that DEG is bound to expand in the future due to the empirical developments in digitalization. Hence, we must 'expect continuing rapid, disruptive changes in information technologies to underpin a reorganization drive in the forefront counties to greater use of risk-based approaches, increased capital intensification in many parts of government, and the extensive use of social media and Web 2.0 applications' (Margetts and Dunleavy 2013: 14). While the critics of DEG fully acknowledge the increasing importance of digitalization, they tend to see it as merely one aspect of the current public sector reforms as opposed to being the key driver (Pollitt and Bouckaert 2017). Many researchers in the public administration community clearly seem to remain more preoccupied with NPM – its diffusion, merits and problems – than with digitalization. To a certain extent, the scholarly debate is still focused on the rise and fall of NPM and has not fully embraced the DEG research agenda. This might change as the empirical development in digitalization becomes ever more pervasive in society and our private lives.

There can also be room for combinations of DEG and other governance paradigms. Niels Ejersbo and Carsten Greve (2016a, b) view the national Danish digital strategy as a crossover between DEG and NWS because the digital strategy requires a strong state presence in its promotion and implementation, and Ines Mergel has voiced some of the same points (personal e-mail correspondence).

Combinations other than DEG/NWS are also possible. The focus on efficiency and effectiveness and streamlined operations possibly suggests a DEG/NPM connection. We also know that many big contracts for digital services development and delivery have been outsourced to big tech companies. This could create a mix between the NPM focus on contracting out and competition and the DEG focus on sophisticated digital service systems. A DEG/NPG combination would investigate how decentralized and distributed services can be supported by decentralized internet solutions and how digital online systems facilitate the co-production of services and co-creation of societal solutions.

Social, economic and political actors coming together in dispersed governance networks may also benefit from digitally facilitated all-to-all communication. Hence, there is a growing interest in the role of digital platforms in collaborative governance (Ansell and Gash 2008), which suggests combining DEG and NPG.

On another point, the unprecedented growth of digitalization means that new services and new digital networks are being created at a rapid pace, which begs the question: Can governments keep up with the technological development? DEG presupposes that the governance of the ongoing digitalization is possible. Some countries are doing well with their national digital strategies and initiatives, as seen in the UN and EU rankings. Yet much of the current discussion concerns the relationship between 'big tech and democracy' (a recent title of a panel at the Harvard Kennedy School on 6 February 2019). The big tech companies are increasingly seen as pursuing their own agendas, and the US Congress and other legislative bodies and executive governments may not be able to keep up and produce proper and precise regulation to counter the constant stream of new initiatives from big tech companies. The recent bout of scandals, from the NSA registration of citizens to Cambridge Analytica and beyond, have alarm bells ringing in governments around the world. The same worries internationally are related to the pending trade war between China and the USA, where the Americans are discouraging people and countries to make use of ICT services provided by Huawei, the Chinese digital provider, which is suspected of collecting information for potential use in cyberwarfare. Governments are struggling to control these multinational tech giants while simultaneously encouraging them to locate massive new data centres in their countries to create jobs and economic growth. The only regulator that seems to have taken up the challenge of regulating the global ICT industry appears to be the EU, which is engaged in developing tighter and tighter regulations of the big tech companies.

DEG is becoming more central to the discussion of how public governance is transformed in the wake of the fierce criticism of NPM, not least due to the growing contemporary diffusion of digital services in all areas of public and private life. Digital solutions are now part of the daily lives of individual citizens, private business operations and the administrative practices of public sector organizations. Most people are using digital platforms, and social media dominates our smart phones and tablets.

The state has been forced to adjust and adapt to the new digital reality and exploit the new opportunities. Digitalization is now actively promoted and implemented throughout the public sector in most states, as witnessed by the EU's Digital Economy and Society Index, the UN's digital rankings, and many other indexes and rankings around the world.

DEG has presented itself as a key concept for how the state can make use of these dramatic technological developments. The three pillars of DEG – reintegration, needs-based holism and digital changes – form the backbone of the governance paradigm. The DEG framework has already been updated once by Margetts and Dunleavy in 2013 and will presumably be updated again as new empirical and theoretical developments occur and are detected and described by public administration scholars.

DEG has been heralded as a path towards a more agile and holistic government. Today, DEG is giving room to more detailed studies in many separate areas of the digitalization of public services, including social media, blockchain technology, the advent and use of big data, and the new threats such as the assault on privacy, intensified surveillance and prevention of cyberattacks, and the commercial behaviour of the big tech companies, which is being kept in check by forceful European Commission regulators. DEG is a welcome addition to the discussion of public governance paradigms, as it challenges us to consider what public governance is like in the digital era compared to earlier analogue eras, where public administration was characterized more by paperwork, bureaucratic agencies in clear and identifiable physical locations, and direct lines of authority. As witnessed by the focus of key research institutes (e.g. the Oxford Internet Institute), DEG is now a part of a wider academic (and practical) area of digital studies that is expanding into the digital economy and international politics.

7. Public Value Management

BACKGROUND

An emerging public governance paradigm entitled Public Value Management (PVM) argues that 'public interventions are defined by the search for public value' (Stoker 2006: 47). While public managers play a pivotal role in discovering and realizing public value, they tend to involve a range of social and political actors in the discussion of what public value is, and in the efforts to produce public value outcomes (Moore 1995; Williams and Shearer 2011).

With its emphasis on the key role played by public managers in public value production, PVM continues the managerial revolution in the public sector that was captured and accelerated by New Public Management (NPM). However, while agreeing with NPM that public managers play a crucial role in developing and implementing organizational strategies and achieving results, PVM insists that public sector organizations are different from private for-profit organizations. Hence, the PVM perspective objects to the idea inherent in NPM that the public sector should be run as a private company. Public governance may hinge on the strategic interventions of public managers, but strategic management in the public sector differs substantively from strategic management in private firms, because public organizations aim to produce social value to society rather than profits to shareholders (Moore 1995, 2000).

The 'public value' concept has a distinct intellectual trajectory in the public management literature. The original idea was conceived by Harvard professor Mark Moore (1995), who focused on strategic management in public service organizations and was interested in how managers create public value. It was later applied in its plural form as 'public values' by Bozeman (2007), who was studying the empirical presence and function of the public values pervading the public sector. A third and more recent usage is found in the work of John Bryson, Barbara Crosby and their colleagues (Bryson and Crosby 2005; Bryson et al. 2015, 2016), who synthesize the two previous concepts into a broader notion, 'public value governance', which explains the inclusion of the public value management perspective in this book. The current debate aims to explore the extent to which public value can be seen as the centrepiece in a new public governance paradigm.

The discussion regarding the status of PVM as a public governance paradigm is about more than its ambivalent relation to NPM. In its original formulation (Moore 1995), it is hard to distinguish PVM from the governance paradigm later referred to as the Neo-Weberian State (NWS) (Pollitt and Bouckaert 2004), although the PVM focus on the role of managers in decentral public service organizations makes it less centralistic than NWS. To further complicate matters, later versions and elaborations of PVM appear to pull PVM further away from NWS and more in the direction of New Public Governance (NPG), which focusses on collaborative governance in and through networks and partnerships and turns public managers into metagovernors (Sørensen and Torfing 2009). As such, PVM may appear to be a transient stepping stone to other public governance paradigms rather than a new and stable model for how to govern and be governed. As we shall see, however, some researchers have worked intently to develop PVM into a governance paradigm in its own right; not least by trying to integrate the different perspectives on public value production (Bryson and Crosby 2005). Our comparative analysis of the different governance paradigms in Chapter 9 also indicates that PVM can be seen as a distinct and relatively coherent and comprehensive set of norms and ideas about how to govern, organize and lead the public sector, thereby constituting a distinct public governance paradigm.

The societal background for the development of PVM was the general recognition in the 1990s that public organizations needed to be more dynamic, entrepreneurial and agile and do more to satisfy the service users than was prescribed by classical forms of bureaucracy (Ferlie and Ongaro 2015). Public legitimacy is not secured alone through predictable rule-bound decision-making and endless rationalization campaigns aimed at enhancing cost efficiency. The public sector must also demonstrate its ability to solve policy and service problems in new and innovative ways that meet the social needs of citizens and benefit wider society. According to the PVM, the responsibility for adapting and developing public services to this end lies with entrepreneurial public managers who must act as creative explorers and adept strategists in different political, democratic and organizational settings in order to discover and produce new and better public value outcomes.

While Porter (1985) reflected on the strategic choices of private firms operating in a competitive environment, Moore (2000) compares the conditions for strategic value management in for-profit, non-profit and government organizations. He asserts that 'although the need for an organizational strategy is common across organizations in the three sectors, the form that such strategies take and the analytic tasks used in developing them differ in important ways' (Moore 2000: 184). Both non-profit and government organizations differ from private for-profit organizations, because they define value in terms of a social mission rather than in terms of profit and because their revenues come from sources other than customer purchases. Despite the shared organizational features that distinguish them from private firms, non-profit and govern- mental organizations differ in important ways, as the social mission of the latter is specified in legislation and subject to political and democratic debate in the parliamentary assembly, and their revenues do not come from charitable contributions and voluntary donations, but rather from compulsory taxation. Nevertheless, public and non-profit organizations both have a 'double bottom line', as they must both enact their underlying social mission *and* achieve financial sustainability. Some authors go so far as to state that multiple goals and multiple stakeholders are the defining characteristics of public organizations (Stoker 2006: 47–9). The argument is that a wide range of stakeholders should legitimately be included and involved in government activity.

How to balance the perspectives of different stakeholders is an important question for PVM. Stakeholders refer to 'any group or individual who can affect or is affected by the achievement of the organization's objectives' (Freeman 1984: 46). Moore (1995) argues that public organizations have many stakeholders with divergent preferences but that it is possible to move from initial disagreement on values to a balance whereby the focus is on the value for both society as a whole and each specific stakeholder. PVM can be seen as an answer to the question of how we should succeed with public value creation, although stake- holders have different value preferences.

The real achievement of the PVM paradigm is its emphasis on public value, which serves to remind us that government exists to serve its community (Dewey 2009). Neoliberal critics and the advocates of NPM reforms used to compare the allegedly ossified, rigid and wasteful public sector (see Downs 1967; Niskanen 1971) with the dynamic, flexible and efficient private sector. The neoliberal attack on the public sector – epitomized by US President Reagan's famous statement that 'government is not the solution, but the problem' – created an enduring inferiority complex within the public sector. Where the private sector was constantly praised for its ability to use competition and innovation as vehicles for accelerating the production of private value that was validated by scores of customers and subsequently appropriated as profits by shareholders, public organizations were depicted as unimaginative and unproductive parasites feeding off of the value created by the private sector (Benington and Moore 2011: 7–8). Moreover, neoliberalism readily asserted that private contractors are far better at producing low-cost, high-quality services in response to the changing individual needs of private users and that the implementation of a strict performance management system in public service organizations was necessary to secure goal attainment and reduce slack (Hood 1991). Finally, rules aimed at ensuring equity, transparency, democratic accountability and the rule of law were seen as red tape preventing efficient problem-solving and service delivery (Osborne and Gaebler 1992).

On this background, the truly positive impact of Moore's initial contribution is his insistence that the *raison d'être* of the public sector is not the production of private value to be validated by customers in private markets and appropriated as profits by shareholders, but rather the creation of politically mandated public value for citizens and society at large (Moore 1995). The discovery of public value rescues a sense of public purpose and community orientation in public organizations, nurtures the idea that public managers are closer to being mission-driven 'knights' than self-interested 'knaves' (Le Grand 2003), and insists that political and democratic debate trumps markets when it comes to validating public value outcomes.

The PVM paradigm goes against the grain of NPM by insisting that the public sector is a unique type of organization that combines a distinct revenue base (public taxes) with a distinct value form (public value). However, it agrees with NPM that public managers play a crucial role in securing the production of efficient and effective outcomes of public governance. However, public managers are not portrayed as unimaginative, self-interested slackers who must be forced to manage effectively via elaborate auditing systems and high-powered incentive schemes. Like managers in the private sector, public managers are seen as inventive, community-oriented and mission-driven explorers. In this way, the PVM paradigm helps to restore the self-worth of public managers, who have been 'talked down' by NPM (Rhodes and Wanna 2007: 407).

The idea that public managers are well-intentioned guardians of the public interest brings the PVM paradigm close to the NWS paradigm, which aims to bring classical bureaucratic values and professional virtues back into public management. However, the implicit managerialism found in the early work of Moore (1995, 2000) has been criticized for exaggerating the autonomy, entrepreneurship and political astuteness of public managers (Stoker 2006; Gains and Stoker 2009; Rhodes and Wanna 2009). In his later work, Moore responds to his critics by recognizing the contribution of users, civil society organizations and other private actors to public value production (Benington and Moore 2011; Moore 2013). The appreciation of the contribution of a broad range of private actors to public value production echoes the argument first advanced by Ostrom (1973, 1996). More recently, other researchers have taken the argument further still, by claiming that the public value concept is a game-changer that prompts us to recast the public sector as an arena for the co-creation of public value outcomes (Bryson 2011; Page et al. 2015; Bryson et al. 2016; Crosby et al. 2017). As we shall see, this claim aligns the PVM paradigm with the NPG focus on collaborative governance (Stoker 2006).

SOURCES OF INSPIRATION, THEORETICAL POSITIONS AND EXEMPLARY COUNTRIES

Moore's original version of PVM draws inspiration from strategic management theories regarding the private sector (Ferlie and Ongaro 2015; Alford and Greve 2017). One of the main contributors to this growing field of study is Porter (1980, 1985), who describes how private firms pursue competitive advantage by choosing between different strategies. Firms operating across different market segments may choose between a low-cost strategy aimed at selling products at prices that are lower than those of their competitors and a differentiation strategy aimed at providing a broader, more specialized selection of products to particular segments than their competitors. Firms operating in a segmented niche market may choose a focus strategy aimed at capturing all of the customers in a small and specialized market segment through product innovation or brand marketing. Failing to choose one of the three strategies available to private firms carries the risk of getting stuck in the middle and losing competitive advantage.

The PVM paradigm aims to bring strategic management into the public sector but argues that public service organizations are very different from private firms (Moore 1995, 2000). Public services are financed by taxes and serve social purposes formulated by entrepreneurial public managers, but they are authorized in and through dialogue with elected politicians, relevant stakeholders and user groups.

The core concept of public value is defined in terms of the social purpose of public policies and services. It is measured in substantive rather than fiscal terms and embedded in mission statements that supposedly guide the daily operations of public organizations (Moore 2000). Rather than reflecting the professional norms and competences of the public employees or the nature of the tasks carried out by public organizations, the public value concept captures the positive impact that public interventions may have on societal problems and social needs. It is a multi-dimensional construct shaped by the collectively expressed and politically mediated preferences of public managers and elected politicians, as well as users, citizens and organized stakeholders (O'Flynn 2007: 358). The inherent tension between the contribution of public sector officials to the definition and identification of the public good and the influence of users, citizens and civil society organizations is well captured by the definition of public value as something that adds value to the public sphere and is valued by the public (Benington and Moore 2011).

Research on public value has been growing in recent decades (van der Wal et al. 2013), and it is possible to identify three different positions or schools. The first school links public value to strategic management in public organizations (Moore 1995, 2000). Public managers must act strategically to explore and formulate public value propositions and produce public value outcomes. They must formulate and mobilize political support to the value-based mission of their organization, develop an organizational strategy that is feasible, robust and sustainable, and ensure that the organization's operational capacity fits the overall strategy. Public managers must also undertake the task of getting feedback on how well the strategy is performing and be prepared to adjust or change it in response to obstacles, malfunctions or unforeseen events. This school constitutes the core of the PVM paradigm, as public value is seen as the driver and compass of strategic managers aiming to develop the public sector and provide efficient and effective services in response to changing needs and societal conditions.

The second school looks at the public values that exist in the public sector rather than the production of public value for citizens and society at large. It defines public values in the plural sense as those providing the normative consensus of the rights, benefits and prerogatives to which citizens should be entitled, the obligations of citizens to society, the state or one another, and the principles upon which governments should be based (Bozeman 2007: 17). Scholars belonging to this school seek to identify and catalogue different public values, explore their empirical prevalence in different countries and at different levels of government, reflect on how they fit together, and how they change over time (Bozeman and Jørgensen 2007; Jørgensen and Vrangbæk 2011). Although this school takes an empirical and descriptive approach to the study of public values, it also has a strong normative aspect (Bozeman and Moulton 2011). The argument is that the public sector must adhere to its basic public values in order to preserve its integrity and that NPM, with its marketization and contractualization of public governance, poses a genuine threat to public values such as equity, transparency and the rule of law (Bozeman 2002; Bozeman and Jørgensen 2002). The second PVM school is connected to the extensive literature on public service motivation, defined as 'an individual's orientation to delivering services to people with a purpose to do good for others and society' (Hondeghem and Perry 2009: 6). In this literature, values are seen as 'conceptions, explicit or implicit, distinctive of an individual or characteristic of a group, of the desirable which influences the selection from available modes, means, and ends of action' (Kluckhohn 1951: 395). According to this perspective, Public Service Motivation (PSM) can be seen as an individual's motivation to perform services directed towards other people and society in general, doing good in the way they themselves understand to be desirable (i.e. their values). Andersen et al. (2013) argue that PSM can metaphorically be seen as the fuel in the car, while values set the direction.

Like the first PVM school, the third school is also concerned with public value production through strategic management, but it downplays and decentres the role played by public managers. The basic assumption is that public managers aim to produce public value outcomes but that they operate in shared-power settings in which no one is in charge and nobody is in control (Bryson and Crosby 2005; Bryson et al. 2015). Here, the ambition is to build a coherent theoretical framework of public value governance. Public organizations defy the standard description (i.e. well-organized hierarchies based on centralized control), as they increasingly take the form of complex networks in which problems and solutions are explored and mutually adjusted in the pursuit of the common good. Public organizations are engaged in public governance, which involves knowledge sharing, coordination and collaboration with a broad range of relevant and affected actors from the state, market and civil society. In this context, leaders in the public sphere – governmental and non-governmental alike – become policy entrepreneurs who aim to solve complex problems by means of: (1) fostering an initial agreement among public and private stakeholders to do something about an undesirable condition; (2) defining the problem while considering alternative problem frames; (3) searching for solutions in deliberative and collaborative forums; (4) developing proposals that can win support in relevant decision-making arenas; (5) formally adopting policy proposals; and (6) jointly implementing and evaluating new policies, programmes and plans while solving emerging disputes in court-like settings. Bryson and Crosby (2005) are not only recommending that we take a collaborative governance approach to PVM but that we also

aspire to provide an integrated framework for understanding and analysing PVM. As such, they argue that public managers must tackle
public problems in a shared-power world by co-creating public value
outcomes with a broad range of stakeholders who are part of cross-
boundary networks that are held to account vis-à-vis a broad set of
public values around which there is normative consensus. In this
perspective, public values provide the foundation for public managers
aiming to produce public value through multi-actor collaboration.

The attempt to link public value production to multi-actor collaboration builds on the fundamental idea that the public value focus is a
game-changer that transforms the modus operandi of the public sector.
Far from being the privilege of well-intentioned public managers, public
value production often involves a broad range of public and private
actors, including public employees, users, citizens, civil society organizations and private firms, all of whom can contribute valuable experiences, ideas, forms of knowledge and resources to the process through
which public value is discovered, defined and achieved. Moore (1995,
2000) recognizes the role that private actors play in authorizing public
value propositions and co-producing public services, and Benington and
Moore (2011) go on to talk about the emergence of a 'new pattern
of co-creation' (ibid.: 15). Upon closer inspection, however, the 'co-
creation' of public value outcomes is reduced to the 'co-production' of
predetermined public services. The reduction of co-creation to co-
production becomes particularly clear when we are told that 'clients play
a crucial role in co-production' and that the success of government
agencies depends on 'millions of individuals accepting the obligation and
doing the duty' (ibid.: 269). While service users may play an active role,
they are not perceived as creative explorers of new public value solutions.

The notion of an intrinsic connection between public value production
and co-creation based on cross-boundary collaboration between a
plethora of public and private actors is by no means new. Almost half a
century ago, the Ostroms insisted that the public sector produces public
goods rather than private goods, claiming that it was unlikely that a
single integrated hierarchical organization was the best way to produce
public goods (Ostrom and Ostrom 1971). Instead, we should expect the
existence of multi-organizational arrangements in the public sector.
Elinor Ostrom later reported findings from an empirical study showing
that the performance of local police is better when the police co-produce
services with local citizens and community actors (Ostrom and Whitaker
1973). In her later work, she reported on studies of sanitation problems
and primary education that show how the co-production of public goods
and services through contract-based collaboration between public and

private actors is crucial for achieving public value outcomes in developing countries (Ostrom 1996). While this leaves us with a sense of co-production as an exceptional add-on to the traditional way in some areas and countries, Osborne et al. (2016) claim that co-production is inherent to public service production due to the service-dominant logic that turns end-users into vehicles of discretionary processes of service production. Finally, Osborne and Strokosch (2013) supplement the traditional focus on 'consumer co-production', which aims to empower users in discrete service delivery processes, with a new focus on 'participatory co-production' in which users participate in the strategic planning of the entire service delivery system and 'enhanced co-production' aimed at involving relevant and affected actors in developing new and innovative public solutions. From here, there is only a tiny step to embracing the idea that co-creation aims to include a broad range of public and private actors with relevant assets in collaborative efforts to solve common problems and produce public value outcomes (Torfing et al. 2016).

In a re-appropriating gesture, Stoker (2006) builds a bridge between the managerial perspective of the first PVM school and the co-creation perspective of the third PVM school. As such, he claims that Moore's public value perspective describes a new management style that supports the emergence of networked governance. Public organizations aim to create public value outcomes, but they increasingly recognize the need to exchange and pool resources with other public and private actors. While the network approach provides a solution to the governance challenge in shared power settings, it has lacked a clear understanding of the role of public managers and what drives them. The PVM perspective provides such an understanding.

The original development of the PVM paradigm by Moore (1995) was not based on systematic empirical observations of public management practices in different countries but rather on case studies from North America. It is therefore difficult to identify a single emblematic PVM country. However, the strategic pursuit of public value outcomes by public managers tends to rest on three conditions. First, there must be a strong belief in the role of public managers and their ability to advance and pursue public value propositions through strategic action. A strong managerial discourse favouring heroic leadership is found in countries in which NPM has had a considerable impact, but a managerial focus on the pursuit of public value is also found in countries with more of an emphasis on bureaucracy as a governance paradigm and in countries approximating the NWS paradigm. Second, the strategic pursuit of public value by public managers requires a high degree of managerial autonomy, which is atypical for countries based on the Westminster model and more likely to be found in pluralist political systems with politically appointed top-level managers capable of pursuing their own agendas within a system based on checks and balances. Finally, public leadership based on PVM will tend to thrive in countries that aim to shift the balance from bureaucratic steering towards a more agile and proactive management based on professional values. These basic conditions are typically found in the USA, which is also the country from which Moore draws most of his examples. Moreover, Moore's work has been particularly well received in the UK and in British Commonwealth countries (Bryson et al. 2015: 2). Much of the executive management programme in the Australia and New Zealand School of Government (ANZSOG) is built around Moore's strategic triangle and approach to creating public value. However, public service organizations in other countries with more or less favourable conditions may also draw inspiration from the PVM paradigm, especially the Scandinavian countries and the Netherlands, in which bureaucracy, professional rule and NPM co-exist, which provides favourable conditions for PVM and its attempt to combine strategic management with a strong public value orientation.

MAIN GOVERNANCE IDEA: GOALS AND MEANS

The core idea of the PVM paradigm is that neither traditional forms of top-down steering based on imperative command and centrally determined rules nor new, incentive-driven steering mechanisms based on contracts, performance management and increased competition will bring about the renewal required by the public sector to meet the changing social needs of the citizens and to solve crucial societal problems. Steering must give way to entrepreneurial leadership and management. The public sector can only renew itself and maintain legitimacy if pro-social and proactive public managers in local public service organizations assume responsibility for the continued production of public value while simultaneously securing financial sustainability. They must work in tandem with elected politicians and other relevant stakeholders to define the mission of their organization, inspire their employees through a mixture of transformational and charismatic leadership, and ensure that they have the knowledge, tools and resources needed to realize the social purpose implicit in public governance.

According to Moore (1995, 2000), the identification and pursuit of public value is the central activity of public managers. Public value is important, because it gives purpose and direction to the daily operations of public organizations and speaks to public employees motivated to provide public service. It also helps to generate synergies between different professional groups, actors and interventions that are aligned in and by their joint contribution to the production of public value outcomes. To illustrate, a public school principal who redefines the purpose of the school from 'providing top-rate teaching' to 'stimulating individual learning' may not only succeed to rally the teachers, administrative staffers, the local janitor and the parents behind the mission, but may also succeed in mobilizing local politicians, business firms, sports associations and cultural institutions that can contribute to achieve this objective.

Public managers play a crucial role in exploring, formulating and communicating the public values that ultimately guide public organizations. They can mobilize organizational resources to assess the external environment (e.g. by using PESTEL analysis) and internal organization (SWOT analysis) and reflect on the mutual fit. They can involve dedicated management teams, internal advisers and external experts and consultants in designing a vision that is simple and easily communicated. However, the executive managers are not free to judge any organizational purpose or strategic vision as valuable. Hence, in order to legitimize their public value proposition and to obtain access to financial resources and devolved power, they must involve elected politicians, interest groups and perhaps even their users and relevant citizens in their *authorizing environment* to garner sufficient support for the social purpose and strategy they want their organization to pursue. The authorization of the public value proposition embedded in their vision and mission is a result of a deliberative process in which public managers tend to have the professional knowledge and expertise and the charismatic and reputational power to persuade others. Elected politicians may thus be forced to invoke their democratic mandate in order to veto public value propositions if they think they are off the mark.

When their public value proposition has been authorized through a process of political and democratic deliberation, public managers must focus their attention on the *operational capacity* of their organization in order to ensure that it commands the necessary financial resources, infrastructure, technology, professional competences and means of communication to successfully pursue the public value set out in its vision and mission. Organizational reform, re-budgeting, staff training, team-building, the purchase of new equipment, digitalization and so forth might be required in order to trim the organization and ensure that it fits the purpose. Strong political support from the authorizing environment may help mobilize additional resources.

Together, the relations between public value, the authorizing environment and organizational capacity make up the 'strategic triangle' that helps public managers make sense of the strategic challenges at stake and to reflect on the complex choices they must make. The strategic triangle provides both a heuristic tool for public managers to better understand what strategic management entails and a broader understanding of public governance as a mission-driven interaction between strategic management forums, political decision-making arenas, organizational settings and specific interventions leading to the production of public value outcomes.

Nevertheless, in its original formulation, Moore's public value perspective is inherently managerial. While public managers must seek the upward authorization of their public value propositions in and through dialogue with politicians and other actors who oversee and evaluate the activities of public organizations, the initiative to define and develop what counts as public value lies with the public managers. Moreover, although the value chain perspective implicit to PVM tends to emphasize the co-production of public services and regulations with the users, citizens and relevant stakeholders, it is the downward and inward management of their own organization that enables public managers to produce public value outcomes (Moore 2000: 198). Hence, while the know-how and capabilities necessary to achieve the desired results sometimes lie outside the organization led by the public managers, the organizational capacity of their own organization is usually sufficient to ensure the production of the desired outcomes in terms of regulatory policies, services and products. Together with the formulation and authorization of public value propositions, exploiting the organizational assets of their own organization and occasionally supplementing these assets with input from stakeholders in the external environment is the key responsibility of public managers.

The construction of the governance diamond for the PVM paradigm is relatively simple. PVM scores medium on the degree of centralized control. While the strategic planning and production of public value outcomes is a task for executive public managers, they tend to be located in decentralized public service organizations (e.g. public libraries, hospitals, schools), and they must lead upwards by selling their public value propositions to elected politicians and higher-level public managers. Hence, compliance with formal legislation is important, but when it comes to guiding the daily operations of public service organizations, organizational vision and mission plays a crucial role in motivating public employees and driving their actions.

PVM scores medium to high on the degree of horizontal coordination. Like NPM, the managerial focus on public value production through the value chain, which connects executive public managers with end-users, bears evidence of an intra-organizational rather than inter-organizational perspective on public governance. Still, the focus on broad public value goals rather than programmes and administrative tasks invites other public agencies to contribute to public value production and involves them in concerted action. Public value formulations often cut across boundaries both within and between organizations. To illustrate, preventive healthcare will tend to engage different public agencies in a collaborative effort to produce value for citizens and societies. The emphasis on horizontal coordination varies between the different PVM schools. It is highest in the third PVM school, which links public value creation to governance networks and co-creation.

PVM scores very high on the use of value articulation, since the pursuit of public value is seen as the ultimate vehicle and driving force of public governance. The purpose of the public sector is to produce public value outcomes in response to social needs and societal problems and it is the primary task of public managers to generate support to their particular interpretation of the public interest and the common good, to trim their organization so that it fits its social mission, and to motivate public employees to use their skills and competences to deliver public goods, alone or together with users, citizens and relevant stakeholders. Value articulation is a key mechanism in all of these efforts. Still, the overlap between the value articulation dimension and the PVM paradigm is not complete, as PVM makes use of a specific form of value articulation as public managers formulate and communicate public values that enjoy political support and are assumed to benefit a particular group of citizens as well as society at large. Other public values inherent to the public sector may not be articulated, and some value proposition advanced by public managers may be rejected by elected politicians and the private stakeholders, who are a part of the authorizing environment of public organizations. Moreover, the outcome of the mission-driven activities of public organizations may not be considered as valuable by the target group and the general public.

PVM scores medium on the use of incentives in governance. Conditional incentives are only used to signal the importance of particular values and not as general instruments to influence the behaviour of self-interested actors. Financial sustainability is a prerequisite of the production of public value outcomes and might require strict budget control and some use of penalties and rewards, but transformational leadership is generally preferred to transactional leadership; in other words, incentives are used to support the articulation of public values.

The final axis is societal involvement. Stakeholders play an active role in all PVM schools. In Moore's (1995) original formulation, societal for-profit and non-profit stakeholders and elected politicians discuss and endorse the mission statements formulated by public managers. In Moore's later work (Benington and Moore 2011), end-users are invited to co-produce individual service solutions based on the so-called IKEA model, which leaves some final tasks to the user. However, the lights shine on the charismatic, entrepreneurial and somewhat heroic public managers and their teams of analysts and advisors. A broader inclusion of societal actors in partnerships and networks is found in the third PVM school, which seeks to involve all of the relevant actors in all phases of public governance. As such, problem definition, solution design and implementation are subject to societal involvement. In sum, we have categorized PVM as high on societal involvement. The classification of PVM on the five dimensions of the public governance diamond is shown in Figure 7.1.

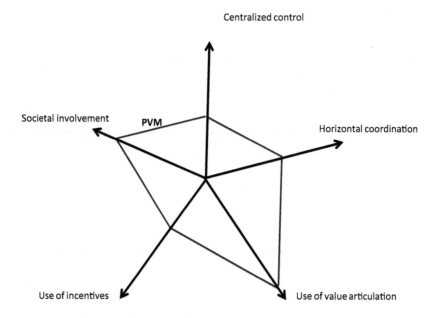

Figure 7.1   The PVM governance diamond

EMPIRICAL RESULTS

There are no systematic empirical studies assessing the ability of public managers to develop and gain the authorization of their value propositions, trim their organization so that it fits its social mission, and to produce the public value outcome with and through their employees. However, there are numerous reports of successful public managers who come close to the entrepreneurial types portrayed by Moore (1995), both in the grey and white bodies of literature. US studies include Doig and Hargrove (1987), who portray an array of public innovation leaders; Cooper and Wright (1992) and Riccuci (1995), both of whom focus on executive public managers; and Vinzant and Crothers (1998) and Theoharis (2009), who deal with street-level leadership. On top of this, Moore (1995) adds his own case-based examples. Australian studies include Rowse's (2002) work on the merits of H.C. Coombs, Furphy's (2015) study of the rise and accomplishment of a group of executive administrators during World War II, and Hunt's (2010) profiling of 54 senior executive managers. While the European literature praising value-based public leadership is more limited, some European scholars present empirically illustrated guidelines for the contribution made by public leaders to public value production (Denhardt and Denhardt 2015).

The problem with the case-based studies of leadership for the public good is not only the selection bias but also the tendency to search for personal traits that enable managers to do what they do, achieve their goals and to enhance public value. The problem is that large-N studies of the contribution made by public managers to public value creation are sparse. However, in a study of Texan school superintendents, O'Toole et al. (2005) found that the superintendents consider Moore's public value triangle to be constitutive of what they do. In a similar study of the German Federal Employment Agency, Meynhardt and Metelmann (2009) found that the middle-managers think along the lines implicit to the public value triangle. Last but not least, Lowndes et al. (2006) have analysed the mobilizing potential of the public value perspective in a multi-method study that concludes that: 'In general terms it is clear that participation was more likely in those local authorities where institutional arrangements were informed by the precepts of public value management' (ibid.: 552). This conclusion supports the idea of co-produced public value outcomes at the end of the value chain, where public employees interact with users, citizens, civil society organizations and/or private firms.

To further sustain the relevance and impact of the PVM perspective, perhaps we should consider the studies of the impact of transformational leadership, which is an important aspect of PVM and the studies of value congruence between public managers and their employees. Studies of transformational leadership indicate a positive impact on job satisfaction (Voon et al. 2011; Sayadi et al. 2017) and organizational performance (Jacobsen and Andersen 2015). Value congruence studies show that transformational leadership and the public value commitment of public managers are positively correlated with the public employees' public service motivation (PSM) (Wright et al. 2012), but also that the causal association is mediated by need satisfaction (Jensen and Bro 2018). New studies suggest that transformational leadership positively affects value congruence in public service organizations, but only when employees see their jobs as having an impact on the well-being of others and society at large (Jensen 2017).

While supportive of the PVM paradigm, the studies of transformational leadership only capture a particular aspect of PVM. The full paradigm is difficult to evaluate empirically, because there are many variables and propositions in the different PVM schools (Bryson and Crosby 2005; Bryson et al. 2015). However, the PVM framework has been used as a tool for analysing public sector reforms and public governance. Bossert and colleagues (1998), for example, have used the strategic triangle to study health reform; Erridge (2007) has tested the PVM framework in a study of employment procurement; Bruijn and Dicke (2006) have studied strategies for safeguarding public values in liberalized utility sectors; and Kingsley (2004) and Grimsley and Meehan (2007) have analysed the development of the internet and e-government from a public value perspective.

In sum, there is some evidence of the relevance of the PVM paradigm for public managers and their exercise of public leadership as well as in the study of public governance reforms. More studies combining qualitative process studies with quantitative studies of empirical prevalence are needed, as are studies testing the analytical value of the PVM paradigm against competing public governance paradigms.

DEBATE AND DILEMMAS

There is an ongoing debate regarding the status of PVM as a public governance paradigm in its own right. Speaking against giving paradigmatic status to PVM is the fact that the empirical analysis of different and shifting public values has not yet been integrated with Moore's managerial action approach, which tells public managers what to do in order to produce public solutions that are valuable for the public (and which the public seem to value). Bryson and Crosby (2005) have aimed to integrate both of these perspectives within a broader PVM framework that takes a collaborative approach to public value production. Despite the inherent risk of creating a synthetic framework that loses sight of the distinctive contributions of the different PVM schools, the work of Bryson and Crosby clearly enhances the paradigmatic status of PVM.

Looking more closely at the three different schools, the problem is that the second PVM school hardly produces any recommendations about how to govern the public sector, let alone society and the economy, and that the third PVM school, with its emphasis on governance networks and the co-creation of public value outcomes, is difficult to distinguish from NPG. That leaves us with the first PVM school, which constitutes a rather thin governance paradigm in the sense that it focusses almost exclusively on the actions of public managers and has little to say about how we structure, organize and design the public sector as a whole and how it relates to and governs the social and economic sectors. Strategic management is undoubtedly important, and the strategic triangle provides a much needed and usable tool for public managers to think through how strategic management may be pursued in the public sector. The emphasis on public value creation, the generation of political support and the need to build the right organizational competences and capabilities certainly provides an antidote to NPM's corporatization of the public sector, but it falls short of providing a comprehensive vision of how to govern and be governed.

The greatest asset of Moore's version of PVM is its discovery of public value production as the central tenet of the public sector. Anchoring public management in the ambition to enhance public value creation reasserts the unique purpose of the public sector: to serve the community. Moore also draws attention to the political and democratic debates through which public value is authorized and which public managers lead by formulating, sharing and maintaining a particular vision and mission (Jacobsen and Andersen 2015). The argument is that the insistent pursuit of a social mission can drive an efficient, effective, equitable and fair production of public values through the mobilization of and collaboration with public employees, users, citizens and other stakeholders.

Despite speculation that the PVM paradigm will be the new or next big thing in public administration (see Alford and Hughes 2008; Talbot 2009), a number of criticisms have been waged against it.

First, Rhodes and Wanna (2007) criticize Moore for the unclear status of PVM as a paradigm, concept, heuristic devise and management tool, as well as his stretched definition of public managers, which seems to include administrators, politically appointed staff and elected politicians. They also note the conspicuous absence of reflections on conflicts and power imbalances among the allegedly good-hearted public and private actors – and on the dark side of public administration, which sometimes involves hidden agendas, budget-maximizing and bureau-shaping (Dunleavy 2014). Their main criticism, however, is that the PVM paradigm has little relevance to parliamentary democracy based on the Westminster model, wherein civil servants are subordinate to elected politicians and therefore have limited autonomy as policy entrepreneurs and value brokers. Rhodes and Wanna (2007) concede that PVM may play a role in North American government but generally consider PVM as a way of governing that downgrades the role of party democracy, the primacy of politics and ultimately representative democracy. Alford (2008) comes to Moore's rescue, refuting each of the points raised by Rhodes and Wanna. In particular, he claims that the strategic triangle gives the authorizing environment – which comprises elected politicians, among others – a crucial role to play in placing 'a legitimate limit on the public manager's autonomy to shape what is meant by public value' (Alford 2008: 359). He also problematizes the idea of a sharp line of demarcation between politics and administration that seems to inform the arguments made by Rhodes and Wanna.

Second, Dahl and Soss (2014) criticize Moore for mimicking neo-liberalism and being captured by a private firm logic that poses public value as analogous to shareholder value; views public value as something that is produced; and conceives democratic dialogue and engagement as instrumental to reaching the production goals. On this point, Moore's work runs the risk of furthering the de-democratizing and market-enhancing consequences of neoliberalism. The vaccination for this inherent risk is greater emphasis on the relational aspects of public management and the embeddedness of public managers in broad-based governance networks that play a role in formulating, authorizing and delivering public value. This cure implies a jump from the first to the third PVM school.

A third critique is raised by Jacobs (2014), who argues that the formation of consensus about public values is seriously difficult to obtain in countries with deep-seated value conflicts, intense partisanship, fierce ideological struggles and multiple veto actors. Despite many of these characteristics applying to North America, however, there are numerous examples of entrepreneurial public managers who formulate and pursue public values in and through their organization. This normative entre-preneurialism might be made possible by the relatively weak political control from above.

We shall conclude this chapter with a discussion of three dilemmas inherent to the emerging PVM paradigm. The first concerns the classical tension between democracy versus effectiveness and efficiency. In a turbulent world, we want public service organizations to be agile and capable of adapting to new needs, problems and conditions in order to enhance public value production. As Moore suggests, this may require entrepreneurial and proactive public managers who take a leading role in reinvigorating the public sector. Still, democracy is also a crucial public value, and the more that public managers engage in the formulation of public value propositions and act as value brokers, the more difficult it becomes for elected politicians to exercise political leadership. Moore tends to conceive of elected politicians as a board of directors that authorizes the public value propositions advanced by public managers and otherwise lets managers manage. This role prescription produces a weak democratic and political leadership. One way of escaping the tension between democratic leadership and the administrative pursuit of effective and efficient value production is for politicians and public managers to team up and work closely together throughout the policy process. This solution is time-demanding for both parties, however, and may contribute to a further blurring of the line separating politics and administrations and thus create accountability problems since it becomes unclear who is responsible for what.

The second dilemma relates to the style of management deployed by public managers. Moore seems to favour a value-based transformational leadership but still insists that the outcomes of public service organ-izations should be measured in order to secure high performance. When public value outcomes are meagre, public managers will have to take action and, after many years of NPM, they may resort to the use of sticks and carrots, which are the classical tools of transactional leadership. While transformational leadership thrives on trust-based dialogue and collaboration up and down the chain of command, some types of transactional leadership (contingent sanctions and to some extent contin-gent material rewards) are based on different assumptions about human nature (arguing that self-interested motives will normally dominate over prosocial motives). In contrast, the use of non-pecuniary rewards, such as praise, may reinforce transformational leadership (Nielsen et al. 2018).

The final dilemma takes us right to the heart of the public value concept: a multidimensional construct that comprises a variety of govern-mental values, values relating to the rights and duties of citizens, as well as the outcomes that are deemed valuable for users and wider society. As for the latter, there will often be a conflict between what is good for society and good for the individual users (see, e.g., Jensen and Andersen 2015). A student graduating from a master's degree programme in public administration will value a high grade, but if all students get high grades it undermines the ability of potential employers to select the best candidate based on merit. Likewise, reducing smoking by putting a ban on smoking in public is undoubtedly good for society as it prevents second-hand smoke and reduces public health costs, but individual smokers may value their ability to smoke in public. The PVM paradigm needs to find ways to deal with such value conflicts between what is good for the individual and what is collectively valued.

As the discussion above indicates, even an emergent governance paradigm such as PVM, which brings forth a relatively clear and attractive vision of public managers as the solicitors of public value, is not spared from important criticisms and objections and is ridden with dilemmas that call for reflection and action.

8. New Public Governance

BACKGROUND

New Public Governance (NPG) is the name of a new governance regime that a growing number of researchers and practitioners perceive as a possible alternative (or significant supplement) to New Public Management (NPM) (Bogason 2001; Osborne 2006, 2010; Torfing and Triantafillou 2013; Morgan and Cook 2014). Like NPM, NPG draws different empirical trends together to construct a new governance paradigm, which in this case seems to provide the antidote for the problems associated with NPM. Building on a different action theory that stresses social orientation, mutual dependence and institutional conditions, it focusses on the enhancement of input and output legitimacy through cross-boundary collaboration between public and private actors in networks and partnerships, and it recommends the use of trust-based steering and management that enhances public service motivation and expands the room for employee discretion and dialogue with users, citizens and stakeholders in order to mobilize local resources.

The appraisal of bottom-up governance processes involving a plethora of public and private actors may conflict with the fundamental normative premise of liberal democracy that authoritative political decisions are taken by sovereign political representatives and implemented top-down by public bureaucracy without interference from private stakeholders. However, the new theories of interactive governance that underpin NPG tend to emphasize the need for metagoverning networks and partnerships through a combination of institutional design, political framing, process management and active participation (Torfing et al. 2012) and urge public actors to ensure the democratic anchorage of networks and other collaborative arenas through which public goals, solutions and outcomes are shaped. Metagovernance is defined as the attempt to influence the processes and outcomes of interactive governance without reverting too much to hierarchical forms of command and control (Sørensen and Torfing 2009). It can be exercised by elected politicians and public managers and helps to connect the formal institutions of government with less formal collaborative governance processes, thereby aligning NPG with core aspects of liberal democracy. Indeed, it is argued that elected politicians are not only capable of influencing the process and outcomes of interactive governance by acting as metagovernors; they may also benefit from the input they receive by engaging in a sustained dialogue with citizens and relevant stakeholders, who often possess relevant experiences, forms of knowledge, creative ideas and valuable resources that help to define policy problems and design and implement new and bold solutions (Sørensen and Torfing 2018).

The compatibility of NPG with classical forms of bureaucracy is further ensured by its focus on public service organizations and the co-production of public services through continuous interaction between private users and public service providers (Osborne and Strokosch 2013). However, rather than giving precedence to the internal processes in public bureaucracy, NPG emphasizes the interorganizational relations through which public agencies relate to other public or private organizations as well as to users and citizens. According to Osborne (2010), in societies in which NPG is predominant, the state is both plural and pluralized. Power is widely distributed among a broad range of public and private actors, and nobody is in control. Hence, multi-actor collaboration is a basic requirement.

In sum, while NPG aims to provide an alternative to the competitive logic and performance management inherent to NPM, it is relatively compatible with bureaucracy and liberal democracy, although it aims to rethink what democracy can mean in a world of shared power and interactive governance (Warren 2002; Rosanvallon 2011).

The societal background for the development of NPG is the general tendency towards a functional differentiation of society. Systems theory claims that modern society is characterized by a seemingly irreversible trend towards organizational differentiation that produces a growing number of functionally defined organizations, institutions and communicative sub-systems, all of which have a high degree of autonomy despite their structural coupling and co-evolution (Luhmann 1995; Jessop 2002). As such, there is a tendency to solve emerging societal problems through the creation of new autonomous organizations and institutions, which together form new systems or sub-systems. The result is a fragmented society and a differentiated polity that renders communication, coordination and societal problem solving exceedingly difficult.

The fragmentation problem has been aggravated by NPM reforms that encourage the contracting out of public services to a myriad of private service providers and then seek to reduce the increasing complexity in the field of public governance and service production through the creation of special-purpose agencies dedicated to solving a specific public task (Rhodes 1997). In addition, the strong focus of NPM on managerialism, budget discipline, performance targets and the use of conditional rewards and punishment leads to a strengthening of the administrative silos. Researchers and public managers supporting the main principles of NPM have themselves been alerted to the problem of the growing fragmentation and compartmentalization of the public sector. The typical solution has been to advance a combination of corporate management and joined-up government. The corporate management approach puts an executive director in charge of several related silos in order to promote intra-organizational coordination in highly differentiated organizations. Joined-up government aims to solve cross-boundary problems and challenges via interorganizational collaboration (Ling 2002). Executive orders and performance management have been the key instruments to promote joined-up government (Bogdanor 2005; Pells 2015). The centralized problem-solving strategy has created great opposition further down in the administrative system and has not been particularly successful, as it tends to create top-heavy organizational rigidities that limit the agility needed in the face of crisis and turbulence (Jun 2009).

NPG perceives the growing fragmentation as a huge challenge for public governance and recommends the formation of cross-boundary collaboration in networks and partnerships as the primary vehicle for pluri-centric coordination and interactive governance (Rhodes 1997; Osborne 2010). NPG goes further than NPM in insisting that crosscutting networks should be formed bottom-up based on the recognition of mutual resource dependencies and that collaborative governance networks should transgress the boundaries of the public sector and involve relevant and affected actors from the economy and civil society. Governance in and through public–private networks and partnerships provides an alternative to traditional bureaucratic steering based on hierarchical command and control and the new forms of market-based allocation based on competition and rivalry (Kooiman 1993; Kickert et al. 1997; Jessop 2002; Sørensen and Torfing 2007). Public–private partnerships can be viewed as a specific organizational form within the broader network governance agenda. They appear in many forms and sizes, including long-term infrastructure partnerships, innovation partnerships, urban development partnerships, service partnerships and policy partnerships (Hodge et al. 2010; Brinkerhoff and Brinkerhoff 2011; Greve and Hodge 2013). Whereas NPM tends to view public–private partnerships as contractual arrangements aiming to enhance efficiency and reduce public expenditure, NPG emphasizes their relational and negotiated character and their contribution to creative problem-solving in the public sector.

A new conception of the key challenge for public governance informs the NPG promotion of networked governance. Whereas NPM saw the public monopoly on societal regulation and service production as the key challenge and prescribed a combination of deregulation, marketization and customer-orientation as the main cure, NPG focusses on the pervasiveness of wicked and unruly problems (Rittel and Webber 1973). These problems call for the formation of collaborative networks in which relevant and affected actors exchange and pool knowledge and resources in order to create innovative solutions that disrupt conventional wisdoms and habitual practices (Roberts 2000; Ansell and Torfing 2014). Simple problems can sometimes be solved by relatively simple solutions, but the large number of complex societal problems, such as climate change, gang-related crime, soaring youth unemployment and traffic congestion and food deserts in big cities seldom have simple solutions. NPG sees problems as 'wicked' if complex causalities with many feedback loops make them difficult to define and if their unique character and implicit goal conflicts preclude clear-cut solutions. Wicked problems are frequently unruly in the sense that there are deep political conflicts, a discounted evaluation of future solutions and a mismatch between the nature of the problem and the level at which we try to solve it. The exorbitant costs of a policy solution and its negative externalities may add to the unruliness of societal problems (Hofstad and Torfing 2017). While the wickedness of problems refers to cognitive constraints, their unruly character points to political and institutional complications. Combining these two dimensions enables us to discern alternative types of complex problems (Alford and Head 2017).

NPG supporters criticize NPM for not delivering on its initial promises. The absent or meagre results and unintended negative implications of NPM may be explained either by the institutional barriers and political resistance to its implementation, the emergence of unintended negative effects due to the presence of unacknowledged conditions, or flaws in the underlying programme and change theory. The wholesale contracting out of all of the public services in a particular service area to private contractors exacerbates the risk of a supply crisis if private service providers go bankrupt in contrast to a mixed model, where a significant part of the public service production is maintained in-house, thus preserving the skills, competences and capacities for public service provision (Girth et al. 2012). Depending on the context, the payment of bonus wages to high-performing public employees may crowd out their intrinsic task-related motivation and their PSM, both of which provide important drivers of service quality (Andersen et al. 2012). Finally, the core steering principles of NPM have been criticized for being too narrow. Hence, Morgan and Cook (2014) criticize NPM for building on the reductionist assumption that one principal strategic actor (public managers) should pursue one single goal (efficiency) using tools from one particular sector (the private sector). In continuation of the critique of the NPM attempt to run the public sector as a private business, NPM is blamed for its intra-organizational focus on leadership and management that is deemed inadequate in a world that is becoming increasingly open and pluri-centric (Osborne 2010). According to NPG, we need to adopt an interorganizational view of public governance aimed at mobilizing a broad range of public and private actors (e.g. politicians, public managers, professionals, private firms, civil society organizations, citizens, users) in the pursuit of a broad selection of goals (e.g. efficiency, effectiveness, quality, equity, democracy) in a public sector that produces public value for society at large rather than profit for private investors.

Part of the background for NPG is that resource mobilization and resource exchange are seen as a welcome alternative to the continued attempts to exploit the increasingly scarce public resources in the face of increasing demands for high-quality services. Cost-efficient resource exploitation has already been achieved via across-the-board budget cuts supported by rationalization techniques such as LEAN, which allow public managers to pick the low-hanging fruit by means of correcting obvious design problems and removing slack (Radnor and Osborne 2013). After several decades, it has become increasingly difficult to make further cuts without hampering core service functions and making cuts to welfare services. NPG argues that the mobilization of new resources from both inside and outside of public organizations offers an escape from this impasse. Resources can be mobilized and productivity increased through trust-based leadership and management aimed at bringing the resources and energies of local agencies and public employees into play (Nyhan 2000). Emphasis on their corporate social responsibility and the formation of public–private partnerships may allow public agencies to gain access to the resources, ideas and technologies of private firms. Inviting them to co-create public service systems may help to enhance the public value contribution made by voluntary organizations and to solicit creative inputs from social entrepreneurs in civil society (Osborne and Strokosch 2013). Finally, the cultivation of an active citizenship and strategies for recruiting volunteers may turn citizens from demanding consumers into the co-producers of public solutions. There are more resources outside the public sector than inside it, and the strategic mobilization of these resources is paramount to public sector success in times of fiscal constraint. To illustrate, there is little hope of dealing with climate change without massive contributions from private investors, social housing corporations and private citizens. Likewise, the ability of public schools to stimulate learning will be greatly enhanced if schools open up and involve private firms, cultural institutions and sports clubs that can provide inspirational real-life settings for schoolchildren to test their skills and competences and learn new things.

NPG shares the critical stance towards the marketization aspect of NPM with the Neo-Weberian State (NWS) paradigm, but it is also critical of the implicit managerialism (performance management) and explicit centralization of NWS. Leadership and management are considered important drivers of renewal in the public sector, but there is good reason to doubt that public leaders can singlehandedly produce the kind of innovative solutions required merely by relying on their public value commitment and their exercise of strategic leadership. Even the most heroic of leaders need input, feedback and support from their surroundings. Without strong networks, alliances and partnerships, they will hardly be able to influence anything in the 'organized anarchy' (Cohen and March 1986) that characterizes public organizations. Leadership and management are therefore considered a distributed practice aimed at dispersing responsibilities to a broad range of actors at different levels and in different sectors and organizations (Bolden 2011). Leadership and management also represent an integrative endeavour seeking to bring together a broad range of actors who can contribute to the design and implementation of innovative solutions (Crosby et al. 2017). Finally, while NWS supporters praise the core principles of bureaucracy and seek to revive its core values, NPG advocates warn us that public bureaucracies tend to be more inward- than outward-looking and that the combination of centralized control and rule-based steering poses a real threat to innovation (Ansell and Torfing 2014).

NPG supporters are generally positive towards the new opportunities offered by new digital technologies. They may help to enhance democratic participation, support knowledge sharing and communication in dispersed governance networks, and stimulate public innovation in both the back and front office by inviting private firms, NGOs and citizens to exploit and experiment with big data (Dunleavy 2006). Unlike the protagonists of Digital Era Governance (DEG), however, NPG does not perceive digitalization as a game-changer in transforming how we organize, govern and lead the public sector. While digitalization may improve the speed, quality and reach of public communication and support the networked co-production of public services (Meijer 2011), it is unlikely to transform governance as such.

If there is a game-changer, it is the discovery of the unique contribution of the public sector to the production of public value. Hence, as seen in Chapter 7 (Stoker 2006), the focus on public value in PVM opens up for the appreciation of the important role of networked governance. Public value is therefore both validated and produced by a broad range of public and private actors engaged in public dialogue and collaborative interaction (Crosby et al. 2017).

SOURCES OF INSPIRATION, THEORETICAL POSITIONS AND EXEMPLARY COUNTRIES

NPG is inspired by institutional theory and new theories of network governance, metagovernance, co-production and collaboration innovation (Osborne 2010). Its point of departure in the new institutionalism, which began to flourish in the 1980s and 1990s, means that NPG breaks with the instrumentalist and utilitarian views of social action associated with rational choice theory, which tends to see social and political actors as rational individuals driven by self-interested and largely unfettered utility maximization. Some strands of the new institutionalism retained the possibility of rational action based on the calculation of the consequences of alternative courses of action, but they insisted that rational action is conditional on institutional rules and norms that rule some alternatives 'in' and others 'out' and which change the rewards and penalties structure (Ostrom 1991; Scharpf 1994). Other strands of the new institutionalism claim that rational action only constitutes a limited part of our repertoire of social actions and that social and political actors generally act on the basis of a situational interpretation of what the institutional context prescribes to be appropriate action (March and Olsen 1989, 1995). The result of the ongoing reflections regarding the nature of social and political action is the assumption of mixed motives. Hence, it is implicitly assumed that institutionally conditioned attempts at pursuing a particular set of interests exist side by side with scripted actions that are shaped by shifting interpretations of what institutional rules, norms, values and roles prescribe as appropriate action for particular actors in specific situations.

As the name indicates, NPG is heavily inspired by the new governance research that emerged in the early 1990s and which has continued to grow in importance (Kooiman 1993, 2003; Ansell and Torfing 2016). The new governance research is rooted in Ostrom's discovery of the viability of collaborative responses to the threat of the depletion of common pool resources (Ostrom et al. 1994), which triggered a scholarly search for alternatives to hierarchies and markets (Mayntz 1993a, b). Another important source of inspiration is Heclo's (1978) discovery of policy sub-systems in the US Congress, which stimulated the interest in policy networks and their influence on public policy (Marsh and Rhodes 1992). Both of these historical roots of the new governance research emphasized the role of collaborative action in networks of interdependent actors.

The basic assumption in the new governance research is that the formal institutions of government and the political-administrative chain of command that links voters to elected politicians, government officials and public service providers play a limited role in governing society and the economy. The hierarchical model of top-down government based on laws, regulation and centralized control is becoming less and less effective in our increasingly complex, fragmented and multi-layered societies. The problematization of the privileged role of government in governing society and the economy has stimulated interest in governance, defined as the formal and informal processes through which a plethora of public and private actors formulate and achieve joint objectives through collective action (Torfing et al. 2012). Whereas the old bureaucratic paradigm merely focused on the formal political and administrative institutions and NPM aims to shift the balance between government and market in favour of the latter, NPG draws attention to the need for collaborative interaction between public and private actors. The state is therefore decentred, as public authorities are increasingly seen as merely one of several actors engaged in governing society and the economy in accordance with common goals and objectives. NPG scholars describe this development as a shift from government to governance. It is, nevertheless, important not to misinterpret this bold statement as meaning that there was only government in the past and that there will only be governance in the future. There have always been elements of interactive governance, and the formal institutions of government will continue to play an important role alongside and in relation to networked forms of governance. That which is new, however, is the analytical shift from the traditional focus on formal institutions to a new focus on less formal processes of multi-actor collaboration. This gravitational shift draws our attention to the manifold public and private actors contributing to public governance through sustained interaction in more or less formal and informal forums for discussion and arenas of decision-making. The decentring of governance mobilizes new resources, energies and ideas, but it also requires dedicated effort to align actors and connect forums and arenas with each other and with government actors.

Governance research highlights the importance of networks, partnerships and other relational governance arrangements that cut across organizations, sectors and levels and contribute to public governance (Koppenjan and Klijn 2004; Hodge and Greve 2010). The functional impact alone cannot explain the formation of networks and partnerships. Interactive governance arrangements are either self-grown from below or formed by public authorities; in both cases, their condition of emergence is the mutual resource dependency between the social and political actors that ties the various actors together in a more or less institutionalized exchange or pooling of knowledge, ideas and resources (Kickert et al. 1997). As such, governance networks are defined as a stable horizontal articulation of interdependent but operationally autonomous actors who govern society and the economy through self-regulated negotiations that take place within a relatively institutionalized framework (Torfing et al. 2012). Although NPG and governance network researchers tend to agree on the definition of governance networks, it is possible to draw distinctions in their respective approaches. These theoretical approaches vary in terms of whether they conceive the social and political actors to be driven by rational calculations or cultural norms and in terms of their differing views on the ability to overcome conflicts in public governance and facilitate the smooth coordination of social and political action (Sørensen and Torfing 2007). The two dominant schools in the field of governance network research are known as interdependency theory (Kickert et al. 1997; Rhodes 1997; Jessop 2002) and governability theory (Mayntz 1993a, b; Scharpf 1994). Interdependency theory is closely associated with historical institutionalism, whereas governability is associated with rational choice institutionalism. While the two schools both perceive social and political actors as equipped with a bounded rationality, they disagree on whether public governance is essentially conflict-ridden or consensus-based. The less dominant schools are normative integration theory (March and Olsen 1995), which has a strong affinity with sociological institutionalism, and governmentality theory, which emerged from poststructuralist theories of power. While these schools agree that social and political action are shaped by the institutional and discursive contexts, they disagree on whether social and political interaction is mostly smooth and civilized or pervaded by conflicts and power struggles. Despite their different ontologies, all four theories of network governance subscribe to the basic view that networked interactions are playing an increasingly crucial role in public governance and thereby creating a dispersed and decentred power structure that spans multiple levels, sectors and organizations.

Governance networks can contribute to effective governance by means of mobilizing relevant resources and enhancing pluri-centric coordination. They can also contribute to democratizing governance by involving relevant and intensely affected actors in public decision-making, stimulating public deliberation and strengthening democratic legitimacy on the output side of the political system, where solutions are designed and implemented. New research has also demonstrated how multi-actor collaboration in networks and partnerships possibly spurs the development of innovative service and policy solutions (Hartley 2005; Bommert 2010; Ansell and Torfing 2014; Torfing 2016). The argument is that the understanding and definition of the problem at hand, the circulation and integration of creative ideas, the selection and testing of promising solutions, mobilization and coordination of resources, the formation of joint ownership over new and bold solutions and the diffusion of these to other organizations and sectors is improved through networked interaction between social and political actors, who together possess all of the innovation assets necessary to formulate and implement disruptive solutions (Hartley et al. 2013).

Given the merits of governance networks, the challenge is that they do not emerge spontaneously when needed, they might lead to destructive conflicts and stalemates, they are often subject to collaborative inertia due to the presence of high transaction costs, and they sometimes spin out of control and produce undesired solutions (Huxham and Vangen 2005). Moreover, participatory selection bias, informal decision-making and large power asymmetries may undermine their democratic quality (Papadopoulos 2003). These challenges have stimulated the interest in how elected politicians or public managers (or professional facilitators acting on their behalf) can influence the relatively self-regulated processes and outcomes of governance networks without reverting to traditional forms of command and control that will either scare off the participating actors or create fierce opposition. The attempt to influence interactive governance processes by means of more indirect and subtle forms of network management is known as metagovernance (Kooiman 1993, 2003; Jessop 2002; Sørensen and Torfing 2009). Metagovernance involves the governance of more or less self-governing governance networks that produce concrete acts of governance. As such, metagovernance is a kind of third-order governance. The research describes the different tools for metagoverning governance networks, including the institutional design of network arenas, overall goal- and framework steering, process management aimed at solving or mitigating conflicts, and direct participation aimed at influencing the agenda, the problem definition and the decision-making principles (Kickert et al. 1997; Sørensen and Torfing 2009).

The key challenge for political and administrative metagovernors is to neither govern too much nor too little. If governing too much, they risk pacifying the participating actors; if too little, destructive conflicts might evolve. Hence, carefully calibrated metagovernance leaves room for active participation and distributed action while nipping irresolvable conflicts in the bud. Another challenge is to avoid the elected politicians being marginalized and sidelined by the public managers, who often have more time, resources and knowledge to invest in the exercise of metagovernance and therefore tend to monopolize the metagovernance of interactive governance arenas, thereby becoming powerful gatekeepers regulating the interplay between elected politicians and societal actors (Koppenjan et al. 2009). To solve this problem, we must identify the strictly political metagovernance tasks that call for the exercise of political rather than administrative metagovernance (Sørensen and Torfing 2016).

More recently, NPG has been associated with attempts at spurring co-production and co-creation in the public sector (Alford 2009, 2014, 2016; Osborne et al. 2016; Torfing et al. 2016). While co-production emphasizes the contributions made by citizens to the production of their own pre-designed welfare services, co-creation refers to the process through which two or more public and private actors collaborate to redesign the entire service system or create new and innovative public solutions (Osborne and Strokosch 2013). As such, co-creation is another word for collaborative innovation. There have always been elements of co-production and co-creation in the public sector, but NPG aims to spur the co-production of services and to turn co-creation into a main governance strategy in order to accelerate creative problem-solving and the production of public value outcomes (the notion of public value tends to link NPG to PVM). Elevating the practice of co-creation to a mode of governance requires the formation of physical and digital platforms that enable public and private actors to hook up and produce joint solutions (Ansell and Gash 2017). The emphasis on digital platforms in sustaining co-created governance provides a bridge between NPG and DEG (Margetts and Naumann 2017).

Despite its immediate appearance, NPG cannot be reduced to interactive governance and the co-creation of public solutions. Other important elements of NPG include the development of new forms of democratic participation aimed at reconnecting elected politicians and their critical (but increasingly assertive) followers (Nabatchi and Leighninger 2015); the use of soft governance tools based on values, norms and standards (Salamon 2000); new ways of ensuring goal achievement in public service organizations through an increasing reliance on trust-based steering and management (Nyhan 2000); and the development of new forms of bottom-up accountability (Kettl 2015). Countering the *homo economicus* model that lies at the heart of principal–agent theory and the introduction of performance management in the public sector,

NPG opts for a new way of governing local service institutions and managing frontline personnel. Inspired by the new stewardship theory (Schillemans 2013), NPG asserts that there is a high degree of goal alignment between the public leaders at the executive level and the public employees producing and delivering services to citizens at the operational level. The high degree of goal alignment means that there is no need for zealous control mechanisms backed by rewards and punishments, but rather for trust-based dialogue and coordination in order to realize the joint ambition of serving the citizens and solving important societal problems and tasks. The institutionalization of a sustained governance dialogue between managers and professional employees challenges the centralized control inherent in classical bureaucracy and the professional autonomy implicit to professional rule.

Some researchers adopt a service-centred perspective on NPG (Osborne et al. 2013). They tend to see public service production as a natural starting point for collaboration among public agencies and between public employees, users, volunteers and social entrepreneurs. Indeed, in their role as service users, citizens are the nodal point of discretionary service production and have a clear interest in being actively involved in the production process and in contributing, because it enhances the quality and effect of the service they receive. This claim finds support in recent research that demonstrates the positive impact of parental participation in the co-production of their children's learning in public schools (Andersen and Jakobsen 2013). Other actors than service users may also be involved. Volunteers are citizens who co-create services for other citizens based on altruism, and social entrepreneurs and civil society organizations are often motivated to engage in co-produced service provision out of concern for social equality and service quality. Other researchers adopt regime-centred perspectives on NPG (Morgan and Cook 2014). They describe NPG as a new way of fulfilling the prerequisite functions of the political-administrative system, including the articulation of demand and support (input), the transformation of these to concrete governance solutions (throughput), the implementation of the new solutions in practice (output), and the evaluation of the outcome in order to improve future solutions (feedback) (Torfing and Triantafillou 2013). All of these functions seem to require interaction between a plethora of public and private actors, and sustained collaboration may further qualify and improve the results. The two different perspectives on NPG are by no means in conflict with each other; rather, they seem to offer complementary perspectives on the micro and macro levels of public governance.

It is difficult to point to a particularly exemplary or frontrunner country that epitomizes NPG. Network governance and co-creation is ubiquitous, and the same goes for the attempt to show local institutions and public employees more trust. If we consider the cases displayed by key NPG researchers, however, the Netherlands, Denmark and the UK seem to display particularly strong NPG tendencies. The co-existence of a strong, well-managed state and a strong, well-organized civil society seems to provide favourable opportunities for the emergence of network governance, partnerships and processes of co-creation. A high level of social capital points in the same direction. A low degree of work structuration and a short power distance between top and bottom in public service organizations tend to support the development of trust-based steering and management. In Denmark, many local municipalities have embraced the idea of co-creation and they also appear to 'walk the walk' in many instances. This finding reflects the high degree of devolution in the Danish welfare state, where the local municipalities provide the lion's share of the universalistic welfare services. The devolution of public service production means that governance decisions are made close to the citizens, which seems to stimulate local participation in collaborative arenas for networked governance.

The European Union (EU) focuses extensively on interactive governance through networks and partnerships. Elements of NPG already had an impact on the White Paper on European Governance, published by the European Commission in 2001, and continues to frame the debate on European governance. Some researchers claim that the EU is basically a networked polity (Kohler-Koch and Larat 2009), and network governance is generally seen as an integral aspect of the EU committee system, the Open Method of Coordination and the structural and social funds (Esmark 2007). The attempt to enhance input and output legitimacy is the key driver of collaborative governance in the EU. Hence, to counteract the ensuing democratic deficit, there has been an increasing number of attempts to involve citizens and organized stakeholder groups in EU policy-making (Boucher 2009). The formation of the European Citizens' Consultations (ECC) in 2009 is an ambitious and pioneering example of this (Leyenaar and Niemöller 2010).

If we are looking outside Europe, US President Barack Obama's Open Government Initiative (OGI) is largely an example of NPG and its potential coupling with elements of DEG. Other countries were able to associate themselves with the OGI, which might have helped to diffuse some of its core ideas.

NPG and the key aspect of networked governance are not restricted to the Western hemisphere; there are also elements of NPG in non-Western countries. As such, there have been interesting discussions about how network governance and partnerships can be combined with Confucian ideas about harmony, moderation and balance (Tao et al. 2010). Some scholars claim that China is experimenting with networks as a mode of governance (Xia 2007), and empirical examples can be found at the local and district levels (Yifen 2007; Fulda et al. 2012). With its strongly authoritarian government and the lack of constitutional guarantees for the formation of independent civic organizations, China provides a tough testing ground for the successful development of NPG.

MAIN GOVERNANCE IDEA: GOALS AND MEANS

The core assumption of NPG is that complex problems and tasks in a fragmented and multi-layered society with a differentiated polity are solved better through networked collaboration than through hierarchical control or market-based competition. As such, it is asserted that wicked and unruly problems call for negotiated solutions based on trust, knowledge sharing and commitment to creative thinking and social experimentation. The argument for this is that hierarchical problem-solving strategies based on the formal authorization of centrally placed decision-makers or policy experts who are entrusted to define the problem and come up with a swift solution often miss the target because they fail to draw on the experiences, views and ideas of relevant and affected actors at the lower levels of (or outside) the organization. Competitive problem-solving strategies compensate for this failure by mobilizing a broad range of social and political actors who compete to find the best possible solution and, in so doing, challenge formal authorities and established hierarchies. Although this strategy clearly broadens the solution space, there is an imminent risk of the competing actors exhausting their resources and wasting precious time and energy on rivalry and destructive conflicts that prevent knowledge sharing and mutual learning (Torfing 2016). On this background, Roberts (2000) argues that networked collaboration is the best strategy for bringing relevant and affected actors together in trust-based learning processes that may spur the development of joint solutions to common problems through the constructive management of the ideational and interest-based differences between the actors (see also Gray 1989).

While networked governance and the co-creation of public value outcomes enable resource mobilization and spur innovation in a public sector that confronts major societal challenges and growing expectations to the quality of public services, it has limited resources at its disposal.

Interactive governance is not only intended to enhance cost efficiency but also to improve the effectiveness, quality and democratic legitimacy of public governance.

Instead of subordinating private actors to hierarchical rule or encouraging competition between public agencies and private contractors, NPG aims to promote collaboration based on resource interdependency by highlighting the 'collaborative advantage', defined as what the actors can achieve together but none of them can achieve by themselves (Huxham and Vangen 2005). However, knowledge sharing, coordination and collaboration in networks are not only relevant for the public sector's external relations to societal actors but also for its internal relations and functioning. The public sector is fragmented and lacks vertical and horizontal alignment, coordination and dialogue. The bureaucratic governance paradigm created lengthy vertical chains of command based on centralized control, and it enhanced the professional specialization and compartmentalization along the horizontal axis. NPM reasserted the bureaucratic separation between politics and administration and introduced the principle of arms-length governance, according to which public service organizations and private contractors should be governed by overall objectives and economic budget frames and evaluated using an elaborate system of performance management coupled to high-powered incentives. Although centralized control is further strengthened when rule compliance is supplemented with performance control, the risk of decoupling between top and bottom in the public sector increases dramatically due to frontline agencies tending to construe the control-based performance management system as a consequence of a growing distrust in the local competences, capacities and motivations, and because the distance between the executive and operational levels of the organization is growing. The vertical unhinging of the chain of command running from elected politicians, via executive managers, to frontline agencies and personnel is supplemented by a growing horizontal separation of line agencies. Each of the managing directors is given a specific budget, a number of employees and a list of key performance indicators, and they are expected to deliver results within the budget frame. Annual budget cuts motivated by the expectation of continuous productivity gains make it difficult for public organizations to make ends meet. In this situation, interagency collaboration quickly becomes an unaffordable luxury. The lack of coordination, alignment and dialogue along both the vertical and horizontal axes threatens the overall cohesion of the public sector; attempting to solve the problem by further tightening the performance system only exacerbates the situation. To reverse this trend and enhance cohesion, NPG recommends that the public sector drills holes in the bureaucratic silos and creates platforms and arenas for dialogue up and down the chain of governance, transforming itself into an arena for co-creation in and through overlapping internal and external networks.

The location of NPG in the governance diamond in Figure 8.1 is relatively clear and simple. Compared to the other governance paradigms, NPG scores very low on the degree of centralized control due to its emphasis on horizontal interaction in networks, which tends to reduce central steering to a subtle and indirect metagovernance aimed at designing collaborative platforms and arenas, framing the interaction, facilitating collaborative processes and influencing outcomes (Torfing et al. 2012). Governance networks operate in the 'shadow of hierarchy' (Scharpf 1998), because the public hierarchies are ready to take control if the networks fail to deliver solutions. Nevertheless, the shadow is weak since the attempt to marginalize or overrule governance networks will be met with strong opposition and deliberate attempts to obstruct the hierarchical solution, which will lack legitimacy. NPG thus perceives centralized steering as being limited by the self-governing character of networks and partnerships in the decentred and differentiated polity.

NPG scores very high on horizontal coordination and strongly recommends horizontal coordination in cross-boundary networks. Fragmented steering landscapes and bureaucratic silos are considered key challenges with respect to solving wicked problems that cut across the administrative division of labour. The prescribed cure for this problem is bottom-up coordination and collaboration based on interdependency. Eliminating administrative silos requires the transformation of the organizational culture so that it becomes simple, easy and appropriate to contact relevant persons in other administrative units and perhaps form a network that can facilitate coordination and joint problem-solving. Ideally, administrative departments and agencies should be involved in a plurality of overlapping networks that cut across levels and organizations and facilitate a constant flow of information, knowledge and resources between organizational levels and units.

NPG scores medium on the use of value articulation, because participation in interactive governance processes is motivated by the mutual dependency of the social and political vis-à-vis the construction of common solutions that are pursued because of their normative value for the involved actors and society at large. To illustrate, the co-creation of local climate solutions is propelled by the joint recognition among a plethora of public and private actors that none of them can save the planet on their own. The normative goal of enhancing sustainability by reducing CO_2 emissions ties the local actors together in a kind of community of destiny that spurs joint action. NPG thus aims to bring relevant and affected actors together in order to create innovative, effective and democratic solutions that realize joint aspirations to enhance social, economic and environmental sustainability. With this background, it is interesting how the UN urges the new global sustainability development goal to be realized through public–private collaboration in networks and partnerships. In short, NPG assumes that the dream of the good society will motivate social and political actors to join forces and engage in interactive governance. Still, it can be difficult to align the network actors' values when they come from organizations with different value sets and diverging interests and because no single actor has the authority to define the values for the entire network. Horizontal coordination and alignment – rather than the articulation of common values – is therefore ultimately considered to be the most important driver of governance.

NPG scores low to medium on the use of incentives, since positive and negative incentives are generally seen as playing a marginal role in governance processes. The vertical relations between the actors involved in public governance are supposed to be based on mutual trust and the constructive management of differences. The horizontal relations are supposed to be based on interdependency rather than competition. However, incentives are not completely absent from NPG. Both interdependency theory and governability theory refer to the use of incentives to encourage networking and solve collective action problems (e.g. free-riding and decision traps) that are not solved by the creation of social and political environments with a high degree of moral obligation and normative control. Incentives can render participation in and contributions to joint solutions in networks more appealing than solutions obtained by going it alone. In addition, competition between different networks and partnerships for funding and political attention might spur innovation and excellence in governance solutions.

The final axis is societal involvement. Here, NPG scores very high as a broad range of societal actors (e.g. users, citizens, civil society organizations, private firms) are seen as potential participants in networks, partnerships and other collaborative governance arrangements. Professional organizations and private contractors are not supposed to be alone in participating in and contributing to the production and delivery of public services. All of the societal actors with relevant resources and competences and a high degree of affectedness can contribute to solving wicked problems and producing innovative, effective and democratic outcomes (Pestoff et al. 2013).

The location of NPG on the five dimensions of the public governance diamond is presented in Figure 8.1.

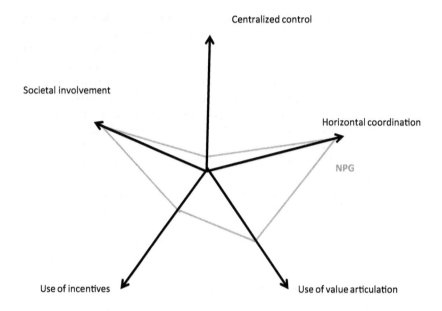

Figure 8.1　The NPG governance diamond

EMPIRICAL RESULTS

Whereas several of the constitutive elements in NPG are well-known features of the public sector, the strategic ambition to spur the development of these features is new and has only been around for little more than a decade. The short lifespan explains why there are hardly any surveys documenting the prevalence of NPG. A recent Danish survey administered to municipal directors for social welfare and technical services provides a small exception, as it shows that NPG measured in terms of eight different items on a five-point Likert scale apparently receives much more attention in local government agencies than NPM, which was also measured using eight different items (Torfing and Køhler 2016). The sequence of the public governance items was randomly selected, and the municipal directors were asked how much attention the organization paid to various governance items. Only the NPM-related item of management by objectives emerged with a positive percentage difference, whereas all of the NPG items had positive percentage differences. However, we know little as to whether the ideas associated with NPG are realized in practice. As such, there is a clear lack of studies evaluating the empirical prevalence and outcomes of NPG. Hence, at present, the demand for hard evidence is difficult to meet. Nevertheless, we are not totally clueless. If we consider each of the different aspects of NPG, there are a number of empirical studies that can provide hints regarding the results that are achieved.

On the input side of the political system, NPG aims to cultivate a more active citizenship. Hence, it claims that the educational and anti-authoritarian revolutions have made the citizens more competent and assertive and therefore ready for more direct and active participation than is commonly offered by representative democracy and more constructive and responsible engagement with the public sector than that which is facilitated by the free choice of service provider that has been introduced by NPM. Here, there is ample evidence of the growing demand among citizens for the development of active and direct forms of participation and involvement in the co-production of public solutions (Bang and Sørensen 1999; Warren 2002; Norris 2011; Dalton and Welzel 2014; Brandsen et al. 2018). NPG aims to meet this growing demand via the expansion of new forms of citizen engagement based on 'thick partici-pation' (Nabatchi and Leighninger 2015). A considerable number of case studies seem to indicate that citizen engagement in dialogue-based forms of participation enhances the democratic empowerment and social capital of the citizens and creates a more democratic decision-making process (Fung and Wright 2003; Rosenberg 2007; Fung 2009; Smith 2009).

Co-production and co-creation are gaining ground at the public service production level (Pestoff et al. 2013; Torfing et al. 2019), although most services are still produced by public agencies with little contribution from users, citizens and volunteers. Some studies show that co-production helps to enhance efficiency and redesign entire service-delivery systems (Alford 2008; Dunston et al. 2009). In the field of policy-making, there is a growing appreciation of the role of networks in providing flexible cross-cutting coordination along the vertical and horizontal axes of the public sector (Scharpf 1999; EU 2001; Marks and Hooghe 2004; Rhodes 2000). Studies of crisis management and emergency response show that intera-gency networks facilitate communication and coordination and help to build resilience (Kapucu 2006; Boin and Lodge 2016; Hermansson 2016).

On the output side of the political system, NPG aims to promote the use of new tools of governance that rely less on legal rules and high-powered incentives and more on voluntary agreements on common, values, norms and standards, intensive communication, self-evaluation and professional dialogue (Salamon 2002). Empirical studies show that the use of new governance tools depends on negotiations and pragmatic, context-sensitive choices (Lascoumes and Le Galès 2007) and that many of the new governance tools build on the principle of 'regulated self-regulation' (Sørensen and Triantafillou 2013). The EU is frequently using new soft forms of governance based on non-binding goals and standards. Studies of the Open Method of Coordination show that, under certain conditions, soft governance tools can produce the desired effects. However, these studies also reveal that the impact of soft governance tools is greater when combined with hard governance tools (Borrás and Jacobsson 2004; Trubek and Trubek 2005). Still, there are few studies in this area, and it is difficult to draw any clear and steadfast conclusions.

Turning to the analysis of the administrative implementation of service and policy solutions, the pendulum seems to swing from growing monitoring and control to more dialogue- and trust-based management and evaluation systems that tend to enhance policy learning (Bovens et al. 2008; Moynihan 2008), improve the efficiency of public governance (Aucoin and Heintzman 2000), mobilize professional competences (Bentzen 2016) and draw on the experiences of users and citizens (Papadopoulos 2003). However, the research in this area tends to focus more on scrutinizing the new forms of dialogue- and trust-based management than measuring their effects. Important exceptions are found in the empirical research on trust-based management, which has identified positive effects, such as less need for monitoring and control (Malhotra and Murnighan 2002), a higher degree of workplace well-being and intrinsic task-motivation among public employees (Nyhan 2000), and more open and cross-cutting collaboration (McEvily et al. 2003). The remarkable achievements of *Buurtzorg*, the Dutch homecare service firm, illustrate the conclusions from the research on trust-based management aimed at minimizing centralized control based on rules, regulation and performance management. Created in 2007 by four homecare nurses who wanted to help make elderly persons requiring assistance more self-sufficient, *Buurtzorg* now has more than 10,000 employees working in self-organizing teams with limited central support and only two top managers. The new homecare firm, which delivers eldercare services on behalf of local municipalities, has received awards as the best workplace in the Netherlands. The number of sick days for the self-managing nurses has been reduced to a minimum, and the number of emergency hospitalizations of the elderly has been reduced by a third. The secret behind the positive results is freedom and responsibility. To avoid overstretching the conclusions, however, we must remember that some studies conclude that excessive trust can backfire by increasing cheating on both efforts and service quality (Gargiulo and Ertug 2006). Control might have a positive impact, as demonstrated by Bengtsson and Engström (2014), who reveal how the introduction of a new system for control in relation to Swedish NGOs has had a positive impact on performance. Perhaps the truth lies in finding the right balance between trust and control (Weibel 2007) or in discovering how public management based on a high level of trust in the motivation and competences of public sector professionals can be exercised in ways that that are compatible with legitimate control over outputs and outcomes (Bentzen 2016).

The empirical research on NPG has spent a lot of time, energy and resources studying the proliferation of networks and partnerships at local, regional, national and transnational levels (van Heffen et al. 2000; Betsill and Bulkeley 2004; Marcussen and Torfing 2007; Koliba et al. 2010). There are numerous studies of how governance networks and partnerships contribute to making public governance more effective (Börzel and Risse 2005; Sørensen and Torfing 2007; Provan and Kennis 2008), more democratic (Fung 2004; Torfing et al. 2009) and more innovative (Newman et al. 2001; Ansell and Torfing 2014; Torfing and Triantafillou 2016). However, most of this research aims to identify the institutional and managerial conditions for effective, democratic and innovative governance (Sørensen and Torfing 2009, 2017) rather than providing precise evidence of the impact. Most studies are qualitative single-case studies, and there is a clear lack of comparative case studies and quantitative medium or large-N studies with precise estimations of the impact of collaborative governance in networks and partnerships. Fortunately, impact studies seem to be gaining ground in the study of public–private partnerships (see Carpintero and Petersen 2013).

In the emerging field of collaborative innovation, a new study aims to measure the degree of collaboration, innovation and crime-prevention impact in 24 local projects in Copenhagen. Each of the three basic variables was measured through carefully validated quantitative and qualitative self-scoring on multiple dimensions that are used to construct three additive indexes. The result of the multiple regression analysis was that collaboration affects the crime-prevention impact, but that this effect results from the enhancement of innovation (Torfing and Krogh 2017). Nevertheless, empirical studies are required that would allow us to draw causal inference while paying attention to context variation in order to provide a genuine assessment of the impact of the collaborative forms of governance recommended by NPG.

DEBATE AND DILEMMAS

NPG aims to transform the public sector from being primarily a legal authority (classical bureaucracy) or a service provider (NPM) to a platform and arena for co-creation (NPG) that invites the relevant and affected actors to participate in defining problems and tasks, and designing and implementing new and bold solutions that hit the target. However, while local governments eager to make ends meet and deal with the growing number of wicked problems might be tempted to go down this road, central government agencies that are concerned about compliance and budget control and sceptical towards excessive experimentation may want to maintain their centralized control on the basis of rule-based regulation combined with strict performance management. The battle is on, but the frontline in this battle is becoming increasingly blurred by the fact that central governments also feel the pressure to involve a plethora of public and private actors in interactive forms of governance, and local and regional governments realize that the participatory, trust-based and deliberative forms of governance might get out of hand without a certain number of controls.

When considering cutting-edge developments, it is interesting to note that core NPG elements such as interactive governance, co-production and co-creation are not only applied in the development of innovative solutions to complex problems and when there is a pressing need for coordination. There are examples of the co-production of building permits that constitute a classic example of public authority. Hence, some local municipalities engage in dialogue with permit seekers before they submit their application and give them opportunity to respond to intended decisions before they are formally announced in order to dispel misunderstandings and perhaps make last minute changes to the application in order to enhance the chance of success. The result of the active involvement of the applicants appears to be increasing user satisfaction and reducing the number of complaints. There are also examples of local municipalities experimenting with the creation of social support networks (typically consisting of, e.g., relatives, neighbours, school teachers, sports coaches) for at-risk children and youth as an alternative to removing them from their home and placement in foster care. The network of trusted and engaged persons offers emotional and social support on a daily basis and helps the children and youth to navigate in a world of disappointment, dysfunctionality and tough demands. Finally, the field of market-based contracting out of public services has seen the growing use of relational contracts, which replace costly monitoring and control mechanisms with continuous collaboration and coordination between the public purchasers and private providers. We lack evidence of the prevalence of these examples of how core features of NPG are spreading into bureaucratic and market-based domains. It is interesting to note that collaborative and dialogical forms of network governance are apparently having an impact on what we think of as clear examples of state rule or market regulation.

The first argument in favour of a turn to NPG is that the public sector is caught in the cross-fire between increasing expectations to public services amongst citizens and scarce public resources, which calls for resource mobilization in order to avoid the gradual erosion of public welfare. A second and equally important argument in favour of NPG is that no single public or private actor has all of the knowledge, resources and ideas to solve the complex societal problems that we are confronting. The exchange and pooling of resources and ideas provides an attractive alternative to the reliance on the in-house resources of either public authorities or private service contractors.

The argument against NPG is first and foremost that interactive governance, at least from the perspective of central government agencies, seems to produce complex, ungovernable and risk-prone processes of collaboration and innovation. There is an imminent risk that the many different actors – all of whom have different agendas, interests and demands – may fail to reach an agreement, may agree on unimaginative solutions based on the least common denominator, or may produce innovative solutions that are attractive but very expensive and vulnerable to societal change (Torfing et al. 2012). As noted above, metagovernance is called for, but the exercise of metagovernance requires that the would-be metagovernor holds a central position in the governance network, enjoys sufficient authority so that the network actors listen, holds enough resources to lower the transaction costs of collaboration, and has sufficient organizational backing to be able to monitor, support and participate in the network.

Another problem is the lack of guarantee that the service-users, citizens and civil society actors are motivated to participate in the co-production and co-creation of public solutions. Participation in public governance and service production by volunteers and stakeholders is often characterized by large fluctuations, and participation is low and unconstructive in some instances. Moreover, citizens may not have the capacity for effective participation. Participatory selection bias favouring the participation of white, retired middle-class people (often with a public sector background) over citizens with few resources and a busy life with small children or private business ownership tends to create a democratic deficit. Finally, if citizens perceive themselves as taxpayers with an undisputable right to certain levels of service, or as customers who are free to demand high quality for as little as possible and with no need to contribute to the solution themselves, they will not want to participate at all despite their skills and competences and their ability to contribute constructively to the production of public value outcomes.

A third argument against the interactive forms of governance associated with NPG is the collective action problems that may arise when actors with different resources and interests aim to find joint solutions to common problems. Free-riding – where actors aim to take advantage of joint solutions without contributing to them – is common in social contexts with weak hierarchical or social control. Moreover, in the absence of strategic alignment aimed at ensuring that all actors are equally committed to achieving the same overall goals, individual actors may pursue their own individual strategies that create suboptimal collective outcomes. Finally, yet significantly, the price of reaching agreement on a joint solution through iterative rounds of give and take may be the formation of a muddy compromise that nobody really wants and that fails to provide a clear direction for public governance.

A fourth problem is that the democratic control over networked processes and outcomes is complicated, as the interactive governance processes often lack public transparency and sometimes take place in 'smoke-filled rooms' and with the participation of actors who deliberately aim to avoid public attention and oversight. On top of this problem with a lack of transparency, it is notoriously difficult to hold networks and partnerships to account for policy failures and governance disasters, because it is unclear who supported which decisions, why and how. The sanctioning of network actors who are deemed responsible for bad or failing solutions is also difficult, because they are often appointed rather than elected and they may have a monopoly on representing an important stakeholder group (Esmark 2007; Papadopoulos 2007; Koliba et al. 2011).

Finally, the overall benefit of resource mobilization, interactive governance and the trust-based co-creation of public solutions is uncertain because the involvement of a plethora of public and private actors, including users and citizens, in public governance and service production may increase public expenditure. Even when the actors create innovative solutions that outperform the existing ones, there is no guarantee that the new solutions will cost less or that they replace the old ones. Public innovation may lead to the production of a large number of add-ons. While NPG supporters will claim that the goal- and framework-steering of collaborative governance and the initial alignment of expectations to innovative outcomes of multi-actor collaboration can reduce this problem, the critics may not be so sure.

Dealing effectively with the problems and challenges associated with a turn towards NPG requires the development of new institutional designs and new forms of leadership that are more attuned to cross-cutting collaboration and trust-based self-organization. In the last 30 years, public managers have been told to focus on their own organization and employees and to ensure that they deliver on the pre-determined perform-ance goals. In the context of NPG, they will have to lead cross-cutting collaboration aimed at producing new and innovative solutions. Switch-ing roles in this manner is by no means easy and requires the develop-ment of collaborative competences, including convener, communication and facilitation skills, storytelling and other framing capacities, and talents for coaching, trust-building, boundary-spanning and brokering.

Three actor-related dilemmas in relation to the implementation of NPG spring to mind. The first concerns the elected politicians. Active engage-ment in interactive processes and collaborative arenas will most likely enable elected politicians to strengthen their political leadership (Ansell and Torfing 2017). Dialogue with citizens and private stakeholders will enable politicians to better understand the problems at hand, to design new and better solutions and to mobilize broad-based support for their implementation. While this might sound well and good, the dilemma is that the interactive policy processes that help to qualify their political leadership tend to undermine their position as sovereign decision-makers who have been given a mandate to take important decisions on behalf of the people. The key question is how much elected politicians lose and gain from the development of a more interactive political leadership based on systematic and sustained dialogue with relevant and affected actors. If the politicians are those who have initiated the collaborative interaction with citizens and private stakeholders and they also take the final decisions based on recommendations from collaborative forums and arenas, they may indeed be able to have their cake and eat it too.

The second dilemma is that public managers and employees alike often find that cross-sectoral and interorganizational collaboration helps to better solve the problems and challenges they are encountering, but that their ability to lead cross-cutting collaboration and actors over whom they have no formal authority is limited. The collaborative interaction with other actors may produce a solution, but there is no guarantee that it is in accordance with the overall political-administrative goals. In fact, the formulation or reformulation of the goal might be a key part of the collaborative endeavour. Public managers and employees will therefore have to accept that goals are subject to negotiation and that the only yardstick is whether the outcomes of interactive governance create public value for the citizens and society at large. Even here there are no definite answers. Public managers might collaborate with a broad range of actors in order to challenge their own thoughts and ideas and to produce more innovative solutions. The problem, however, is that collaborative innovation processes sometimes go wrong or lead to failures. Hence, the dilemma for public managers is that they must lead risk-prone innovation processes while continuing to deliver stable results and meet their performance targets.

The final dilemma is that the citizens might want to participate in public governance and service production in order to influence the public solutions – but without necessarily taking any responsibility for them. Although participation often breeds ownership over joint solutions, citizens and private stakeholders tend to reserve the right to criticize public solutions even if they themselves have contributed to shaping their content. The solutions might include the involvement of citizens in designing and implementing solutions in which influence and responsibility go hand in hand, for example by involving them in co-design and/or co-delivery. However, not all citizens and users are both willing and able to participate in the co-design of public service solutions (Andersen, Kristensen and Pedersen 2012).

In sum, NPG seeks to present itself as an antidote to NPM; it is a new governance paradigm aimed at responding to the societal challenges and shortcomings of previous governance paradigms. At the same time, however, it generates a new set of problems, challenges and dilemmas that politicians, public managers and employees – working together with active and assertive citizens – will need to find new ways of tackling.

9. Comparing governance paradigms

EVOLUTION, DEVOLUTION AND REVOLUTION – THE PENDULUM

When comparing the different governance paradigms, it may be useful to see how they are connected and have developed over time. Governance paradigms point both back in time and into the future. We have argued that the bureaucratic paradigm characterized by the combination of hierarchy and formal rules is the oldest paradigm dating back to ancient civilizations and recently renewed by Max Weber and Woodrow Wilson.

However, bureaucracy has been historically layered with professional rule by civil servants, mandarins and the like. Professional rule gained momentum in the twentieth century, when the professionals became the backbone of public service production. Today, professional rule is particularly strong in professions such as medicine and amongst civil servants with legal backgrounds.

New Public Management (NPM) surfaced in the late 1970s and early 1980s and was gradually supplemented by Public Value Management (PVM), Digital Era Governance (DEG) and New Public Governance (NPG). Whether all of these new paradigms are the result of evolution or revolution depends upon the historical interpretation and explanation. Even if the Weberian bureaucracy developed gradually, as a paradigm it represented a radically new and coherent way of organizing the public sector compared to the chaotic and clientelistic principles of medieval public organization. Similarly, professional rule dramatically challenged the principles of hierarchical top-down steering through command and formal rules. NPM might be seen as a revolution in the governance of the public sector in challenging central welfare state values and being promoted by neo-liberal and neo-conservative political forces that challenged the post-war consensus. Still, it may also be interpreted as a way of dealing with the fiscal challenges of the welfare state in order to make it survive. Similar can be said of NPG, whereas DEG is clearly the result of an evolutionary learning process, although it continues to revolutionize public service production by introducing new digital technologies.

The development and discovery of the governance paradigms presented and discussed in this book can be understood in many ways. To mention just a few, we are able to distinguish between political, functional and institutional explanations. Political explanations claim that current and new paradigms are a result of decisions taken by political elites that in turn are informed by the dominant ideology of the ruling government party or government coalition. This implies that paradigms change as a result of political changes. Functional explanations argue that governance paradigms provide a plausible answer to specific problems and challenges that are accumulated in relation to the dominant governance paradigm. Institutional explanations say that dominant paradigms may travel in time and space and become hegemonic, because they reflect what is currently thought of as an appropriate way forward within a particular institutional context. Most paradigms have a claim to universality due to their generic traits, which presumably cover and work well in different situations and contexts. Our argument is that they are historically contingent constructs that emerge, develop and adapt over time, and that they are combined with other governance paradigms in response to political changes, new societal challenges and new technological discoveries. A synthesizing combination of these explanations would look at paradigmatic evolution and revolutions as a response to political and administrative learning processes. The pendulum metaphor captures this explanation even if it is a bit simplistic and tends to descale the overlaps and mixed nature in empirical manifestations of the paradigms. The pendulum may be associated with reactions to changes and thus capture some of the dynamics in the development of new paradigms.

The pendulum metaphor has long been used to account for the historical development of governance paradigms (e.g. Aucoin 1990; Norman and Gregory 2003). Some would argue that, deep down, all of the new administrative reforms and management fads presuppose some well-functioning government institutions based on legal authority, hierarchical rule and bureaucratic ethics (Klausen 2014). We have already mentioned the New PA and the Blacksburg Manifesto, both of which hold such a view. The NWS can also be seen as a specific and historical expression of such a stance, as it aims to protect the core principles of bureaucratic government from the marketization reforms spurred by NPM.

Social science is rife with attempts to explain how competing organizing principles can be combined when trying to build nations and organizations. This literature refers to contingent combinations of exit, voice and loyalty (Hirschman 1970), politics and markets (Lindblom 1977) and markets, bureaucracies and clans (Ouchi 1980). Olsen (2006) argues that ideological struggles sometimes develop over the determination of what exactly constitutes desirable forms of administration. Although he admits that bureaucratic organization is not the answer to all of the challenges of public administration, he argues that we should rediscover Weber's analysis of bureaucratic organization. Olsen sees bureaucratic organization as part of a repertoire of overlapping, supplementary and competing forms of governance that are co-existing in contemporary democracies, and he claims that the same applies to market organization and network organization.

In line with this, Rhodes (2015) argues that the pendulum has swung too far towards NPM and NPG and that it needs to swing back towards bureaucracy and the traditional skills of professional bureaucrats. He argues that counselling, stewardship, practical wisdom, probity, judgment, diplomacy and political nous are important and must be brought back in. Arguing that it is not a question of traditional skills versus NPM and NPG, he stresses the importance of context dependency (which skills fit in a particular context). This is in line with the idea of the layering of paradigms implicit in Olsen's (2006) argument. Christopher Hood (1998) used 'cultural theory' and grid-group theory in the tradition of the anthropologist Mary Douglas (1999) to argue for a more complex dynamic between four different styles of organization and public management (fatalist, hierarchical, individualist and egalitarian).

In sum, context-dependent learning and societal dynamics seem to drive complex transformations of public governance paradigms that include evolutionary and revolutionary developments, institutional layering processes, back-and-forth pendulum swings and shifting emphases on ideological re-orientation and pragmatic adaptation.

COMPARING THE PARADIGMS

When comparing the different governance paradigms, we have focused on what the competing paradigms assume to be needed to improve the public sector, and we have highlighted the specific tools and ways of organizing, governing and leading the public sector that each paradigm holds dear. We have referred to the cherished components of the governance paradigms as strategies, programmes and institutional templates.

We developed the public governance diamond used in the previous chapters to create an overview of the variation of the paradigms on some important dimensions that are frequently discussed in the public governance literature. The previous chapter has scored the different governance paradigms on the five axes of the public governance diamond. We shall now compare the result of the scoring of each governance paradigm on the five dimensions more directly. The ranking of the seven governance paradigms on the various dimensions based on the scoring presented in the previous chapters is presented in Table 9.1. Ranking the different governance paradigms in this way is no easy task, and it can and should be discussed. It builds on arguments presented above, but there is an element of discretion in placing the governance paradigms on the axes of the public governance diamond.

Table 9.1   *The relative ranking of the seven paradigms on the five dimensions of the governance diamond (ranked highest to lowest)*

Centralized control	Horizontal coordination	Use of value articulation	Use of incentives	Societal involvement
The degree of centralized control in the vertical chain of command	The degree of horizontal inter-organizational coordination and collaboration	The degree to which public governance is based on articulation of understanding of the desirable (values)	The degree to which public governance is based on conditional positive and negative pecuniary and non-pecuniary incentives	The degree to which societal for- and/or non-profit actors (including citizens) are involved in public governance
Bureaucracy	NPG	PVM	NPM	NPG
NWS	DEG	NWS	DEG	PVM
DEG	PVM	Professional rule	NWS	NPM
PVM	NWS	NPG	PVM	Professional rule
Professional rule	NPM	Bureaucracy	NPG	DEG
NPM	Bureaucracy	DEG	Bureaucracy	NWS
NPG	Professional rule	NPM	Professional rule	Bureaucracy

Let us briefly consider the arguments behind the ranking of the different governance paradigms on the five axes.

The 'centralized control' dimension concerns the degree of top-down control in the vertical chain of command. We place bureaucracy at the top, because both rules and hierarchies (with supervisors and subordinates) strongly promote a top-down steering logic. In the ranking, bureaucracy is followed by the Neo-Weberian State (NWS), which still emphasizes the role of classical hierarchy but also recommends greater responsiveness towards citizens and seeks to facilitate a two-way dialogue up and down the chain of command in order to promote a well-informed and negotiated leadership. DEG can be both very centralized (if digital solutions are used to centralize functions at the national level) and relatively decentralized (if used to enhance bottom-up participation), but the structure and use of digital solutions will often be decided by central decision-makers. PVM is less centralized due to the important role played by individual public managers in public service organizations and the emphasis on the translation of values to frontline staff, but it is more centralized than professional rule, where the centralization only emerges through the creation of organized professions and, thus, professional associations. NPM recommends decentralization, for example, in and through the 'steering, not rowing' statement, but NPG is even lower on centralized control, because it aims to enhance the trust-based management of frontline personnel and recommends the inclusion of all types of decentralized actors and through the recommendation of network governance, which clearly distances it from centralized decision-making.

Horizontal coordination concerns the degree of recommended horizontal inter-organizational coordination and collaboration. NPG aims to drill holes in the silos created by bureaucracy and NPM and actively recommends horizontal coordination through networks and partnerships. DEG follows suit, because one of the key arguments for digitalization is improved real-time coordination between (sub-) agencies. PVM recognizes the need for horizontal coordination at lower levels in public organizations but still positions the public manager (in the vertical hierarchy) as the key translator and articulator of public values. One of the differences between NWS and classical forms of bureaucracy is how NWS recognizes the need for horizontal coordination. Still, if not through organizational mergers, NWS has few ideas and suggestions about how this coordination can be achieved. The responsibility of each (heroic) manager in NPM places this paradigm lower than the other new paradigms, although it considers the coordinating role of the executive group of leaders and managers as pivotal. The idea of centralized hierarchical coordination is also found in classical bureaucracy. Here, however, the preference for a clear division of labour between bureaucratic agencies seems to outweigh the attempt to provide horizontal coordination. Finally, professional rule almost goes against horizontal coordination, because it recommends reliance on the professional norms and specialized knowledge of separate occupations. This can seriously hamper coordination between fields dominated by different professional groups that are infused by different norms and values and speak different 'languages'.

Although specific norms and values inform each of the paradigms, they differ in terms of whether they recommend an active use of value articulation in public sector governance. PVM sees the articulation of values as the most important governance mechanism and is accordingly placed highest on this dimension. NWS also emphasizes the importance of using values actively in public governance, especially highlighting the observance of traditional bureaucratic virtues and the value communicated by strategic managers. Professional rule attaches importance to value articulation, but only a very specific type of values held by a particular professional group. NPG acknowledges the role of public values in networks and in governance more generally, but the use of value articulation is less central to the paradigm than in PVM, NWS and professional rule. For bureaucracy, specific values such as rule of law, neutrality and loyalty are important, but the paradigm pays relatively little attention to how they should be articulated to improve public governance. This lack of attention to value articulation is even more the case for DEG. The logic informing NPM clashes completely with the active use of value articulation, because this paradigm builds on a model of man wherein individuals are seen as self-interested utility optimizers, indicating that value articulation would have no effect.

The use of incentives concerns the degree to which the paradigms recommend the deployment of conditional positive and negative pecuniary and non-pecuniary incentives. Here, NPM is a clear top scorer, as the abovementioned model of human behaviour suggests that individuals can only be governed through contingent rewards and sanctions. DEG is open to the use of incentives as a governance tool but does not explicitly recommend doing so in all cases. NWS is aware of the importance of managers exercising transactional leadership but does not see incentives as a one-size-fits-all solution for public organizations. The focus on the uniqueness of public organizations is even higher for PVM, which also seems aware of the potentially negative effects of using incentives. This is also the case for NPG, where the model of human behaviour is much more complex, highlighting that individuals and groups are motivated by both prosocial and extrinsic motives. According to the bureaucracy paradigm, incentives should only be contingent on merit, and professional rule directly opposes the use of incentives (especially pecuniary rewards), because such inducements are seen as clashing with the logic of professionalism.

Societal involvement concerns the recommendations in the governance paradigms regarding the degree of involvement of societal for-profit and/or non-profit actors. NPG scores highest here, because the involvement of relevant and affected actors is one of the key governance mechanisms recommended by the paradigm. The stakeholder perspective in PVM indicates a high score on this dimension, although the involvement of societal actors is mainly part of the process through which public value propositions are authorized and less pronounced in the implementation process. NPM recommends a very specific involvement of external actors, namely of private firms through outsourcing and privatization. Professional rule also suggests a rather specific and somewhat narrow involvement, namely of the professional associations that contribute to the development and exchange of professional norms and values. DEG can be seen as relatively indifferent on this dimension, while NWS emphasizes the importance of democratic accountability and vertical responsibility and loyalty much higher than citizen involvement (and other societal actors), indicating a score on the dimension that is lower than the other paradigms (expect for classical bureaucracy, where the public sector is seen as self-sufficient and does not need the involvement of external societal actors).

After having compared the seven governance paradigms on the five different dimensions, it is worth remembering that each paradigm has a relatively coherent core. Hence, in the final instance, bureaucracy focusses on hierarchy and formal rules; professional rule builds on the relative autonomy of professions with particular forms of knowledge and norms; NPM emphasizes the use of competition and transactional leadership; NWS aims to integrate organizations and ground them in public bureaucratic virtues; NPG is synonymous with the co-creation of solutions in networks and partnerships and through citizen engagement; DEG aims to exploit digital technologies and big data to create efficient, integrated and holistic service delivery; and PVM is associated with the pursuit of public value outcomes by proactive public managers. The differences in the core principles of each paradigm determine their respective scores on the five axes of the governance diamond.

We can now proceed to the grand comparison of all seven governance paradigms on the five axes capturing the analytical dimensions that bring out the differences between the paradigms. These differences should not be overexaggerated. Still we find that ideal-type comparisons make sense as a heuristic tool from which the layering, the overlaps and the specific historical and empirical expressions – some close to the ideal type, others further away from such an ideal – may be discovered, discerned and discussed.

Plotting all of the different governance paradigms into the same governance diamond in Figure 9.1 illustrates how they move in different directions and produce very differently shaped diamonds.

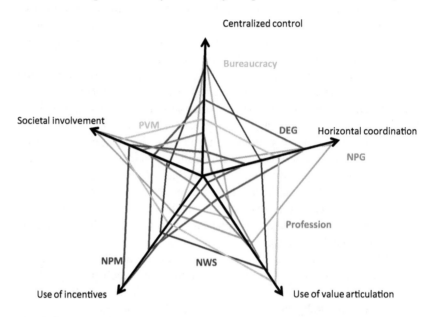

Figure 9.1   Grand comparison of all the different governance diamonds

The full-blown governance diamond model reveals the characteristic profiles distinguishing the governance paradigms from each other as well as the complexity of the social reality that public leaders and employees are facing in their everyday work. The contrasted and conflicting diamond shapes that emerge in the governance diamond co-exist and make it difficult for public leaders and employees to discern what is appropriate to think and do when it comes to organizing, governing and leading public sector activities. We return to discuss this challenge in Chapter 10.

A few interesting observations can be made from the grand comparison of the governance paradigms.

First, the governance paradigms differ from each other, each having their characteristic profile. The different diamond shapes move in different directions. They are complementary and together they cover almost all of the available space in the governance diamond.

Second, the historical development of the paradigms from classical bureaucracy and professional rule via NPM to NWS, PVM, DEG and

NPG shows itself in terms of a series of 'corrections' compared to the previous paradigms that sent the subsequent paradigms in new directions, thus transforming the shape of the diamond.

Third, the shape of the diamonds of three old paradigms (bureaucracy, professional rule and NPM) are very different, indicating that they are the results of revolutionary ruptures, whereas the newer governance paradigms have more congruence in their diamond shapes, thus indicating more moderate and evolutionary modifications.

Fourth, the diamond shapes of NWS and PVM cover the largest areas, suggesting that they are moderate, ambitious and inclusive. But this is also indicative of how they are founded on eclecticism and combine elements from multiple governance paradigms. In contrast, bureaucracy, NPM and NPG have very different diamond shapes that point in different directions and will therefore be difficult to combine in practice.

Having compared the paradigms on the five dimensions of the governance diamond, we want to narrow the focus and compare the paradigms regarding their stipulations about the roles of key public actors, such as the elected politicians and public employees. We return to the role of the politicians in Chapter 10. Here, we compare the paradigms in terms of their assumptions about public employee behaviour.

PARADIGMATICALLY DIFFERENT ASSUMPTIONS ABOUT HUMAN BEHAVIOUR

When seeking to understand the institutional setup and mental frames that the different governance paradigms offer to and impose on public managers, there is a key question concerning the consistency of their ontological or anthropological stance. Do they harbour a coherent view on what drives human beings in general and public employees in particular? To what extent are others – distant others in particular – to be trusted? To what extent is it possible to delegate authority to them? What motivates them, makes them comfortable, annoyed etc.? Such questions lie at the heart of leadership and management and notably of managing relations. If we are to believe the governance paradigms and their more or less explicit or implicit assumptions, what are we then to expect from the public employees and private stakeholders with whom they collaborate? And on that background, how will public managers choose to manage? To 'live' a governance paradigm and be loyal to its core ambition and principles would imply managers acting in accordance with its inherent assumptions about human behaviour.

Identifying the inherent behavioural assumptions of the various governance paradigms is no easy task, as they are not always completely explicit. In some of the paradigms, such as classical bureaucracy, professional rule, NPM and NPG, the assumptions about human behaviour are relatively clear, but this does not hold for the rest of the paradigms. Nevertheless, the behavioural assumptions implicit to the governance paradigms can be reconstructed, even if they are not entirely explicit.

Understanding the behavioural assumptions is important because they provide the micro foundation for the governance mechanisms recommended by the different governance paradigms. The behavioural assumptions are particularly important for middle managers, who will have superiors with particular expectations of their managerial behaviour, which is grounded in assumptions about human behaviour. These assumptions can also become self-fulfilling prophecies and thus reinforce themselves, which is what happens when a particular behaviour is counted and rewarded or penalized. A behaviour that is counted will tend to be looked upon as important, a behaviour that is rewarded will be seen as attractive, and one that is penalized will be frowned upon and not repeated. Other behaviours that are not counted and which might be equally or even more important to organizational goal achievement may be neglected. Similarly, looking at someone and approaching them with trust or mistrust may change long-term behaviour by setting off positive or negative spirals of trust-building or increased mistrust.

The assumptions about human behaviour implicit to the different governance paradigms may be more or less in accordance with and appropriate in different circumstances. This is true with respect to managers and employees alike. For instance, there may be important differences between countries and between different parts of the country – between north and south, urban and rural – not to mention the different sectors in a given country which validate or invalidate the assumptions. Cultural differences may also render a particular set of behavioural assumptions more or less appropriate. Some countries and sectors are characterized by a high degree of trust, social capital and prosocial sentiments, whereas others are not. Such deep societal structures are not easily changed, so introducing a new paradigm that breaks with the logic of appropriateness in a particular context will be difficult – and perhaps not a particularly clever thing to do.

The same goes for smaller units, such as organizations or task-specific agencies that may have behavioural norms that resonate better with some behavioural assumptions than others. Organizational cultures are hard to change and are difficult to combine with particular behavioural assumptions and the actions based on these assumptions.

While assumptions about human behaviour may fit (more or less) nicely with national and organizational cultures and path-dependencies, there is no guarantee that they fit with the ideas, sentiments and entrenched behaviour of each and every human being in the public sector. Hence, what works well as an assumption about the behaviour of one public employee may not work for another employee. This also applies to managers: some will share the behavioural assumptions of a particular paradigm and feel comfortable acting upon them, whereas others do not. In this way, a new governance paradigm may also challenge managers in their beliefs about the right way to go about managing their organization and employees. As such, governance paradigms may either confirm or challenge the ideas and behaviours of public managers.

Having duly noted the different circumstances upon which the behavioural assumptions are brought to bear, we offer a brief interpretation of the key assumptions about human behaviour imbedded in the ideal-typical governance paradigms.

The basic assumption in *classical bureaucracy* is that the employees are motivated to work diligently and conscientiously to maintain law and order and that they will put the public interest over their own. Consequently, they are to be trusted to take impartial, discretionary decisions in local institutions governed by laws and administrative regulations and occasional orders from above that help them to prioritize their work and understand the formal rules. These assumptions form the backbone of the hierarchical order and the horizontal specialization characterizing modern industrialized societies and their drive towards efficient and effective governance. In classical forms of bureaucracy, employees are recruited because of their educational and intellectual skills and merits. They are paid justly and evenly for their performance. Moreover, it is assumed that they are capable of understanding and implementing the norms of Weberian bureaucracy, including legality, impartiality, due process, accountability, regularity, and orderly and non-corrupt behaviour. Once the politicians have made laws, the public managers are responsible for implementing them through the chain of command and based on detailed instructions given to their employees and the regular auditing of their behaviour.

The basic assumption about human behaviour informing *professional rule* is that employees are motivated by acting professionally and do a good job that they can be proud of and which will ultimately be to the benefit of the citizens. This assumption implies that professionals are recruited on the basis of their skills and merits and that they are trusted to govern themselves based on their skills, expertise and professional norms about how particular tasks are carried out and how the professionals ought to carry themselves. Accordingly, managers may delegate authority to their employees when it comes to most of the micro-level task-related decisions that must be made on a daily basis and involve dealing with citizens and customers. Professional employees are guided by profession-specific norms and values, and the socialization that they receive in their formal education and on-the-job training creates a professional culture which is at once empowering and prohibiting. It is empowering and effective to know what to do and how to act in different situations in accordance with well-known standards, but it is often prohibitive to think of one's own profession as 'God's gift to the world'. Like bureaucracy, professional rule challenges managers when interdisciplinary and cross-sectional cooperation is needed. Managerial control is often looked upon with great scepticism by professionals, whereas supervision may be thought of as attractive.

As described in Chapter 4, the *New Public Management* paradigm comprises two different rationales: an economic rationale aimed at reaping the fruits of competition and a managerial rationale focussed on goal and framework steering and performance management. The assumptions about human behaviour point in rather different directions. The managerial aspect of NPM is worried about the opportunistic behaviour of subordinate agents driven by personal interests and duly recommends that public employee behaviour be monitored and the results carefully assessed. At the same time, it pays considerable attention to the contingency of specific situations and contexts that must be analysed in order to take the right managerial decisions, for example about how to deal with shirking, optimal span of control, and whether to make or buy public service. The degree of delegation would be contingent upon the situation, the capabilities of the employees and the possibility for effective control with results, but it would typically rest on the assumption that most employees are well motivated by bureaucratic and/or professional ethics or by an interest in being rewarded and avoiding penalty. The economic component of NPM has a more clear-cut understanding of human behaviour as primarily motivated by self-interest. They are seen as egoistic and opportunistic. Economic greed is seen as natural and a source of dynamic change and entrepreneurship. Consequently, high-powered economic incentives are supposed to be highly motivating for human behaviour. In contrast, employees are not to be trusted, as they are likely to exploit trust to obtain one-sided benefits at the expense of the public sector as a whole. Furthermore, since public employees are naturally inclined to work for themselves, it is a good idea for managers to clearly stipulate what they are expected to deliver and subsequently to monitor and sanction their contractual obligations and the achievement of results. Much of the research on NPM has focussed on performance management based on 'regulation inside the state' (Hood et al. 1999), and the critics claim that the attempt to curb opportunistic behaviour by means of control has created an audit society in which only measurable tasks are viewed as legitimate (Power 1998).

Being a hybrid governance paradigm, the assumptions about human behaviour guiding the *Neo-Weberian State* combine elements drawn from classical bureaucracy, professional rule and NPM. Bureaucratic and professional ethics are supposed to motivate public managers and employees and self-interested behaviour is considered as a minor, albeit not entirely negligible, problem. In any case, public management under NWS depends on the delegation of responsibility to employees who respect hierarchical authority and formal rules and respond to and are motivated to do their best by the creation, communication and insistence on specific organizational value statements that remind the employees of the important public tasks they are performing.

To the extent that *Digital Era Governance* is a governance paradigm based on assumptions about human behaviour, we might expect DEG to view people as the extension of the machine (as in Taylorism) so that the expectation (as in classical bureaucracy and professional rule) would be that employees are loyal to the system and professionally competent to engage in man–machine interaction and reap the benefits from that. However, DEG unto itself does not seem to have a very explicit built-in behavioural model of human action. Digital technologies and big data are seen as a vehicle for making the public sector more efficient, transparent and coordinated. From this description, we can infer that human beings are first and foremost communicators; they produce, code, send, retrieve, manage, interpret and act on data that is constantly circulating and exchanged between large numbers of actors from different organizations. The social and political actors are not discussed in terms of their pursuit of personal or societal interests, but rather in terms of their will to communicate. The actors are communicating with other actors and with machines in large networks in which individual actors are less important. That said, the basic condition for the development of a data- and fact-driven public sector in which information exchange in real time improves the quality of decisions and services is that public managers and employees have enough public service motivation to use digitaliz-ation to improve the public sector and to prevent the dark side of digitalization from growing too strong.

Considering next *Public Value Management*, we find no explicit assumptions about human behaviour. However, public managers are clearly portrayed as explorative innovators who constantly monitor the performance of the organizations and scan the environment for problems, challenges and opportunities that can be exploited in the formulation of public value propositions that are subsequently modified and endorsed in and through a democratic dialogue with elected politicians and relevant stakeholders and implemented by service organizations and frontline personnel who are driven by the public values that they are supposed to achieve. Public value commitment and the wish to excel and receive recognition as a public leader are combined in the production of public value outcomes.

New Public Governance assumes that political and social actors have mixed motives and that their behaviour is driven partly by the pursuit of interests and partly by prosocial forms of motivation focussed on doing good and producing solutions that benefit individual citizens and society at a whole. Still, the persistent emphasis on networks, partnerships, collaboration and co-creation and the recommendation of trust-based leadership styles and steering-based stewardship bear witness to the inclination of NPG to favour prosocial motives. Under the right circumstances, people can develop enough trust and empathy to collaborate and produce innovative solutions to wicked problems and to facilitate professional and task-focussed interaction between managers and employees who are more or less aligned with respect to the overall goals and ambitions that drive their actions.

In summary, we may say that the formal or informal contact between managers and employees is of crucial importance in all of the governance paradigms (with the possible exception of the economic aspect of NPM). The manager–employee relationship is critical for public organizations to achieve their objectives. This relation is not particularly close in classical bureaucracy and NPM, as managers rely on formal rules and incentive systems to ensure compliance. The manager–employee relationship is very close – perhaps sometimes too close, not least in professional rule, especially when the managers have the same professional background as their employees. This relationship is also rather close in PVM, where public managers are busy trying to align their employees with the value statements of the organization and NPG in which trust-based dialogue replaces control-based performance management. DEG and NWS are more difficult to place in this respect.

Another clear dividing line between the different governance paradigms is whether they subscribe to a *homo economicus* model of human behaviour as based on self-interest or whether they assume that social and political actors are driven by prosocial motives. Setting DEG aside, there seems to be an uneven distribution of governance along a continuum from self-interest to pro-social motivation. NPM is alone in its relatively one-sided celebration of the economic model. Classical bureaucracy, NSW and PVM are placed at the other end of the continuum, and professional rule and NPG are both also leaning towards that pole as well. The only reservations are that professional rule is concerned with the pursuit of the collective interest of the professionals and that NPG conceives networks as stable articulations of interdependent actors with diverging interests that they may pursue in and through their more or less collaborative interaction.

Lastly, it should be mentioned that the co-existence of different assumptions about human behaviour in public organizations may create confusion among managers and employees alike, who ask themselves: are we here to do a good job and produce value for citizens and society at large or are we here to be rewarded when we work hard and avoid penalty when we shirk? The relative dominance of different behavioural assumptions and the governance tools that they deem valid may also affect the ability of public organizations to attract new personnel and influence the type of employees they recruit. Hence, the analysis of the paradigmatic stipulations about human behaviour is not only of academic interest.

10. Managing a public sector with competing and co-existing governance paradigms

In this chapter, we will discuss what it means to be a public manager in a context defined by the competing and co-existing governance paradigms that we have discussed in the previous chapters. In order to know what to do in a particular governance context, it is imperative for public managers to decipher and understand the logic of appropriate action that defines how to govern and be governed in the situation like the one in which they are placed. One or more governance paradigms may prescribe what public managers are expected to do in a particular context.

The focus in this book primarily has been upon the 'working logic' and 'rationale' of the paradigms. So far, we have paid little direct attention to the actors such as the politicians, the managers and the employees, let alone the interest groups and stakeholders in and around the public sector. We fully realize that each of these actors are both directly and indirectly affected by the paradigmatic setups chosen in each specific setting. The public sector is by definition politically led, and as we have mentioned several times during the book it is the politicians that decide for specific public sector reforms and governance paradigms. The decisive role of the elected politicians cannot be underestimated. In this book, however, we have been more interested in understanding the way in which the paradigms frame the function of the public sector. In this final chapter we wish to focus specific attention on managers who have the responsibility of implementing public sector reforms and make the institutional setup of the specific combination of paradigms work in their setting. However, we also briefly will discuss how the roles of the politicians and assumptions about relationships between them and the managers are affected by the paradigms respectively, just as we briefly discussed the assumptions held about the employees in Chapter 9. But our main aim in this chapter is to present a managerial view on the paradigms.

First, we emphasize that the particular governance context of a given manager is always specific and embedded in layered and hybrid manifestations of different governance paradigms that are changing over time. Thus, far from being stable and predictable, this institutional governance context is a moving target that must be decoded on an ongoing basis. Second, we take a closer look at the role of elected politicians vis-à-vis public managers and employees in each of the paradigms to determine whether there is alignment and internal consistency. This is important, because public managers are part of a politically led system, and the role consistency cannot be taken for granted. Furthermore, managers are expected to guide employee behaviour, and how they do so is supposed to be in accordance with the rationale of the assumptions grounded in the paradigms in order to harvest the full potential of the paradigm. Third, we look more closely at the expectations in each of the paradigms about management behaviour. What are seen to be the main challenges? And which recommended tools are used to handle these challenges in the various paradigms? Finally, we consider the managerial dilemmas that are generated by the incoherent and inconsistent co-existence of the governance paradigms and try to illustrate these dilemmas with a few examples.

CONTEXT: A MOVING TARGET

How do governance paradigms condition the actions of public managers? How are they to understand their managerial situation and act in accordance with their specific governance context and the expectations inherent to the different and shifting governance paradigms that we have analysed in this book?

First, it is important to note that any governance paradigm constitutes a normative and institutional framework defining the room for managerial discretion, including expectations regarding decision-making, managerial behaviour and the evaluation criteria used to judge whether or not managers are performing well (i.e. in accordance with the inherent codes of conduct).

Second, the exact manifestation of a given paradigm or set of paradigms is uniquely dependent on the specific context (Christensen and Lægreid 2001; Pollitt 2013). For each and every public manager, there will be a specific set of national, regional or local circumstances defining specific constellations of governance paradigms that are shaped historically and sustained by particular path dependencies. The specific constellations of governance paradigms provide the guiding principles, norms and values, which together prescribe what is considered appropriate managerial conduct. Furthermore, for each public manager there are given sets of conditions, such as available resources, particular stakeholder coalitions and specific sets of situational challenges.

Finally, and yet importantly, it should be clear by now that these governance paradigms are ideal types and rarely found in pure form. In the real world, we find them more or less close to or far from the ideal type, and they are to be mixed in different ways so that their co-existence at a given time and place creates a layered and hybrid governance system that would be more or less incoherent and inconsistent and characterized by rivalry among the proposed rationales for decision-making and evaluation criteria for performance. What we find are specific manifestations of governance ideas travelling in time and space and translating into contextually embedded layered and hybrid forms.

The governance paradigms we have presented and discussed in this book evolve historically in different national, regional and local contexts as the pendulum of what is thought of as necessary and appropriate swings back and forth and in new directions over time. As mentioned in Chapters 1 and 9, changes in governance regimes come about for different reasons, at least three of which deserve reiteration. Elections and the periodic changes among the power holders may foster changes in governance regimes, because new political coalitions have new ideas about the principles which should be guiding the public sector (this is the political explanation). Changes also occur due to changes in the actual challenges and possibilities in society in general and the public sector in particular (the functional and rational explanation). Finally, various critiques, learning processes and the diffusion of ideas and experience allow for gradual changes in managerial focus and behaviour (the evolutionary and institutional explanation). This may vary considerably from sector to sector and over time. What we are trying to understand – and what the managers should conform to, make use of proactively and handle – is indeed a moving target.

Altogether, the composite, malleable and changing governance context challenges the ability of managers to interpret and understand what is going on and what is expected of them. It challenges their ability to manoeuvre in and between the paradigms and to translate these expectations into local (strategic) narratives, which may be thought of as meaningful amongst their employees and main stakeholders; that is, meaningful enough to produce the expected changes in behaviour and the expected effects on performance.

MATCH OR MISMATCH BETWEEN ROLES IN THE PARADIGMS?

One of the basic assumptions in organization theory and notably in strategic management is the idea of fit and alignment; that is, the external fit between situation, strategy and internal alignment (also called design-fit) between various parts and elements of organizational systems and the strategies they pursue. Following this assumption, the key questions become: does the chosen strategy – the chosen governance paradigm(s) – fit the situation? And is there an internal coherence within and across paradigms? We are not going to discuss whether the chosen governance paradigms fit the current challenges of the particular situation, since the number of different situations is infinite. Suffice it to expect that national and local governments have made informed and reflected choices about how to govern, organize and lead the public sector. As such, we simply assume that governments have decided to lean on a particular governance paradigm that both supplements and partly supplants existing governance paradigms in different ways.

What we want here is to explore the internal consistency. There are important questions concerning the kind of consistency and consequences of these consistencies for the involved participants. Theories of innovation and organizational development and change often assume that diversity and conflicts are important drivers of creativity. We agree with this. The assumptions about fit and alignment, however, emphasize that there must be a minimum of unanimity and harmony for systems to function. If actors, departments and organizational subsystems are not aligned, they cannot work together efficiently, and the entire system is therefore expected to suffer from various kinds of dysfunction. While agreeing with these assertions, we note that large systems may tolerate a certain degree of inconsistency. To further explore the consistency within governance paradigms, we will focus on their role prescriptions. We might therefore ask ourselves about the coherence and match between the political and administrative actors within each governance paradigm: what is the design-fit between the actors in each of the ideal type paradigms we have presented thus far?

What is the match between the roles of the politicians, managers and employees in each paradigm? Managers are situated in hierarchies between political leadership and employee autonomy. It is important for them to decode and understand the roles of the politicians and employees in each paradigm to know what is expected of them and to harvest the full potential of a given paradigm. We have already discussed the underlying assumptions about human behaviour in the previous chapter (Chapter 9). We now briefly discuss the governance context provided by the ideas about how to govern, organize and lead in politically led public organizations as regards the match between the roles of politicians and public employees.

Bureaucracy builds on the idea of a strict division between politics and administration under the leadership of elected politicians. The employees in the administration are supposed to be skilled and loyal and to implement the will of the politicians in a politically neutral manner. The politicians are supposed to govern by way of lawgiving and policy-making, meaning that the overall goals and frames are set for the administration and that the available funds are prioritized and allocated. The politicians can supposedly rely on the ethics of the bureaucrats, and the roles of the politicians and the bureaucrats match well, even when politicians try to involve themselves directly in administrative matters. What may disturb the balance is when bureaucrats cross the demarcation line between the two spheres; that is, when they stop acting in accordance with the ideal division of labour between the two, and the bureaucrats try to politicize public decisions or aim to fill the space left by poor or absent political leadership.

Professional rule has no explicit role for politicians, the assumption being that there is a division of labour between the politicians, administrative bureaucracy and professionals in which the professionals have high discretion over implementation and service production. We might say that there is a perfect match between the roles of the politicians, managers and employees when the rules of division are respected by each party. The employees in the decentral public institutions are to be trusted in so far as they will act in accordance with the norms of the profession, as are the administrative bureaucrats (who are, so to speak, leading themselves). Problems arise when politicians try to have a say about how managers are to manage their subordinates, and how bureaucrats and frontline personnel should do their job. Notably, when political directives and bureaucratic rule clash with professional norms and values, conflicts erupt and public managers face dilemmas.

New Public Management builds on the assumption that there should be an even stricter division of labour between politics and administration in which the leaders are allowed to lead. NPM may actually be seen as a reaction to the actors struggling to stick to the roles defined by classical bureaucracy. In the famous metaphor used in the American version of NPM, there should be a division of steering and rowing in order to make the public sector more business-like and to let the managers manage (Osborne and Gaebler 1992). There is an ideal match between the stipulated roles of the politicians doing the steering in boards and the managers doing all of the executive work (as in the ideal of the private sector). Once again, however, the managers will experience dilemmas when borders are crossed, when roles become blurred and when they are asked to implement NPM decisions via the hierarchies of bureaucracy; decisions that do not match the expectations of the decentral employees, who have their loyalty and values deposited in professional rule. Politicians will often vote for NPM governance models without realizing the full consequences of their new role. This is seen when they engage in selected administrative matters or try to profile themselves on particular issues instead of playing the roles of visionary, frame-making and goal-setting politicians. When the perfect match turns into a detrimental and demotivating mismatch, there is not the supposed alignment between the paradigm and the roles played by politicians, managers and employees.

As with bureaucracy and professional rule, we may argue and conclude that to the extent that the actors do not understand and play by the rules of the paradigm, we find a kind of built-in structural disposition for hypocrisy; namely in the apparent decoupling between the ideal and reality, between what is said and what is done. This simultaneously renders managerial and strategic manoeuvring more difficult and more important.

Being a hybrid of NPM, bureaucracy and professional rule, the *Neo-Weberian State* paradigm suffers from some of the same inadequacies seen in the previous paradigms when the roles of politicians, managers and employees are being challenged and the actors cross the demarcation lines in the division of work.

While the *Digital Era Governance* paradigm has no clear stance on the roles played by politicians, it may suffer from the same malfunctions of mismatch and misalignment we have found in the other paradigms. Alternatively, *Public Value Management* provides the politicians with an additional role apart from being legislators and policymakers. The politicians are supposed to act as visionary leaders and communicators, and the managers are supposed to address the politicians to get them to accept the public value propositions advanced by the managers. Like the others, this paradigm assumes that things will work well enough for the actors to stick to their roles. Conversely, this match may be disturbed when politicians, managers and employees do not respect and understand the logic and rationale of the paradigm and regress to previous roles. The famous discussion between Rhodes and Wanna (2007, 2008) and John Alford (2008) revealed this tension in the literature on creating public value.

The *New Public Governance* paradigm challenges the roles established by the other paradigms. The politicians, managers and employees are supposed to share their power with the citizens and invite them to participate in decision-making processes and to become part of the service production. Decision-making power is decentralized and distributed in networks rather than concentrated at the apex of organizational hierarchies. Public and private actors are expected to collaborate with each other on an equal footing and to exchange and pool their knowledge, resources and ideas in the co-creation of public value outcomes. However, in representative democracies governments will remain in charge. They will make the final decisions and hold the administrative managers and the public employees to account. At the same time, it is uncertain whether the citizens can step outside their roles as customers and clients and are willing to participate in time-consuming networking and co-creation processes. Finally, interest organizations and civil society associations may continue to act as pressure groups pursuing a particular set of interests. In this way, all of the actors may regress to previous roles in order to cope with the uncertainties produced by the inclusion of citizens and groups of citizens.

The roles and expectations vary across the governance paradigms. In some of them, the role expectations of politicians, managers and employees are relatively consistent; problems only emerge when recommendations are not followed. In other governance paradigms, the role expectations are unclear or less consistent. Confronted by the internal inconsistencies and the emerging real-life conflicts together with the various combinations of governance paradigms, managers may struggle to find their way.

MANAGERIAL CHALLENGES WITHIN THE PARADIGMS

Before engaging in the discussion of the specific and inherent governance challenges facing the managers in each of the paradigms, it is useful to clarify the criteria for managerial success anchored in and produced by each paradigm. In so doing, we should interest ourselves in at least three different criteria for success: survival, goal attainment and legitimacy amongst various stakeholders. These three criteria are interwoven to the extent that survival in office depends on the ability of managers to deliver what is expected of them, which different stakeholders in turn define differently. The problem is that the latter may have divergent goals in mind. We might arrive at the neutral implementation of hierarchical decisions as the criterion for success in classical bureaucracy; high professional quality under professional rule; efficiency and effectiveness on key performance indicators in NPM; bureaucratic performance and content citizens in NWS; the exploitation of technological (digital) possibilities and integration in DEG; negotiated stakeholder value and public value outcome in PVM; and a combination of input and output legitimacy in the NPG paradigm. Obviously, managers cannot do everything at once without losing control and legitimacy to at least some of the stakeholders. They must be able to manoeuvre between and address various criteria for success and to communicate with their constituency accordingly to gain recognition and legitimacy. But since their authorizing environment (as PVM would put it) varies and changes, the threat of losing out is considerable, and decoupling strategies become difficult to handle. The strategic and communicative manoeuvring power is not only challenging the managers in the interfaces between paradigms, they are equally important within the paradigms.

Despite all its merits, *classical bureaucracy* has a number of well-known, built-in shortcomings. The main challenge to public managers in classical bureaucracy is to execute the political will. In order to do so, they must recruit the right staff, allocate resources and develop competences in an efficient and effective manner and produce rules and regulations to guide the employees. They must also ensure that these rules and regulations are followed and that accountability is established without producing red tape, mistrust and demotivating repression. Bureaucracy is the tool of the power-holders, and managers are therefore to respect their democratically elected principals, to understand the policy processes and to know how to give the right policy advice while at the same time functioning as the guardians of democratic and bureaucratic values and prevent the abuse of power (also by political power holders). Even if bureaucracy is installed in order to guard public and civil rights and to safeguard the citizens against abuse by the state, bureaucracy is not necessarily responsive to citizens' needs from the outset. As such, bureaucracy tends to seek its legitimacy within itself instead of gaining it by adding value to the citizens and being service-minded in the modern sense of these words (producing public goods and notably services that are considered immediately valuable by the citizens). The challenges also relate to the fact that bureaucracy calls for management by the rules and leaves less leeway for discretionary decisions. Bureaucratic systems also have a built-in fear of failure by producing errors and a tendency to produce skilled incompetence and fancy footwork when dealing with the errors (zero error tolerance). All of this makes bureaucratic systems inefficient and less capable of reinvention and innovation. Furthermore,

vertical and horizontal divisions of labour may be efficient because
working processes are specialized, but they hinder work across boundaries, making bureaucracy less flexible than more organic systems.
Managers working within this paradigm are supposed to be skilled in
abiding by laws and regulations and to be role models for orderly
management. They are supposed to give clear orders and ensure that they
are followed, which would work well in the best of all worlds. However,
since the cure for bureaucratic shortcomings seems to be more bureaucracy – to try harder, or single-loop learning if you like – the redesign of
bureaucracy takes place only gradually and typically may struggle to
reinvent itself in the light of new challenges. That's where the other
paradigms come in. While the potential for breaking with bureaucracy is
considerable in most of the other paradigms, the professional rule lives
well with bureaucracy as its 'extended arm', although the collegial rule
and norm-based governance within professional groups disrupts the chain
of command upon which bureaucracy is based.

When *professional rule* is the guiding and dominant paradigm, managers are challenged by the strong position of the employees (i.e. by the
very fact that the employees are professionals). On top of that, managers
are challenged by the professional associations, which sometimes also act
as unions. From the outset, professional rule lives well with bureaucracy
(in so far as there is a division of labour between the employees and the
bureaucratic system which is serving the professionals and setting the
frames). Still, the employees and their associations or unions may find
bureaucracy illegitimate and troublesome due to its constraints on professional power and discretion. When professional rule is the governing
paradigm, power is pulled away from the hierarchy and the managers and
situated among the employees. The authority and legitimacy of the
system and the managers are questioned by employees who generally do
not think they need managers in as much as they see themselves as being
capable of managing themselves and achieving the desired ends:
professional-quality services. They do not think that they need bureaucratic rules and regulations; and notably not the rigid registrations that
are supposed to 'feed the system' but instead take away time, energy and
the focus of the employees. Managers are also challenged by the
tendencies towards sectorization and the lack of respect and understanding with which different professions are looking at other professions. The
easiest way for the managers to gain legitimacy within this governance
paradigm is to be or become part of the dominant profession and its
value-setting, because there is an almost immediate recognition and
adoption of someone who is similar to oneself and committed to the

same (professional) norms and values, which is facilitating the production of services in accord with professional standards. This is the base for the legitimacy of 'hybrid' managers; that is, managers who have been recruited from amongst the professionals themselves and who have gained managerial competences through experience and managerial education. The hybrid manager may bridge the cleavages and information asymmetries between the managerial and professional spheres and logics in so far as the hybrid manager speaks and understands the languages in both worlds. What the employees expect (to the extent that they expect anything) is 'professional management': management focussing on the object and efforts of the employee as a professional. The employees may also view various forms of facilitative and democratic and/or distributive management as legitimate.

The *New Public Management* paradigm is supposed to deal with the shortcomings of both classical bureaucracy and professional rule. The managers must relate to the implementation of initiatives aimed at making the public sector more efficient, effective, responsive to user needs and service-minded. The proposed tools for dealing with these challenges are the well-known management techniques associated with contingency theory, including human resource management, design theory, management by objectives and change management, as well as all of the modern management recommendations and fads, such as quality management, performance management, the learning organization, strategic management and the like. Such endeavours should make the public sector more efficient and effective and at the same time aim at the creation of value for the end user: the customers and or citizens (this is the endpoint of both value-chain management and so-called 'Lean' technologies). While these tools are recommended for the streamlining of public sector service production, we also find recommendations stemming from the economic side of NPM, namely to create new quasi-markets and enhance competition through the use of economic incentives, tendering, contracting out, public–private partnerships and various types of control systems (ideas and imperatives that are usually combined with and work well with strategic management, marketing and communication to gain strategic fit, alignment and the development of organizational identity and branding effects). The managerial challenges stemming from NPM also relate to the paradoxes and dynamics of centralization and decentralization to which we shall make reference shortly.

As a reaction to NPM (and to a certain extent also to the shortcomings of bureaucracy and professional rule), *New Public Governance* can be seen as the pendulum swinging back and in another direction. A key critique in relation to NPM is the lack of trust associated with the combination of marketization and performance management. As discussed in Chapter 9, NPG holds a different view on human behaviour than NPM. NPG aims at infusing trust into the public sector as a whole and especially into the relations that bridge the cleavages between management and employees and between the public sector and citizens. The sectorization of classical bureaucracy and the compartmentalization of NPM is supposed to be bridged by the NPG imperative regarding flat hierarchies, networks and relational coordination. The lack of flexibility associated with bureaucracy and the *besserwissen* (know-it-all) tendency of the professionals are potentially alienating everyone else. This is supposed to become more organic and human when hierarchies are supplemented by networks and power gets distributed by delegation and inclusion. The challenges facing the managers relate to bringing the citizens and civil society back in. According to NPG, managers should try to produce outcome legitimacy by practising integrative and cross-sectoral leadership and initiating projects aimed at including the citizens in service production through various forms of co-production; and in the rethinking and redesign of the public sector through co-creation and collaborative innovation. Thus far, the ideal is some kind of relational coordination and distributed leadership, which includes both employees and citizens in deliberations on managerial decision-making. This has proven to be a challenge for both employees and managers, as their roles are changing and they potentially lose control when letting someone else (e.g. citizens) into their sphere of authority. While management must make these decisions, it is in a somewhat different form, which can better be associated with leadership. This is a leadership that is gaining followership by infusing values into the organization and building social capital, including trust and skills for cooperation, by showing the way and communicating visions and producing convincing and meaningful strategic storytelling.

Where *Digital Era Governance* is gaining ground as a governing paradigm, the managers are confronted with yet another set of challenges related to the structural and mental setup for the implementation of digital solutions. It is not merely a simple technical problem of implementing new digitized solutions to working procedures and data systems that used to be analogue. The managerial challenges have to do with redesigning the entire organizational setup of structural differentiation in the vertical and horizontal division of work and of preparing and encouraging the organization to harvest the full potential of digital processes and the interaction with citizens and customers. Most procedures must be changed, and most employees must gain new competences.

One aspect has to do with the handling of data – when they are to be registered and used – and another has to do with data-safety and securing the citizens' anonymity. The most challenging aspect of digitalization, however, may be the symbolic and mental aspect. What happens when face-to-face encounters are superseded by the digital interface between employees and citizens and between the public sector and its many stakeholders? Potentially, such developments are changing the roles and identities of all of the parties involved, and there has to be a drive to make it function. The managers must therefore be capable of rethinking and reorganizing their area of responsibility, to recruit and develop the needed skills, and to develop new ways of thinking about what the public sector is doing and how it interacts and communicates with its environment.

The *Neo-Weberian State* poses challenges to the managers, who combine what we have analysed as challenges raised by the previous paradigms, including classical bureaucracy, professional rule and NPM, but with a stronger faith in the classical bureaucratic – and Weberian – values and less emphasis on the economic aspects of NPM. The NWS paradigm (even if it holds a distinct governance profile of its own) may live well with DEG, NPG and PVM. As we shall discuss in the next section of this chapter, however, the NWS is challenged when such hierarchies are competing with networks and when centralized initiatives are combined with decentral dynamics. In a sense, it is a true hybrid paradigm of its own, and the managers largely have to be omnipotent in combining both classical virtues, such as accountability and loyalty to the system (hierarchy, democracy and political rule), with the new management techniques from NPM and citizen involvement from NPG. Value management should not be seen as alien to NWS either, even if PVM and NPG may bring employees and managers out of their comfort zone.

To 'live' the *Public Value Management* paradigm, the managers should be capable of reading and understanding at least three important aspects of the public sector. First, managers should respect and be loyal to democracy and the elected politicians. Consequently (as in classical bureaucracy), the managers should be able to understand and play (or fulfil) their role as advisors and facilitators in the policy processes. Secondly, managers should understand and respect the ethics of good public governance (just as in classical bureaucracy) and the practice of modern management (just as in NPM). And third, managers should respect and understand the values and expectations of the citizens (just like in the NPG paradigm) in order to be capable of knowing and producing what is seen as valuable by the citizens and other stakeholders with whom the public sector is cooperating (negotiated stakeholder value). In this vein, the managers may play their part in bridging cleavages between the value systems of politics, bureaucracy and the public at large.

MANAGERIAL MANOEUVRING IN CHANGING AND OVERLAPPING PARADIGMS

In as much as each governance paradigm is a set of instructions for good management and leadership and each of these sets of instructions has its own *raison d'être* based on differences in focus, values and behavioural assumptions, it becomes problematic for public managers when they are co-existing. One of the recurring conflicts in the public sector is the clash between the managerial logic of bureaucracy and the values of the professionals. When bureaucratic governance is historically supplemented by professional rule, where groups of professionals become influential due to their privileged and often monopolized possession of knowledge and competence, managers who are trained and anchored in the bureaucratic paradigm may struggle to obtain support and understanding from the professional group for some of the decisions that are executed top-down and based on political and executive administrative concerns for efficiency, effectiveness and accountability.

The professionals may respect neither the separation between politics and administration nor the rules of bureaucratic hierarchies. Due to the strong belief in the superiority of the profession and possibly also the strength of the public employees' unions, the professionals may have difficulty respecting the division between politics and administration, which stipulates that the elected politicians have the right to decide over the entire public sector, including what the professional employees are to do. The professionals may also struggle to respect the rule of hierarchy according to which a superior is a superior even if they do not belong to the profession. Finally, the professionals may have difficulties recognizing the need for bureaucracy, saying that there should be due process, accountability and rule of law.

Individuals belonging to strong professional groups, such as doctors, nurses and teachers, have their own views about the right thing to do in particular situations and in relation to citizens. For example, when politicians have decided to prioritize and reallocate resources in new ways and to focus on a particular sector or group of citizens and problems, and when managers insist on due process, it may become difficult for the employees to do their job and deliver their services in accordance with the quality standards of their profession. In such cases, the employees must live with the standards of bureaucracy, which they consider to be red tape, and they must manage with fewer resources than they find necessary to do the job properly.

This classical conflict between professional rule and bureaucracy becomes even more explosive when NPM steps onto the scene, because it is typically a programme for downsizing and streamlining the public sector. The bottom line of professional standards is being supplemented and superseded by a new focus on efficiency in the production of outputs and effectiveness in generating desired outcomes. The professional's privileged position of knowing better is being challenged by ideas about service-mindedness; that is, that public employees should be focussed on the wants and needs of citizens and customers. When managers are talking about strategic goals, efficiency and quality standards, and when they urge public employees to serve the citizens better while respecting the economic constraints, most employees tend to think of it as airy talk and may consequently regard the decisions made by their managers as illegitimate. This can lead to hypocrisy in the way the Swedish organizational scholar Nils Brunsson (1989) famously put it.

Historically, public managers have been faced with different expectations, and the ideas characterizing good public management have changed in the face of shifting societal circumstances and governance paradigms. Management by rule and management by profession have become 'professional' management practised by hybrid managers who have management as their profession; a practice whereby management by rule and/or professional standards is often overruled by the importance of keeping the budget, achieving set goals and managing networks so that different stakeholders may feel comfortable and continue to support public policies. Nevertheless, several recent projects have tried to identify the role of the twenty-first century public manager (van der Wal 2017; Dickinson et al. 2018).

Within each governance paradigm, it is relatively clear where authority lies and who is in charge. Classical bureaucracy puts the politicians in charge, while the administrative hierarchy is responsible for implementing their decisions. Professional rule insists on transferring power to the professionals and their associations, whereas the economic aspect of NPM would prefer market rule, and the managerial side of NPM would like the entrepreneurial managers to lead and manage. The Neo-Weberian State puts authority in the front seat, re-establishes the formal division of labour between politicians and administrators and re-invokes the hierarchical rule of public managers, while New Public Governance would like to see networks and network managers rule. In other words, whenever paradigms are combined, the ideas about authoritative and legitimate rule may clash and have to be negotiated. The managers have to adjust to and be capable of manoeuvring in accordance with what different stakeholders within and outside the public sector (politicians, groups of employees and their unions, groups of citizens, NGOs and private enterprises) and the media consider legitimate. Taken together, modern managers must be skilled in interpreting the situation, they must be skilled in negotiating the decision-making process and they must be skilled in communication (apart from being skilled in leadership and management, as in change management, quality management and strategic management).

Over time, these developments have led to a transformation of public management that may be characterized as a kind of professionalization and which has undergone a learning process in which the managers have changed their style and *modus operandi* in order to accommodate the expectations of the various stakeholders. Some of the conflicting pressures that many managers feel as a clash between different aspects of their professional identity and between different and shifting loyalties have led to the construction of new abstract identities and loyalties. Managers may therefore perceive themselves as being managers or leaders; as belonging to different managerial professions; and being loyal to the system, their policy sector or the common good. Moral and ethical dilemmas concerning what to do and how to argue for decisions are never easy to handle but must be dealt with. Now that they are in a managerial position and expected to lead and manage, managers must learn to be comfortable with what they do and who they are.

Each paradigm has its own rationale of importance for public management. For example, one might argue that the NWS added nothing new, as it readily adopted the strategic management perspective of NPM. But the particular combination of bureaucratic rule and bureaucratic values with the managerial aspect of NPM constitutes a particular challenge to public managers in which they must balance decisions and legitimize themselves with reference to two very different – and at times opposing – rationales, both of which are in potential conflict with the values of the professional employees.

Paradigms such as NPG and PVM challenge the comfort zones of the elected politicians and public managers and employees alike, since the basic idea is to invite citizens and relevant stakeholders into processes of policymaking, service production, managerial deliberation and strategic development. Sharing power and inviting others into one's own domain can be frightening and is giving rise to a conflict between unicentric forms of government and pluri-centric forms of governance. The easiest thing to do in such a situation is for the politicians, managers and employees to all retreat to the old and familiar roles of being policy-makers, directive managers and professional employees and to defy the need to share power. Similarly, exploiting the full potential of digitaliz-ation is not merely a matter of technically implementing new platforms; it is also about changing mind-sets about the public sector, its hierarch-ical organization and monopolistic professions. Managers are faced with expectations regarding the facilitation of processes whereby old rules and procedures are challenged and must be reinvented in order to harvest the full potential of inviting new actors into the public sector and using the latest technologies at hand.

The public sector is already characterized by forms of governance that create managerial paradoxes, dilemmas and cross-pressures. The inherent nature of the public sector – with its many wicked problems, the existence of competing interests (articulated by political parties as well as the many stakeholders) and the many bottom lines, goal conflicts and evaluation criteria – inevitably puts managers in situations of confusion and cross-pressure. The existence of differing modernization paradigms pushes this basic condition and setup for public management one step further.

The co-existence of governance paradigms produces layered and hybrid forms of governance and may very well be a sign of organ-izational schizophrenia that gives rise to and deepens managerial dilem-mas. A schizophrenic organization has to live with inconsistent and complementary traits that compete for lending authority and legitimacy to different actors and provide different models for decision-making and public problem-solving.

Public organizations typically want to do (maybe a little too) many different things at the same time, such as simultaneously going for top-down and bottom-up governance and inside-out and outside-in decision-making. The dilemma-filled choices are many. Should we go for further centralization or more decentralization? Give priority to stability or development? Preserve the old and proven or create the new and unknown? Or should we opt for rule compliance or enhanced flexibility? Should the managers or the employees be in charge? Should the appointed managers be loyal to the professional employees or to the system? Are other managers and institutions my friends or my foes? Should we choose to have more collaboration or more competition? Are the economic or the human resources the most important and valuable? Should we accommodate political interests or particular citizen interests? What is of most importance: keeping the budget, acting professionally or ensuring a positive work environment? Is the identity of the appointed manager purely managerial or professional? And so on and so forth. The answers to these questions are context-specific and depend on the present state of the 'moving target' of public governance. What remains, however, is that the managerial dilemmas must be dealt with. They must be handled, no matter how messy, frustrating or disappointing the result may turn out to be (Pollitt and Bouckaert 2017, Chapter 7).

Dilemmas differ. There are situations where some decisions are more correct than others, and the solutions are complementary and cannot be combined. If managers choose one solution, they cannot then return and choose another without losing legitimacy. To illustrate, public managers are either loyal to the system or to their employees, and they either follow the rules or break them. Such dilemmas inevitably produce criticism, as someone is bound to be disappointed.

Other types of dilemmas are typically characterized by confusion as to what to do, and managers must therefore argue for the decision they choose. These dilemmas often involve prioritization (e.g. prioritizing the needs of citizens, politicians or employees). Managers must often cut to the chase and make decisions in a truly undecidable terrain and afterwards find a way of providing a convincing and trustworthy explanation to justify them. There are situations in which managers know the formally correct way to handle a situation but feel inclined to choose a less formally correct and somewhat illegitimate decision, such as disobeying orders out of concern for professional norms, encouraging civil disobedience in order to contest decisions that are detrimental to the environment, or breaking the law or the rules in pursuit of the common good. In any case, public managers must be able to come up with good explanations to justify their actions; and even that might not be good enough.

The paradoxes and dilemmas anchored in co-existing and competing governance paradigms can be illustrated with reference to a couple of well-known examples. Let us briefly mention four undertakings that may contribute to confusion: building networks into hierarchies, working with innovation, constructing corporate-like public sector organizations and cooperation versus competition within the public sector.

While vertical hierarchies and horizontal specialization are long-proven ways of ensuring that responsibilities are distributed efficiently and transparently, this classical organizational design of industrial society is challenged by what is commonly referred to as the new knowledge and network society. The challenge is parallel to how classical bureaucracy and NPM are challenged by NPG and to a certain extent also DEG, both of which aim to reap the fruits of cooperation and speed up processes by facilitating the communication between the relevant and affected actors. Managers being forced to work with networks and to prioritize horizontal collaboration over vertical execution challenges the chain of command, loyalties and managerial focus, meaning that various managerial dilemmas become visible.

Innovation is at the forefront of NPG, the expectation being that new ideas will have a better foundation, be triggered by mutual learning, and enjoy broader support if they are developed bottom-up and with the extensive involvement of users, citizens and stakeholders (including employees). But this may not be the whole truth about innovation. Decisions regarding initiatives to encourage innovative thinking are often taken at the top and are part of strategic decisions that are to be executed in and through new ways of working further down in the organization. Hence, innovation is not merely a matter of either top-down or bottom-up processes. We should also remember that innovation is not just on the NPG agenda, as it was also one of the headlines of NPM (not least in the USA, where the 'reinventing government' phrase was coined). As we have argued, the motives and evaluation criteria of NPM and NPG may very well differ when it comes to evaluating the initiatives, meaning that the managers should be very much aware of how they phrase their endeavours and on what they choose to focus attention. DEG and PSV both make important contributions to rethinking, reinventing and innovating the public sector.

The ideal of seeing public sector organizations as business-like corporate bodies is obviously a key part of NPM. But while the idea of the corporation may go well with the classical bureaucracy, it easily gets into conflict with the aforementioned bottom-up innovation processes, co-creation and collaborative governance. The question is whether massive public agencies can be turned into highly centralized corporate structures while at the same time opening up for decentralizing authority and encouraging local actors to make independent decisions and spur innovation at the bottom of the enterprise. How are managers to act when there are strong incentives to use the same standards throughout the corporation (e.g. a shared vision, strategic storyline and use of corporate culture, corporate IT, corporate human resources, corporate identity), when at the same time they are expected to show initiative and create their own local identity and the like?

These dilemmas between what is shared and what is particular are at the heart of understanding how to approach other parts of the public sector: Are the different administrative units competitors or are they part of the family? Can they be both at the same time? How are decentral managers to decide what to do when the classical bureaucracy, professional rule and NPG (and maybe also NWS, DEG and PVM) are expecting them to cooperate and sacrifice themselves for the rest of the organization, while the NPM paradigm is encouraging them to compete for resources, customers and employees? Precisely how tough may a manager be when negotiating a favourable deal for their own part of the organization, and how appropriate would others find it if a particular part chooses to differentiate and market itself at the expense of others? Similar dilemmas can be found when managers use economic incentives and employees are encouraged to compete amongst – and possibly against – each other.

A manager is always part of and personally responsible for managerial decisions. Integrity is always at stake as managers are also (supposed to be) leaders. When managers try to conform to the inherent expectations of various governance paradigms, they inevitably stumble over dilemmas that they must handle in a way that may be thought of as appropriate by those whom they think are the most important among their stakeholders. But most importantly, how they choose to handle such dilemmas influences not only the legitimacy of their own institution or agency; it may be of importance for the entire organization and might ultimately compromise themselves. Modern public managers must therefore be capable of decoding and understanding the expectations and possibilities of their particular institutional setup, one which inter alia but fundamentally is defined by the co-existence of competing governance paradigms, and to act in a manner so that they are comfortable with and capable of looking themselves in the eye and coming up with viable, meaningful explanations as to why they choose one direction when other options are available.

References

Abbott, A. (1988), *The System of Professions: An Essay on the Division of Expert Labor*, Chicago, IL: Chicago University Press.

Ackroyd, S., I. Kirkpatrick and R.M. Walker (2007), 'Public management reform in the UK and its consequences for professional organization: a comparative analysis', *Public Administration*, **85** (1), 9–26.

Alford, J. (2008), 'The limits to traditional public administration, or rescuing public value from misrepresentation', *Australian Journal of Public Administration*, **67** (3), 357–66.

Alford, J. (2009), *Engaging Public Sector Clients: From Service Delivery to Co-Production*, Basingstoke: Palgrave Macmillan.

Alford, J. (2014), 'The multiple facets of co-production: building on the work of Elinor Ostrom', *Public Management Review*, **16** (3), 299–316.

Alford, J. (2016), 'Co-production, interdependence and publicness: extending public service-dominant logic', *Public Management Review*, **18** (5), 673–91.

Alford, J. and C. Greve (2017), 'Strategy in the public and private sectors: similarities, differences and changes', *Administrative Sciences*, **7** (4), 35.

Alford, J. and B.W. Head (2017), 'Wicked and less wicked problems: a typology and a contingency framework', *Policy and Society*, **36** (3), 397–413.

Alford, J. and O. Hughes (2008), 'Public value pragmatism as the next phase of public management', *The American Review of Public Administration*, **38** (2), 130–48.

Allison, G. (1980), 'Public and private management: are they fundamentally alike in all unimportant respects?', *Setting Public Management Research Agendas*, Washington, DC: United States Office of Personnel Management.

Amirkhanyan, A. and K. Lambright (2018), *Citizen Participation in the Age of Contracting: When Service Delivery Trumps Democracy*, New York, NY: Routledge.

Andersen, L.B. (2014), 'Health care cost containment in Denmark and Norway: a question of relative professional status?', *Health Economics, Policy and Law*, **9** (2), 169–91.

Andersen, L.B. and M. Blegvad (2003), 'Normer eller egennytte? Professionelle og økonomiske incitamenter i dansk børnetandpleje', *Politica*, **35** (2), 125–35.

Andersen, L.B. and L.H. Pedersen (2012), 'Public service motivation and professionalism', *International Journal of Public Administration*, **35** (1), 46–57.

Andersen, L.B. and S. Serritzlew (2012), 'Remunerating general practitioners with fees: between economic incentives and professional norms', *Scandinavian Journal of Public Administration*, **15** (4), 25–43.

Andersen, L.B., B. Bjørnholt, L. Ladegaard Bro and C. Holm-Petersen (2018), 'Achieving high quality through transformational leadership: a qualitative multilevel analysis of transformational leadership and perceived professional quality', *Public Personnel Management*, **47** (1), 51–72.

Andersen, L.B., J.G. Christensen and T. Pallesen (2008), 'The political allocation of incessant growth in the Danish public sector', in H.-U. Derlien and B.G. Peters (eds), *The State at Work, vol. 1: Public Sector Employment in Ten Western Countries*, Cheltenham, UK and Northampton, MA, USA: Edward Elgar Publishing, pp. 249–67.

Andersen L.B., C. Greve, K.K. Klausen, J. Torfing, E. Albæk, J.G. Andersen, K.N. Andersen, N.Å. Andersen, S.C. Andersen, R. Buch, N. Ejersbo, A. Esmark, H.F. Hansen, M.B. Hansen, M.L.F. Jakobsen, M. Jakobsen, K. Löfgren, M. Marcussen, P. Melander, P.B. Mortensen, V.L. Nielsen, D. Pedersen, S. Serritzlew, E. Sørensen and P. Triantafillou (2012), *An Innovative Public Sector that Enhances Quality and Joint Responsibility*, publicly circulated memo.

Andersen, L.B., E. Heinesen and L.H. Pedersen (2014), 'How does public service motivation among teachers affect student performance in schools?', *Journal of Public Administration Research and Theory*, **24** (3), 651–71.

Andersen, L.B., T.B. Jørgensen, A.M. Kjeldsen, L.H. Pedersen and K. Vrangbæk (2013), 'Public values and public service motivation: conceptual and empirical relationships', *The American Review of Public Administration*, **43** (3), 292–11.

Andersen, L.B., N. Kristensen and L.H. Pedersen (2012), 'Public service efficacy', *International Journal of Public Administration*, **35** (14), 947–58.

Andersen, L.B., P. Leisink and W. Vandenabeele (2017), 'Human resources practices and research in Europe', in N.M. Riccucci (ed.), *Public Personnel Management: Current Concerns, Future Challenges*, New York, NY: Routledge, pp. 12–27.

Andersen, S.C. and M. Jakobsen (2013), 'Coproduction and equity in public service delivery', *Public Administration Review*, **73** (5), 704–13.

Andrews, R. (2010), 'Organisational structure and public service performance', in R.M. Walker, G.A. Boyne and G.A. Brewer (eds), *Public Management and Performance: Research Directions*, Cambridge: Cambridge University Press, pp. 89–109.

Andrews, R. (2011), 'New public management and the search for efficiency', in T. Christensen and P. Lægreid (eds), *The Ashgate Research Companion to New Public Management*, Farnham and Burlington: Ashgate, pp. 281–94.

Andrews, R., P. Bezes, G. Hammerschmid and S. Van de Walle (2016), 'Conclusion: a kaleidoscope of administrative reforms in Europe', in G. Hammerschmid, S. Van de Walle, R. Andrews and P. Bezes (eds), *Public Administration Reforms in Europe: The View from the Top*, Cheltenham, UK and Northampton, MA, USA: Edward Elgar Publishing, pp. 273–80.

Ansell, C. and A. Gash (2008), 'Collaborative governance in theory and practice', *Journal of Public Administration Research and Theory*, **18** (4), 543–71.

Ansell, C. and A. Gash (2017), 'Collaborative platforms as a governance strategy', *Journal of Public Administration Research and Theory*, **28** (1), 16–32.

Ansell, C. and J. Torfing (eds) (2014), *Public Innovation Through Collaboration and Design*, London and New York, NY: Routledge.

Ansell, C. and J. Torfing (eds) (2016), *Handbook on Theories of Governance*, Cheltenham, UK and Northampton, MA, USA: Edward Elgar Publishing.

Ansell, C. and J. Torfing (2017), 'Strengthening political leadership and policy innovation through the expansion of collaborative forms of governance', *Public Management Review*, **19** (1), 37–54.

Ansell, C., J. Trondal and M. Ogard (eds) (2017), *Governance in Turbulent Times*, Oxford: Oxford University Press.

Appleby, P. (1945), 'Government is different', reprinted in J.M. Shafritz and A.C. Hyde (1987), *Classics in Public Administration*, Chicago: The Dorsey Press, pp. 158–64.

Aucoin, P. (1990), 'Administrative reform in public management: paradigms, principles, paradoxes and pendulums', *Governance: An International Journal of Policy and Administration*, **3** (2), 115–37.

Aucoin, P. and R. Heintzman (2000), 'The dialectics of accountability for performance in public management reform', in G. Peters and D.J. Savoie (eds), *Governance in the Twenty-First Century: Revitalizing the Public Service*, Montreal: McGill-Queen's Press.

Baldwin, J.N. (1990), 'Perceptions of public versus private sector personnel and informal red tape: their impact on motivation', *The American Review of Public Administration*, **20** (1), 7–28.

Bang, H. and E. Sørensen (1999), 'Hverdagsmagerne – en udfordring til demokratiet og samfundsforskningen', in J.G. Andersen, P.M. Christiansen, T.B. Jørgensen, L. Togeby and S. Vallgårda (eds), *Den demokratiske udfordring*, Copenhagen: Hans Reitzels, pp. 92–112.

Barber, B.R. (2013), *If Mayors Ruled the World: Dysfunctional Nations, Rising Cities*, New Haven, CT: Yale University Press.

Barbosa, A., M. Pozzebon and E. Diniz (2013), 'Rethinking e-government performance assessment from a citizen perspective', *Public Administration*, **91** (3), 744–62.

Barzelay, M. and R. Gallego (2006), 'From "new institutionalism" to "institutional processualism": advancing knowledge about public management policy change', *Governance*, **19** (4), 531–57.

Bass, B.M. and R.E. Riggio (2006), *Transformational Leadership*, Mahwah, NJ: Lawrence Erlbaum Associates.

Bellé, N. and E. Ongaro (2014), 'NPM, administrative reforms and public service motivation: improving the dialogue between research agendas', *International Review of Administrative Sciences*, **80** (2), 382–400.

Bengtsson, N. and P. Engström (2014), 'Replacing trust with control: a field test of motivation crowd out theory', *The Economic Journal*, **124** (577), 833–58.

Benington, J. and M.H. Moore (eds) (2011), *Public Value: Theory and Practice*, Basingstoke: Palgrave Macmillan.

Bentzen, T.Ø. (2016), 'Tillidsbaseret styring og ledelse i offentlige organisationer', PhD dissertation, Department of Social Sciences and Business, Roskilde University.

Bertelsmann Stiftung (2019), *Policy Performance and Governance Capacity in the OECD and EU: Sustainable Governance Indicators 2018*, Berlin: Bertelsmann Stiftung.

Betsill, M.M. and H. Bulkeley (2004), 'Transnational networks and global environmental governance: the cities for climate protection program', *International Studies Quarterly*, **48** (2), 471–93.

Blake, R.R. and J.S. Mouton (1969), *Building a Dynamic Corporation through Grid Organization Development*, Reading, MA: Addison-Wesley.

Bogason, P. (2001), *Fragmenteret Forvaltning: Demokrati og Netværksstyring i Decentraliseret Lokalstyre*, Aarhus: Systime.

Bogdanor, V. (ed.) (2005), *Joined-Up Government*, Oxford: Oxford University Press.

Boin, A. and M. Lodge (2016), 'Designing resilient institutions for transboundary crisis management: a time for public administration', *Public Administration*, **94** (2), 289–98.

Bolden, R. (2011), 'Distributed leadership in organizations: a review of theory and research', *International Journal of Management Reviews*, **13** (3), 251–69.

Bommert, B. (2010), 'Collaborative innovation in the public sector', *International Public Management Review*, **11** (1), 15–33.

Borins, S. (1998), 'Lessons from the New Public Management in Commonwealth nations', *International Public Management Journal*, **1** (1), 37–58.

Borrás, S. and K. Jacobsson (2004), 'The open method of co-ordination and new governance patterns in the EU', *Journal of European Public Policy*, **11** (2), 185–208.

Börzel, T.A. and T. Risse (2005), 'Public–private partnerships: effective and legitimate tools of international governance', in E. Grande and L.W. Pauly (eds), *Complex Sovereignty: Reconstituting Political Authority in the Twenty First Century*, Toronto: University of Toronto Press, pp. 195–216.

Bossert, T., W. Hsiao, M. Barreram, L. Alarcon, M. Leo and C. Casares (1998), 'Transformation of ministries of health in the era of health reform: the case of Colombia', *Health Policy and Planning*, **13** (1), 59–77.

Boucher, S. (2009), 'If citizens have a voice, who's listening? Lessons from recent citizen consultation experiments for the European Union', EPIN Working Paper.

Bovens, M., P. 't Hart and T. Schillemans (2008), 'Does public accountability work? An assessment tool', *Public Administration*, **86** (1), 225–42.

Boyne, G. and J. Gould-Williams (2003), 'Planning and performance in public in public organizations: an empirical analysis', *Public Management Review*, **5** (1), 115–32.

Bozeman, B. (2002), 'Public-value failure: when efficient markets may not do', *Public Administration Review*, **62** (2), 145–61.

Bozeman, B. (2007), *Public Values and Public Interest: Counterbalancing Economic Individualism*, Washington, DC: Georgetown University Press.

Bozeman, B. and M. Feeney (2011), *Rules and Red Tape: A Prism for Public Administration Theory and Research*, Armonk, NY: M.E. Sharpe.

Bozeman, B. and T.B. Jørgensen (2002), 'Public values lost? Comparing cases on contracting out from Denmark and the United States', *Public Management Review*, **4** (1), 63–81.

Bozeman, B. and T.B. Jørgensen (2007), 'Public values: an inventory', *Administration & Society*, **39** (3), 354–81.

Bozeman, B. and S. Moulton (2011), 'Integrative publicness: a framework for public management strategy and performance', *Journal of Public Administration Research and Theory*, **21** (S3), i363–i380.

Brandsen, T., B. Verschuere and T. Steen (eds) (2018), *Co-Production and Co-Creation: Engaging Citizens in Public Services*, Abingdon and New York, NY: Routledge.

Braudel, F. (1982), *Civilization and Capitalism 15th–18th Century*, London: Collins.

Brinkerhoff, D.W. and J.M. Brinkerhoff (2011), 'Public–private partnerships: perspectives on purposes, publicness, and good governance', *Public Administration and Development*, **31** (1), 2–14.

Brint, S. (1993), *In an Age of Experts: The Changing Role for Professionals in Politics and Public Life*, Princeton, NJ: Princeton University Press.

Bruijn, H.D. and W. Dicke (2006), 'Strategies for safeguarding public values in liberalized utility sectors', *Public Administration*, **84** (3), 717–35.

Brunsson, N. (1989), *The Organization of Hypocrisy: Talk, Decisions and Actions in Organizations*, Chichester: John Wiley & Sons.

Bryson, J.M. (2011), *Strategic Planning for Public and Nonprofit Organizations: A Guide to Strengthening and Sustaining Organizational Achievement*, San Francisco, CA: Jossey-Bass.

Bryson, J.M. and B.C. Crosby (2005), *Leadership for the Common Good: Tackling Public Problems in a Shared-Power World*, San Francisco, CA: Jossey-Bass.

Bryson, J. M., F. Ackermann and C. Eden (2016), 'Discovering collaborative advantage: the contributions of goal categories and visual strategy mapping', *Public Administration Review*, **76** (6), 912–25.

Bryson, J.M., B.C. Crosby and L. Bloomberg (eds) (2015), *Public Value and Public Administration*, Washington, DC: Georgetown University Press.

Burau, V. (2005), 'Comparing professions through actor-centred governance: community nursing in Britain and Germany', *Sociology of Health and Illness*, **27** (1), 114–37.

Burau, V. and L.B. Andersen (2014), 'Professions and professionals: capturing the changing role of expertise through theoretical triangulation', *American Journal of Economics and Sociology*, **73** (1), 264–93.

Burau, V., L. Henriksson and S. Wrede (2004), 'Comparing professional groups in health care: towards a context sensitive analysis', *Knowledge, Work and Society*, **2** (2), 49–68.

Burns, J.M. (1978), *Leadership*, New York, NY: Harper & Row.

Burrage, M., K. Jarauch and H. Siegrist (1990), 'An actor-based framework for the study of professions', in M. Burrage and R. Thorstendahl (eds), *Professions in Theory and History: Rethinking the Studying of Professions*, London: Sage, pp. 203–25.

Byrkjeflot, H. (2011), 'Healthcare states and medical professions: the challenges from NPM', in T. Christensen and P. Lægreid (eds), *The Ashgate Research Companion to New Public Management*, Farnham and Burlington: Ashgate, pp. 147–60.

Byrkjeflot, H. and F. Engelstad (eds) (2018), *Bureaucracy and Society in Transition: Comparative Perspectives*, Bingley: Emerald Publishing.

Byrkjeflot, H., C. Greve and P. du Gay (2018), 'What is the Neo-Weberian State as a regime of public administration?' in E. Ongaro and S. van Thiel (eds), *The Palgrave Handbook of Public Administration and Management in Europe*, London: Palgrave Macmillan, pp. 991–1009.

Campbell, J. and J. Hall (2015), *The World of States*, London: Bloomsbury.

Campbell, J.L. and O.K. Pedersen (eds) (2006), *The Rise of Neoliberalism and Institutional Analyses*, Princeton, NJ: Princeton University Press.

Carpintero, S. and O.H. Petersen (2013), 'Finding the optimal level of integration in PPPs: implications for risk sharing in large-scale infrastructure projects', conference paper for the Public Private Partnership Conference, 18th–20th March 2013, Preston, UK.

Chapman, J. and G. Duncan (2007), 'Is there now a New Zealand Model?', *Public Management Review*, **9** (1), 1–25.

Cho, W., T. Im, G.A. Porumbescu, H. Lee and J. Park (2013), 'A cross-country study of the relationship between Weberian bureaucracy and government performance', *International Review of Public Administration*, **18** (3), 115–37.

Christensen, J.G. and R. Gregory (2008), 'Public personnel policies and personnel administration', in H.-U. Derlien and B.G. Peters (eds), *The State at Work, vol. 2: Comparative Public Service Systems*, Cheltenham, UK and Northampton, MA, USA: Edward Elgar Publishing, pp. 192–225.

Christensen, J.G. and T. Pallesen (2008), 'Public employment trends and the organization of public sector tasks', in H.-U. Derlien and B.G. Peters (eds), *The State at Work, vol. 2: Comparative Public Service*

Systems, Cheltenham, UK and Northampton, MA, USA: Edward Elgar Publishing, pp. 7–33.

Christensen, T. and P. Lægreid (2001), *New Public Management: The Transformation of Ideas and Practice*, Aldershot: Ashgate.

Christensen, T. and P. Lægreid (2003), 'Administrative reform policy: the challenges of turning symbols into practice', *Public Organization Review*, **3** (1), 3–27.

Christensen, T. and P. Lægreid (2011), 'Introduction', in T. Christensen and P. Lægreid (eds), *The Ashgate Research Companion to New Public Management*, Farnham and Burlington: Ashgate, pp. 1–15.

Christensen, T. and P. Lægreid (eds) (2016), *The Routledge Handbook to Accountability and Welfare State Reforms in Europe*, London: Routledge.

Christensen, T. and P. Lægreid (2017), *Transcending New Public Management*, Taylor & Francis.

Clarke, A. and H. Margetts (2014), 'Governments and citizens getting to know each other: open, closed and big data in public management reform', *Policy & Internet*, **6** (4), 394–17.

Clarke, J. and J. Newman (1997), *The Managerial State*, London: Sage.

Cohen, M.D. and J.G. March (1986), 'Leadership in an organized anarchy', reprinted in M.C. Brown (ed.) (2000), *Organization and Governance in Higher Education* (5th edn, pp. 16–35), ASHE Reader Series, Boston, MA: Pearson Custom Publishing.

Constantiou, D. and J. Kallinikos (2015), 'New games, new rules: big data and the changing context of strategy', *Journal of Information Technology*, **30** (1), 44–57.

Cooper, T.L. and N.D. Wright (eds) (1992), *Exemplary Public Administrators: Character and Leadership in Government*, San Francisco, CA: Jossey-Bass.

Crosby, B.C., P. 't Hart and J. Torfing (2017), 'Public value creation through collaborative innovation', *Public Management Review*, **19** (5), 655–69.

Crozier, M., S. Huntington and J. Watanuki (1975), *The Crisis of Democracy: Report on the Governability of Democracies in the Trilateral Commission*, New York, NY: New York University Press.

Dahl, A. and J. Soss (2014), 'Neoliberalism for the common good? Public value governance and the downsizing of democracy', *Public Administration Review*, **74** (4), 496–504.

Dahlström, C., V. Lapuente and J. Teorell (2012), 'The merit of meritocratization: politics, bureaucracy, and the institutional deterrents of corruption', *Political Research Quarterly*, **65** (3), 656–68.

Dalton, R.J. and C. Welzel (eds) (2014), *The Civic Culture Transformed: From Allegiant to Assertive Citizens*, New York, NY: Cambridge University Press.

Danish Government (2018), *Danish Cyber and Information Security Strategy*, Copenhagen: Ministry of Finance.

Danziger, J.N. and K.V. Andersen (2002), 'The impacts of information technology on public administration: an analysis of empirical research from the "golden age" of transformation', *International Journal of Public Administration*, **25** (5), 591–627.

Darmstaedter, F. (1948 [2017]), *Bismarck and the Creation of the Second Reich*, London and New York, NY: Routledge.

Day, P. and R. Klein (1987), *Accountability: Five Public Sectors*, London and New York, NY: Tavistock.

De Jong, J. (2016), *Dealing with Dysfunction: Innovative Problem Solving in the Public Sector*, Washington DC: Brookings Institution Press.

Denhardt, J.V. and R.B. Denhardt (2015), *The New Public Service: Serving, Not Steering*, New York, NY: Routledge.

Dewey, J. (2009), 'Search for the great community', in V. Hodgkinson and M.W. Foley (eds), *Civil Society Reader*, Boston, MA: Tufts University Press, pp. 133–53.

Dickinson, H., C. Needham, C. Mangan and H. Sullivan (2018), *Reimagining the Future Public Service Workforce*, Singapore: Springer.

Diefenbach, T. and J.A.A. Sillince (2011), 'Formal and informal hierarchy in different types of organization', *Organization Studies*, **32** (11), 1515–37.

DiIulio, J.J. Jr. (2014), *Bring Back the Bureaucrats*, West Conshohocken, PA: Templeton Press.

DiMaggio, J. and W.W. Powell (1983), 'The iron cage revisited: institutional isomorphism and collective rationality in organizational fields', *American Sociological Review*, **48** (2), 147–60.

Doig, J.W. and E.C. Hargrove (1987), *Leadership and Innovation: A Biographical Perspective on Entrepreneurs in Government*, Baltimore, MD: Johns Hopkins University Press.

Douglas, M. (1999), 'Four cultures: the evolution of a parsimonious model', *GeoJournal*, **47** (3), 411–15.

Downs, A. (1967), *Inside Bureaucracy*, Boston, MA: Little, Brown and Company.

du Gay, P. (2000), *In Praise of Bureaucracy: Weber, Organisation, Ethics*, London: Sage.

du Gay, P. (ed.) (2005), *The Values of Bureaucracy*, Oxford: Oxford University Press.

du Gay, P. (2009a), 'In defence of "Mandarins": recovering the "core business" of public management', *Management and Organizational History*, **4** (4), 359–84.

du Gay, P. (2009b), 'Max Weber and the ethics of office', in P. Adler (ed.), *Oxford Handbook of Sociology and Organizational Studies: Classic Foundations*, Oxford: Oxford University Press, pp. 146–73.

du Gay, P. (2017), 'Introduction: office as a vocation', *European Journal of Cultural and Political Sociology*, **4** (2), 156–65.

Dunleavy, P. (2006), *The Westminster Model and the Distinctiveness of British Politics*, Basingstoke: Palgrave Macmillan.

Dunleavy, P. (2014), *Democracy, Bureaucracy and Public Choice: Economic Approaches in Political Science*, London and New York, NY: Routledge.

Dunleavy, P. and L. Carrera (2013), *Growing the Productivity of Government Services*, Cheltenham, UK and Northampton, MA, USA: Edward Elgar Publishing.

Dunleavy, P. and C. Hood (1994), 'From old public administration to New Public Management', *Public Money and Management*, **14** (3), 9–16.

Dunleavy, P., H. Margetts, S. Bastow and J. Tinkler (2006a), *Digital Era Governance: IT Corporations, the State, and E-Government*, Oxford: Oxford University Press.

Dunleavy, P., H. Margetts, S. Bastow and J. Tinkler (2006b), 'New Public Management is dead – long live digital-era governance', *Journal of Public Administration Research and Theory*, **16** (3), 467–94.

Dunston, R., A. Lee, D. Boud, P. Brodie and M. Chiarella (2009), 'Co-production and health system reform – from re-imagining to re-making', *Australian Journal of Public Administration*, **68** (1), 39–52.

Durant, R. (2012), *The Oxford Handbook of the American Bureaucracy*, Oxford: Oxford University Press.

Eggers, W.D. (2016), *Delivering on Digital*, New York, NY: Rosetta Books.

Ejersbo, N. and C. Greve (2014), *Moderniseringen af den offentlige sektor*, København: Akademisk Forlag.

Ejersbo, N. and C. Greve (2016a), 'Digital era governance reform and accountability: the case of Denmark', in T. Christensen and P. Lægreid (eds), *The Routledge Handbook of Accountability and Welfare State Reforms in Europe*, London: Routledge, pp. 267–79.

Ejersbo, N. and C. Greve (2016b), 'Denmark: towards the Neo-Weberian State in the digital era', in G. Hammerschmidt, S.V.D. Walle, R. Andrews and P. Bezes (eds), *Public Administration Reforms in*

Europe: The View from the Top, Cheltenham, UK and Northampton, MA, USA: Edward Elgar Publishing, pp. 119–28.

Ejler, N. (2017), *Faglig ledelse mellem kerneopgave og styring*, Copenhagen: DJØF Publishing.

Erikson, R., E.J. Hansen, S. Ringen and H. Uusitalo (eds) (1987), *The Scandinavian Model: Welfare and Welfare Research*, New York, NY: M.E. Sharpe.

Erridge, A. (2007), 'Public procurement, public value and the Northern Ireland unemployment pilot project', *Public Administration*, **85** (4), 1023–43.

Esmark, A. (2007), 'Network management in the EU: the European Commission as network manager', in M. Marcussen and J. Torfing (eds), *Democratic Network Governance in Europe*, Basingstoke: Palgrave Macmillan, pp. 252–72.

EU (2001), *European Governance: A White Paper.* http://europa.eu/rapid/press-release_DOC-01-10_en.htm (accessed 7 April 2019).

EU (2009), The Committee of the Regions' White Paper on Multilevel Governance. https://publications.europa.eu/en/publication-detail/-/publication/3cba79fd-2fcd-4fc4-94b9-677bbc53916b/language-en (accessed 7 April 2019).

European Commission (2017), *Advancing Europe's Digital Future: Digital Headlines*, Brussels: European Union.

European Commission (2018), *A Comparative Overview of Public Administration Characteristics and Performance in EU28*, Brussels: European Union.

Evans, P., D. Rueschemeyer and T. Skocpol (eds) (1985), *Bringing the State Back In*, Cambridge: Cambridge University Press.

Evetts, J. (2003), 'The sociological analysis of professionalism: occupational change in the modern world', *International Sociology*, **18** (2), 395–415.

Exworthy, M. and S. Halford (eds) (1999), *Professionals and the New Managerialism in the Public Sector*, Buckingham: Open University Press.

Ferlie, E. and E. Ongaro (2015), *Strategic Management in Public Services Organizations: Concepts, Schools and Contemporary Issues*, Abingdon and New York. NY: Routledge.

Ferlie, E., L. Ashburner, L. Fitzgerald and A. Pettigrew (1996), *The New Public Management in Action*, Oxford: Oxford University Press.

Flynn, N. (2000), 'Managerialism and public services: some international trends', in J. Clarke, S. Gewirtz and E. McLaughlin (eds), *New Managerialism, New Welfare?* London: Sage.

Flyverbom, M. and A.K. Madsen (2015), 'Sorting data out: unpacking big data value chains and algorithmic knowledge production', in F. Süssengut (ed.), *Die Gesselschaft der daten*, Bielefeld: Transcript Verlag, pp. 123–44.

Flyverbom, M., R. Deibert and D. Matten (2017), 'The governance of digital technology, big data and the internet: new roles and responsibilities for business', *Business and Society*, **58** (1), 3–19.

Freeman, R.E. (1984), *Strategic Management: A Stakeholder Approach*, Boston, MA: Pitman.

Freidson, E. (1970a), *Professional Dominance: The Social Structure of Medical Care*, Chicago, IL: Aldine.

Freidson, E. (1970b), *Profession of Medicine: A Study in the Sociology of Applied Knowledge*, New York, NY: Dodd, Mead & Co.

Freidson, E. (1994), *Professionalism Reborn: Theory, Prophecy, and Policy*, Chicago, IL: University of Chicago Press.

Freidson, E. (2001), *Professionalism: The Third Logic*, Chicago, IL: University of Chicago Press.

Fukuyama, F. (1992), *The End of History and the Last Man*, New York, NY: The Free Press.

Fukuyama, F. (2004), *State Building: Governance and World Order in the Twenty-First Century*, London: Profile Books.

Fukuyama, F. (2013), 'What is Governance?', *Governance*, **26** (3), 347–68.

Fulda, A., Y. Li and Q. Song (2012), 'New strategies of civil society in China: a case study of the network governance approach', *Journal of Contemporary China*, **21** (76), 675–93.

Fung, A. (2004), *Empowered Participation*, Princeton, NJ: Princeton University Press.

Fung, A. (2009), *Empowered Participation: Reinventing Urban Democracy*, Princeton, NJ: Princeton University Press.

Fung, A. and E.O. Wright (eds) (2003), *Deepening Democracy: Institutional Innovations in Empowered Participatory Governance*, London: Verso.

Furphy, S. (ed.) (2015), *The Seven Dwarfs and the Age of the Mandarins: Australian Government Administration in the Post-War Reconstruction Era*, Acton: Australian National University Press.

Gains, F. and G. Stoker (2009), 'Delivering "public value": implications for accountability and legitimacy', *Parliamentary Affairs*, **62** (3), 438–55.

Gargiulo, M. and G. Ertug (2006), 'The dark side of trust', in R. Bachmann and A. Zaheer (eds), *Handbook of Trust Research*, Cheltenham, UK and Northampton, MA, USA: Edward Elgar Publishing, pp. 165–86.

Girth, A.M., A. Hefetz, J.M. Johnston and M.E. Warner (2012), 'Outsourcing public service delivery: management responses in non-competitive markets', *Public Administration Review*, **72** (6), 887–900.

Golden, B.R., J.M. Dukerich and F.H. Fabian (2000), 'The interpretation and resolution of resource allocation issues in professional organizations: a critical examination of the professional–manager dichotomy', *Journal of Management Studies*, **37** (8), 2257–88.

Goldfinch, S. (1998), 'Evaluating public sector reforms in New Zealand: have the benefits been oversold?', *Asia Journal of Public Administration*, **20** (2), 203–32.

Goodsell, C. (2004), *The Case for Bureaucracy*, 4th edn, Washington, DC: CQ Press.

Goodsell, C. (2015), *The New Case for Bureaucracy*, Los Angeles, London, New Delhi, Singapore and Washington, DC: Sage.

Gore, A. (1993), *From Red Tape to Results: Creating a Government that Works Better and Costs Less*, New York, NY: Times Books/Random House.

Gray, B. (1989), *Collaborating: Finding Common Ground for Multiparty Problems*, San Francisco, CA: Jossey-Bass.

Greve, C. and G. Hodge (eds) (2013), *Rethinking Public–Private Partnerships: Strategies for Turbulent Times*, London and New York, NY: Routledge.

Greve, C., P. Lægreid and L.H. Rykkja (eds) (2016), *Nordic Administrative Reforms: Lessons for Public Management*, London: Palgrave Macmillan.

Grimsley, M. and A. Meehan (2007), 'E-government information systems: evaluation-led design for public value and client trust', *European Journal of Information Systems*, **16** (2), 134–48.

Grøn, C.H., L.L. Bro and L.B. Andersen (2019), 'Public managers' leadership identity: concept, causes, and consequences', *Public Management Review*, online version first published 8 August 2019. DOI: 10.1080/14719037.2019.1645875.

Gruening, G. (2001), 'Origin and theoretical basis of New Public Management', *International Public Management Journal*, **4** (1), 1–25.

Ha, Y.-C. and M.-K. Kang (2011), 'Creating a capable bureaucracy with loyalists: the internal dynamics of the South Korean Developmental State, 1948–1979', *Comparative Political Studies*, **44** (1): 78–108.

Hafner, K. and M. Lyon (1996), *Where the Wizards Stay up Late: The Origins of the Internet*, New York, NY: Simon & Schuster.

Hall, P.A. and R.C.R. Taylor (1996), 'Political science and the three new institutionalisms', *Political Studies*, **XLIV**, 936–57.

Hammerschmidt, G., S. van de Walle, R. Andrews and P. Bezes (eds) (2016), *Public Administration Reforms in Europe: The View from the Top*, Cheltenham, UK and Northampton, MA, USA: Edward Elgar Publishing.

Hammond, T.H. and P.A. Thomas (1989), 'The impossibility of a neutral hierarchy', *Journal of Law, Economics, and Organization*, **5** (1), 155–84.

Hansen, E.J., S. Ringen, H. Uusitalo and R. Erikson (eds) (1993), *Welfare Trends in the Scandinavian Countries*, Armonk, NY: M.E. Sharpe.

Hartley, J. (2005), 'Innovation in governance and public services: past and present', *Public Money and Management*, **25** (1), 27–34.

Hartley, J., E. Sørensen and J. Torfing (2013), 'Collaborative innovation: a viable alternative to market competition and organizational entrepreneurship', *Public Administration Review*, **73** (6), 821–30.

Hatch, M.J. (1997), *Organization Theory: Modern Symbolic and Postmodern Perspectives*, Oxford: Oxford University Press.

Heclo, H. (1978), 'Issue networks and the executive establishment', in A. King (ed.), *The New American Political System*, Washington, DC: American Enterprise Institute, pp. 87–124.

Heffron, F.A. (1989), *Organization Theory and Public Organization: The Political Connection*, Englewood Cliffs, NJ: Prentice-Hall.

Heidenheimer, A.J. (1989), 'Professional knowledge and state policy in comparative historical perspective: law and medicine in Britain, Germany and the United States', *International Social Science Journal*, **41** (4), 529–53.

Henriksen, H.Z. and B. Rukonova (2011), 'To mind IT or not to mind IT', *Transforming Government*, **5** (2), 155–66.

Hermansson, H. (2016), 'Disaster management collaboration in Turkey: assessing progress and challenges of hybrid network governance', *Public Administration*, **94** (2), 333–49.

Hernes, Gudmund (1976) 'Structural change in social processes', *American Journal of Sociology*, **82** (3), 513–547.

Hirschman, A.O. (1970), *Exit, Voice and Loyalty: Responses to Decline in Firms, Organizations and States*, Cambridge, MA: Harvard University Press.

Hodge, G. and C. Greve (2010), 'Public–private partnerships: governance scheme or language game?', *Australian Journal of Public Administration*, **69** (1), 8–22.

Hodge, G.A., C. Greve and A. Boardman (2010), *International Handbook on Public–Private Partnerships*, Cheltenham, UK and Northampton, MA, USA: Edward Elgar Publishing.

Hofstad, H. and J. Torfing (2017), 'Towards a climate-resilient city: collaborative innovation for a "green shift"', in R.A. Fernandez, S. Zubelzu and R. Martínez (eds), *Oslo Carbon Footprint and the Industrial Life Cycle*, Cham: Springer, pp. 221–42.

Hofstede, G. (1980), *Culture's Consequences: International Differences in Work-Related Values*, London: Sage.

Holborn, H. (1969 [1982]), *A History of Modern Germany: 1840–1945*, Princeton, NJ: Princeton University Press.

Homburg, V. (2008), *Understanding E-Government: Information Systems in Public Administration*, London: Routledge.

Hondeghem, A. and J.L. Perry (2009), 'EGPA symposium on public service motivation and performance: introduction', *International Review of Administrative Sciences*, **75** (1), 5–9.

Hood, C. (1991), 'A public management for all seasons?', *Public Administration*, **69** (1), 3–19.

Hood, C. (1998), *The Art of the State*, Oxford: Oxford University Press.

Hood, C. and R. Dixon (2015a), *A Government that Works Better and Costs Less?* Oxford: Oxford University Press.

Hood, C. and R. Dixon (2015b), 'What we have to show for 30 years of New Public Management: higher costs, more complaints', *Governance*, **28** (3), 265–67.

Hood, C. and R. Dixon (2016), 'Not what it said on the tin? Reflections on three decades of UK public management reform', *Financial Accountability & Management*, **32** (4), 409–28.

Hood, C., C. Scott, O. James, G. Jones and T. Travers (1999), *Regulation Inside Government: Waste-Watchers, Quality Police and Sleaze Busters*, Oxford: Oxford University Press.

Hoogland, J. and H. Jochemsen (2000), 'Professional autonomy and the normative structure of medical practice', *Theoretical Medicine and Bioethics*, **21** (5), 457–75.

Hunt, J. (2010), 'Leadership style orientations of senior executives in Australia: an analysis of 54 Australian top managers', *The Journal of the American Academy of Business*, **16** (1), 207–17.

Huxham, C. and S. Vangen (2005), 'Aiming for collaborative advantage: challenging the concept of shared vision', Advanced Institute of Management Research Paper No. 015.

Iversen, T. and H. Lurås (2000), 'Economic motives and professional norms: the case of general medical practice', *Journal of Economic Behavior & Organization*, **43**, 447–70.

Jacobs, L.R. (2014), 'The contested politics of public value', *Public Administration Review*, **74** (4), 480–94.

Jacobsen, C.B. and L.B. Andersen (2015), 'Is leadership in the eye of the beholder? A study of intended and perceived leadership practices and organizational performance', *Public Administration Review*, **75** (6), 829–41.

Jakobsen, M.L.F. (2009), 'Bureaukratisering som begreb: fra politisk skældsord til videnskabeligt analyseobjekt', *Politica*, **41** (2), 135–49.

Jakobsen, M.L.F. and P.B. Mortensen (2014), *Regelstaten: Væksten i danske love og bekendtgørelser 1989–2011*, Copenhagen: DJØF Publishing.

Jakobsen, M.L.F. and P.B. Mortensen (2016), 'Rules and the doctrine of performance management', *Public Administration Review*, **76** (2), 302–12.

Jensen, K.R. (2017), *Leading Global Innovation: Facilitating Multicultural Collaboration and International Market Success*, Basingstoke: Palgrave Macmillan.

Jensen, U.T. and L.B. Andersen (2015), 'Public service motivation, user orientation, and prescription behaviour: doing good for society or for the individual user?', *Public Administration*, **93** (3), 753–68.

Jensen, U.T. and L.L. Bro (2018), 'How transformational leadership supports intrinsic motivation and public service motivation: the mediating role of basic need satisfaction', *The American Review of Public Administration*, **48** (6), 535–49.

Jessop, B. (1990), *State Theory: Putting Capitalist States in their Place*, Cambridge: Polity Press.

Jessop, B. (2002), *The Future of the Capitalist State*, Cambridge: Polity Press.

Johnson, T.J. (1972), *Professions and Power*, London: Macmillan.

Jørgensen T.B. and D.-L. Sørensen (2012) 'Codes of good governance', *Public Integrity*, **15** (1), 71–96.

Jørgensen, T.B. and K. Vrangbæk (2011), 'Value dynamics: towards a framework for analyzing public value changes', *International Journal of Public Administration*, **34** (8), 486–96.

Jun, J.S. (2009), 'The limits of post: New Public Management and beyond', *Public Administration Review*, **69** (1), 161–5.

Kapucu, N. (2006), 'Interagency communication networks during emergencies: boundary spanners in multiagency coordination', *The American Review of Public Administration*, **36** (2), 207–25.

Kaufmann, H. (1997 [2015]), *Red Tape: Its Origins, Uses, and Abuses*, Washington DC: Brookings.

Ketll, D.F. (1997), 'The global revolution in public management: driving themes, missing links', *Journal of Policy Analyses and Management*, **16** (3), 446–62.

Kettl, D.F. (2002), *The Transformation of Governance*, Baltimore, MD: Johns Hopkins University Press.

Kettl, D.F. (2005), *The Global Public Management Revolution*, 2nd edn, Washington, DC: Brookings.

Kettl, D.F. (2015), *The Transformation of Governance: Public Administration for the Twenty-First Century*, Baltimore, MD: Johns Hopkins University Press.

Kettl, D.F. (2016), *Escaping Jurassic Government: How to Recover America's Lost Commitment to Competence*, Washington, DC: Brookings.

Kickert, W.J.M. (2011), 'Public management reforms in Continental Europe: national distinctiveness', in T. Christensen and P. Lægreid (eds), *The Ashgate Research Companion to New Public Management*, London and New York, NY: Routledge, pp. 97–112.

Kickert, W.J.M., E.-H. Klijn and J.F.M. Koppenjan (eds) (1997), *Managing Complex Networks*, London: Sage.

Kingsley, G. (2004), 'On becoming just another contractor: contract competition and the management of science at Sandia National Laboratories', *Public Performance and Management Review*, **28** (2), 186–213.

Klausen, K.K. (2014), 'Still the century of government? No signs of governance yet!', *International Public Management Review*, **15** (1), 1–16.

Klausen, K.K. and K. Ståhlberg (1998), *New Public Management i Norden: nye organisations- og ledelsesformer i den decentrale velfærdsstat*, Odense: University Press of Southern Denmark.

Kluckhohn, C. (1951), 'Values and value-orientations in the theory of action: an exploration in definition and classification', in T. Parsons and E. Shils (eds), *Toward a General Theory of Action*, Cambridge, MA: Harvard University Press, pp. 388–433.

Knott, J.H. and G.J. Miller (1987), *Reforming Bureaucracy: The Politics of Institutional Change*, Englewood Cliffs, NJ: Prentice Hall.

Kohler-Koch, B. and F. Larat (eds) (2009), *European Multi-Level Governance*, Cheltenham, UK and Northampton, MA, USA: Edward Elgar Publishing.

Koliba, C.J., J.W. Meek and A. Zia (2010), 'Gordian knot or integrated theory? Critical conceptual considerations for governance network analysis', in T. Brandsen and M. Holzer (eds), *The Future of Governance: Selected Papers from the Fifth Transatlantic Dialogue on Public Administration*, pp. 257–80.

Koliba, C.J., R.M. Mills and A. Zia (2011), 'Accountability in governance networks: an assessment of public, private, and nonprofit emergency management practices following Hurricane Katrina', *Public Administration Review*, **71** (2), 210–20.

Kooiman, J. (ed.) (1993), *Modern Governance*, London: Sage.

Kooiman, J. (2003), *Governing as Governance*, London: Sage.

Koppenjan, J. and E.-H. Klijn (2004), *Managing Uncertainties in Networks: A Network Approach to Problem Solving*, London and New York, NY: Routledge.

Koppenjan, J., M. Kars and H.V.D. Voort (2009), 'Vertical politics in horizontal policy networks: framework setting as coupling arrangement', *Policy Studies Journal*, **37** (4), 769–92.

Kotter, J.P. (1996), *Leading Change*, Boston, MA: Harvard Business School Press.

Kragh Jespersen, P. (2005), *Mellem profession og management*, Copenhagen: Handelshøjskolens Forlag.

Krasnik, A., P.P. Groenewegen, P.A. Pedersen, P.V. Scholten, G. Mooney, A. Gottschau, H.A. Flierman and M.T. Damsgaard (1990), 'Changing remuneration systems: effects on activity in general practice', *British Medical Journal*, **300**, 1698–701.

Krejsler, J. (2005), 'Professions and their identities: how to explore professional development among (semi-) professions', *Scandinavian Journal of Educational Research*, **49** (4), 335–57.

Kuhn T. (1962), 'The structure of scientific revolutions', *International Encyclopedia of Unified Science*, **2** (2), xv and 172.

Kuhnle, S. (2000), 'The Scandinavian welfare state in the 1990s: challenged but viable', *West European Politics*, **23** (2), 209–28.

Lane, J.-E. (1993), *The Public Sector: Concepts, Models and Approaches*, London: Sage.

Lascoumes, P. and P. Le Galès (2007), 'Introduction: understanding public policy through its instruments – from the nature of instruments to the sociology of public policy instrumentation', *Governance*, **20** (1), 1–21.

Lazear, E.P. and M. Gibbs (2015), *Personnel Economics in Practice*, 2nd edn, Hoboken, NJ: John Wiley & Sons.

Le Grand, J. (2003), *Motivation, Agency and Public Policy*, Oxford: Oxford University Press.

Le Grand, J. (2010), 'Knights and knaves return: public service motivation and the delivery of public services', *International Public Management Journal*, **13** (1), 56–71.

Leyenaar, M.H. and B. Niemöller (2010), 'European citizens' consultations 2009: evaluation report', Brussels: The King Baudouin Foundation.

Lindblom, C.E. (1977), *Politics and Markets*, New York, NY: Basic Books.

Ling, T. (2002), 'Delivering joined-up government in the UK: dimensions, issues and problems', *Public Administration*, **80** (4), 615–42.

Lips, M. (2019), *Digital Government: Managing the Public Sector in the Digital Era*, London: Routledge.

Lipsky, Michael (1980), *Street-Level Bureaucracy: Dilemmas of the Individual in Public Services*, New York, NY: Russell Sage Foundation.

Lowndes, V., L. Pratchett and G. Stoker (2006), 'Local political participation: the impact of rules-in-use', *Public Administration*, **84** (3), 539–61.

Luhmann, N. (1995), *Social Systems*, Palo Alto, CA: Stanford University Press.

Lundquist, L. (1998), *Demokratins väktare: ämbetsmännen och vårt offentliga etos*, Lund: Studentlitteratur AB.

Lunenburg, F.C. (2012), 'Organizational structure: Mintzberg's framework', *International Journal of Scholarly, Academic, Intellectual Diversity*, **14** (1), 1–8.

Lynn, L.E. (1981), *Managing the Public's Business: The Job of the Government Executive*, New York, NY: Basic Books.

Lynn, L.E. Jr. (1996), *Public Management as Art, Science and Profession*, Chatham: Chatham House Publishers.

Lynn, L.E. Jr. (2008), 'What is a Neo-Weberian State? Reflections on a concept and its implications', *The NISPAcess Journal of Public Administration and Policy*, special issue: *A Distinctive European Model? The Neo-Weberian State*, **1** (2), 17–30.

Malhotra, D. and J.K. Murnighan (2002), 'The effects of contracts on interpersonal trust', *Administrative Science Quarterly*, **47** (3), 534–59.

March, J.G. and J.P. Olsen (1989), *Rediscovering Institutions*, New York, NY: Free Press.

March, J.G. and J.P. Olsen (1995), *Democratic Governance*, New York, NY: Free Press.

March, J.G., M. Schulz and X. Zhou (2000), *The Dynamics of Rules: Change in Written Organizational Codes*, Stanford, CA: Stanford University Press.

Marcussen, M. and J. Torfing (eds) (2007), *Democratic Network Governance in Europe*, Basingstoke: Palgrave Macmillan.

Margetts, H. and P. Dunleavy (2013), 'The second wave of digital era governance: a quasi-paradigm for government on the web', *Philosophical Transactions of the Royal Society*, **371** (1987), 1–17.

Margetts, H. and A. Naumann (2017), 'Government as a platform: what can Estonia show the world?', research paper, Oxford: University of Oxford.

Margetts, H., P. John, S. Hale and T. Yasseri (2017), *Political Turbulence: How Social Media Shape Collective Action*, Princeton, NJ: Princeton University Press.

Marini, F. (ed.) (1971), *Toward a New Public Administration: The Minnowbrook Perspective*, Scranton, PA: Chandler Publishing.

Marks, G. and L. Hooghe (2004), 'Contrasting visions of multi-level governance', in I. Bache and M. Flinders (eds), *Multi-Level Governance*, Oxford and New York, NY: Oxford University Press, pp. 15–30.

Marsh, D. and R.A.W. Rhodes (1992), *Policy Networks in British Government*, Oxford: Clarendon Press.

Mayer-Schönberger, V. and K. Cuckier (2013), *Big Data*, London: John Murray.

Mayntz, R. (1993a), 'Modernization and the logic of interorganisational networks', in J. Child, M. Crozier and R. Mayntz (eds), *Societal Change between Markets and Organization*, Aldershot: Avebury, pp. 3–18.

Mayntz, R. (1993b), 'Governing failure and the problem of governability: some comments on a theoretical paradigm', in J. Kooiman (ed.), *Modern Governance*, London: Sage, pp. 9–21.

Mazzucato, M. (2013), *The Entrepreneurial State*, London: Anthem Press.

McEvily, B., V. Perrone and A. Zaheer (2003), 'Trust as an organizing principle', *Organization Science*, **14** (1), 91–103.

McGivern, G., G. Currie, E. Ferlie, L. Fitzgerald and J. Waring (2015), 'Hybrid manager–professionals' identity work: the maintenance and hybridization of medical professionalism in managerial contexts', *Public Administration*, **93** (2), 412–32.

Meijer, A.J. (2011), 'Networked coproduction of public services in virtual communities: from a government-centric to a community approach to public service support', *Public Administration Review*, **71** (4), 598–607.

Melchiorsen, I.M. (2012), 'En nøgle til afbureaukratisering?', master's thesis, Aarhus: Department of Political Science, Aarhus University.

Mergel, I. (2016), 'Social media institutionalization in U.S. federal government', *Government Information Quarterly*, **33** (1), 142–8.

Mergel, I. (2017). 'Building holistic evidence for social media impact', *Public Administration Review*, **77** (4), 489–95.

Mergel, I. and S. Bretschneider (2013), 'A three-stage adoption process for social media use in government', *Public Administration Review*, **73** (3), 390–400.

Mergel, I., K. Rethemeyer and K. Issett (2017), 'Big data in public affairs', *Public Administration Review*, **76** (6), 928–37.

Meyer, J.W. and B. Rowan (1977), 'Institutionalized organizations: formal structure as myth and ceremony', *American Journal of Sociology*, **83** (2), 340–63.

Meynhardt, T. and J. Metelmann (2009), 'Pushing the envelope: creating public value in the labor market: an empirical study on the role of middle managers', *International Journal of Public Administration*, **32** (3–4), 274–312.

Miller, G.J. (2000), 'Above politics: credible commitment and efficiency in the design of public agencies', *Journal of Public Administration Research and Theory*, **10** (2), 289–327.

Milward, H.B., L. Jensen, A. Roberts, M.I. Dussauge-Laguna, V. Junjan, R. Torenvlied, A. Boin, H.K. Colebatch, D. Kettl and R. Durant (2016), 'Is public management neglecting the state?', *Governance*, **29** (3), 311–34.

Mintzberg, H. (1992), *Structure in Fives: Designing Effective Organizations*, Upper Saddle River, NJ: Prentice Hall.

Mintzberg, H. (2009), *Tracking Strategies: Toward a General Theory of Strategy Formation*, New York, NY: Oxford University Press.

Moe, T.M. (1987), 'Interests, institutions and positive theory', in K. Orren and S. Skowronek (eds), *Studies in American Political Development*, New Haven, CT: Yale University Press, pp. 236–99.

Moore, M.H. (1995), *Creating Public Value: Strategic Management in Government*, Cambridge, MA: Harvard University Press.

Moore, M.H. (2000), 'Managing for value: organizational strategy in for-profit, nonprofit, and governmental organizations', *Nonprofit and Voluntary Sector Quarterly*, **29** (S1), 183–204.

Moore, M.H. (2013), *Recognizing Public Value*, Cambridge, MA: Harvard University Press.

Morgan, D.F. and B.J. Cook (eds) (2014), *New Public Governance: A Regime-Centered Perspective*, London and New York, NY: Routledge.

Moynihan, D.P. (2008), *The Dynamics of Performance Management: Constructing Information and Reform*, Washington, DC: Georgetown University Press.

Murphy, R. (1986), 'Weberian closure theory: a contribution to the ongoing assessment', *British Journal of Sociology*, **31** (1), 21–41.

Nabatchi, T. and M. Leighninger (2015), *Public Participation for 21st Century Democracy*, San Francisco, CA: Jossey-Bass.

Newman, J., J. Raine and C. Skelcher (2001), 'Transforming local government: innovation and modernization', *Public Money and Management*, **21** (2), 61–8.

Nielsen, P.A. (2013), 'Performance information in politics and public management: impacts on decision making and performance', PhD dissertation, Department of Political Science, Aarhus University http://politica.dk/fileadmin/politica/Dokumenter/ph.d.-afhandlinger/poul_aaes_nielsen.pdf (accessed 20 October 2016).

Nielsen, P.A., S. Boye, A.L. Holten, C.B. Jacobsen and L.B. Andersen (2018), 'Are transformational and transactional types of leadership compatible? A two-wave study of employee motivation', *Public Administration*, 1–16 (early view November 22, 2018).

Nielsen, V.L. (2006), 'Are street-level bureaucrats compelled or enticed to cope?' *Public Administration*, **84** (4), 861–89.

Niskanen, W.A. (1971), *Bureaucracy and Representative Government*, Chicago, IL: Aldine Atherton.

Noordegraaf, M. (2007), 'From "pure" to "hybrid" professionalism: present-day professionalism in ambiguous public domains', *Administration & Society*, **39** (6), 761–85.

Noordegraaf, M. (2011a), 'Risky business: how professionals and professional fields (must) deal with organizational issues', *Organization Studies*, **32** (10), 1349–71.

Noordegraaf, M. (2011b), 'Remaking professionals? How associations and professional education connect professionalism and organizations', *Current Sociology*, **59** (4), 465–88.

Noordegraaf, M. (2016), 'Reconfiguring professional work: changing forms of professionalism in public services', *Administration and Society*, **48** (7), 783–810.

Norman R. and R. Gregory (2003), 'Paradoxes and pendulum swings: performance management in New Zealand public sector', *Australian Journal of Public Administration*, **62** (4), 35–49.

Normann, R. (2001), *Service Management: Strategy and Leadership in Service Business*, 3rd edn, Chichester: Wiley.

Norris, P. (2011), *Democratic Deficit: Critical Citizens Revisited*, Cambridge: Cambridge University Press.

Nyhan, R.C. (2000), 'Changing the paradigm: trust and its role in public sector organizations', *The American Review of Public Administration*, **30** (1), 87–109.

OECD (1995), *Governance in Transition: Public Management Reforms in OECD Countries*, Paris: OECD.

OECD (2018), *OECD Better Life Index*, Paris: OECD www.oecd betterlifeindex.org/.

O'Flynn, J. (2007), 'From New Public Management to public value: paradigmatic change and managerial implications', *Australian Journal of Public Administration*, **66** (3), 353–66.

Olsen, J.P. (1986), 'Foran en ny offentlig revolution', *Nytt Norsk Tidsskrift*, **3** (3) 3–15.

Olsen, J.P. (1991), 'Modernization programs in perspective: institutional analyses of organizational change', *Governance*, **4** (2), 125–49.

Olsen, J.P. (2006), 'Maybe it is time to rediscover bureaucracy', *Journal of Public Administration Research and Theory*, **16** (1), 1–24.

Olsen, J.P. and G.B. Peters (1996), *Lessons from Experience*, Oslo: Scandinavian University Press.

Ongaro, Edoardo (2017), *Philosophy and Public Administration: An Introduction*, Cheltenham, UK and Northampton, MA, USA: Edward Elgar Publishing.

Osborne, S. (2006), 'The New Public Governance?', *Public Management Review*, **8** (3), 377–87.

Osborne, S. (ed.) (2010), *The New Public Governance?* London and New York, NY: Routledge.

Osborne, D. and T. Gaebler (1992), *Reinventing Government: How the Entrepreneurial Spirit is Transforming the Public Sector*, Reading, MA: Addison-Wesley.

Osborne, D. and P. Plastrik (1998), *Banishing Bureaucracy: The Five Strategies for Reinventing Government*, New York: Penguin Books.

Osborne, S.P. and K. Strokosch (2013), 'It takes two to tango? Understanding the co-production of public services by integrating the services management and public administration perspectives', *British Journal of Management*, **24** (S1), 31–47.

Osborne, S.P., Z. Radnor and G. Nasi (2013), 'A new theory for public service management? Toward a (public) service-dominant approach', *American Review of Public Administration*, **43** (2), 135–58.

Osborne, S.P., Z. Radnor and K. Strokosch (2016), 'Co-production and the co-creation of value in public services: a suitable case for treatment?', *Public Management Review*, **18** (5), 639–53.

Ostrom, E. (1973), *Community Organization and the Provision of Police Services*, Thousand Oaks, CA: Sage.

Ostrom, E. (1991), 'Rational choice theory and institutional analysis: toward complementarity', *American Political Science Review*, **85** (1), 237–43.

Ostrom, E. (1996), 'Crossing the great divide: coproduction, synergy, and development', *World Development*, **24** (6), 1073–87.

Ostrom, E. and G. Whitaker (1973), 'Does local community control of police make a difference? Some preliminary findings', *American Journal of Political Science*, **17** (1), 48–76.

Ostrom, E., R. Gardner and J. Walker (1994), *Rules, Games, and Common-Pool Resources*, Ann Arbor, MI: University of Michigan Press.

Ostrom, V. and E. Ostrom (1971), 'Public choice: a different approach to the study of public administration', *Public Administration Review*, **31** (2), 203–16.

O'Toole, Jr, L.J., K.J. Meierand and S. Nicholson-Crotty (2005), 'Managing upward, downward and outward: networks, hierarchical relationships and performance', *Public Management Review*, **7** (1), 45–68.

Ouchi, W.G. (1980), 'Markets, bureaucracies and clans', *Administrative Science Quarterly*, **25**, 129–41.

Page, S.B., M.M. Stone, J.M. Bryson and B.C. Crosby (2015), 'Public value creation by cross-sector collaborations: a framework and challenges of assessment', *Public Administration*, **93** (3), 715–32.

Papadopoulos, Y. (2003), 'Cooperative forms of governance: problems of democratic accountability in complex environments', *European Journal of Political Research*, **42** (4), 473–501.

Papadopoulos, Y. (2007), 'Problems of democratic accountability in network and multilevel governance', *European Law Journal*, **13** (4), 469–86.

Parkin, F. (1979), *Marxism and Class Theory: A Bourgeois Critique*, London: Tavistock.

Parsons, T. (1951), *The Social System*, London: Free Press.

Pells, C. (2015), 'Debate: against collaboration', *Public Money & Management*, **36** (1), 4–5.

Perry, J.L. and A. Hondeghem (2008), 'Building theory and empirical evidence about public service motivation', *International Public Management Journal*, **11** (1), 3–12.

Perry, J.L. and L. Wise (1990), 'The motivational bases of public service', *Public Administration Review*, **50** (3), 367–73.

Pestoff, V., T. Brandsen and B. Verschuere (eds) (2013), *New Public Governance, the Third Sector, and Co-Production*, London and New York, NY: Routledge.

Pfeffer, J. and G.R. Salancik (1978), *The External Control of Organizations: A Resource Dependence Perspective*, New York, NY: Harper and Row.

Poel, M., E.T. Meyer and R. Schroeder (2018), 'Big data for policy-making: great expectations but with limited progress?', *Policy and Internet.* Online version first published 15 July 2018. DOI: 10.1002/poi3.176.

Pollitt, C. (2013), *Context in Public Policy and Management: The Missing Link?* Cheltenham, UK and Northampton, MA, USA: Edward Elgar Publishing.

Pollitt, C. (2016a), 'Managerialism redux?', *Financial Accountability & Management,* **32** (4), 429–47.

Pollitt, C. (2016b), *Advanced Introduction to Public Management and Administration,* Cheltenham, UK and Northampton, MA, USA: Edward Elgar Publishing.

Pollitt, C. and G. Bouckaert (2003), 'Evaluating public management reforms: an international perspective', in H. Wollmann (ed.), *Evaluation in Public-Sector Reform: Concepts and Practice in International Perspective,* Cheltenham, UK and Northampton, MA, USA: Edward Elgar Publishing, pp. 12–35.

Pollitt, C. and G. Bouckaert (2004), *Public Management Reform: A Comparative Analysis,* Oxford: Oxford University Press.

Pollitt, C. and G. Bouckaert (2011), *Public Management Reform: A Comparative Analysis of NPM, the Neo-Weberian State, and New Public Governance,* 3rd edn, Oxford: Oxford University Press.

Pollitt, C. and G. Bouckaert (2017), *Public Management Reform: A Comparative Analysis into the Age of Austerity,* 4th edn, Oxford: Oxford University Press.

Porter, M.E. (1980), *Competitive Strategy: Techniques for Analyzing Industries and Competitors,* New York, NY: Free Press.

Porter, M.E. (1985), *Competitive Advantage: Creating and Sustaining Superior Performance,* New York, NY: Free Press.

Powell, W.W. and P.J. DiMaggio (eds) (1991), *The New Institutionalism in Organizational Analysis,* Chicago, IL: University of Chicago Press.

Power, M. (1998), *The Audit Society,* Oxford: Oxford University Press.

Provan, K.G. and P. Kenis (2008), 'Modes of network governance: structure, management and effectiveness', *Journal of Public Administration Research and Theory,* **18** (2), 229–52.

Radnor, Z. and S.P. Osborne (2013), 'Lean: a failed theory for public services?', *Public Management Review,* **15** (2), 265–87.

Raelin, J.A. (1983), *The Clash of Cultures: Managers and Professionals,* Boston, MA: Harvard Business School Press.

Rainey, H.G., R.W. Backoff and C.H. Levine (1976), 'Comparing public and private organizations', *Public Administration Review,* **36** (2) 233–44.

Rhodes, R.A.W. (1997), *Understanding Governance: Policy Networks, Governance, Reflexivity and Accountability*, Buckingham: Open University Press.

Rhodes, R.A.W. (2000), 'Governance and public administration', in J. Pierre (ed.), *Debating Governance*, Oxford: Oxford University Press, pp. 54–90.

Rhodes, R.A.W. (2015), 'Recovering the craft of public administration', *Public Administration Review*, **76** (4), 638–47.

Rhodes, R.A.W. and J. Wanna (2007), 'The limits to public value, or rescuing responsible government from the platonic guardians', *Australian Journal of Public Administration*, **66** (4), 406–21.

Rhodes, R.A. and J. Wanna (2008), 'Stairways to heaven: a reply to Alford', *Australian Journal of Public Administration*, **67** (3), 367–70.

Rhodes, R.A.W. and J. Wanna (2009), 'Bringing the politics back in: public value in Westminster parliamentary government', *Public Administration*, **87** (2), 161–83.

Riccucci, N.M. (1995), *Unsung Heroes: Federal Execucrats Making a Difference*, Washington, DC: Georgetown University Press.

Rittel, H.W. and M.M. Webber (1973), 'Dilemmas in a general theory of planning', *Policy Sciences*, **4** (2), 155–69.

Roberts, A. (2017), *Four Crises of American Democracy*, Oxford: Oxford University Press.

Roberts, A. (2018), *Can Government Do Anything Right?* Cambridge: Polity Press.

Roberts, J. and M. Dietrich (1999), 'Conceptualizing professionalism: why economics needs sociology', *American Journal of Economics and Sociology*, **58** (4), 977–98.

Roberts, N.C. (2000), 'Wicked problems and network approaches to resolution', *International Public Management Review*, **1** (1), 1–19.

Rosanvallon, P. (2011), *Democratic Legitimacy: Impartiality, Reflexivity, Proximity*, Princeton, NJ: Princeton University Press.

Rosenberg, S. (ed.) (2007), *Deliberation, Participation, and Democracy: Can the People Govern?* New York, NY: Palgrave Macmillan.

Rosser, C. (2018), 'Max Weber's bequest for a European public administration', in E. Ongaro and S. van Thiel (eds), *The Palgrave Handbook of Public Administration and Management in Europe*, London: Palgrave Macmillan, pp. 1011–29.

Rothstein, B. and J. Teorell (2008), 'What is quality of government? A theory of impartial government Institutions', *Governance*, **21** (2), 165–90.

Røvik, K.A. (2011), 'From fashion to virus: an alternative theory of organizations' handling of management ideas', *Organization Studies*, **32** (5), 631–53.

Rowse, T. (2002), *Nugget Coombs: A Reforming Life*, Cambridge: Cambridge University Press.

Salamon, L.M. (2000), 'The new governance and the tools of public action: an introduction', *Fordham Urban Law Journal*, **28**, 1611–74.

Salamon, L.M. (2002), *The Tools of Government: A Guide to the New Governance*, New York, NY: Oxford University Press.

Sayadi, Z., M. Dehbannejad, H.R. Pordanjani and O.J. Aghad (2017), 'The impact of leadership style on employee creativity: mediator role of employee trust', *Journal of Economic and Management Perspectives*, **11** (1), 1393–402.

Scharpf, F.W. (1994), 'Games real actors could play: positive and negative coordination in embedded negotiations', *Journal of Theoretical Politics*, **6** (1), 27–53.

Scharpf, F.W. (1998), *Games Real Actors Play: Actor-Centered Institutionalism in Policy Research*, Boulder, CO: Westview Press.

Scharpf, F.W. (1999), *Governing in Europe: Effective and Democratic?*, Oxford and New York, NY: Oxford University Press.

Schillemans, T. (2013), 'Moving beyond the clash of interests: on a stewardship theory and the relationships between central government departments and public agencies', *Public Management Review*, **15** (4), 541–62.

Schön, D. (1973), *Beyond the Stable State*, New York, NY: W.W. Norton.

Schott, C., D. van Kleef and M. Noordegraaf (2016), 'Confused professionals? Capacities to cope with pressures on professional work', *Public Management Review*, **18** (4), 583–610.

Schott, C., D. van Kleef and T. Steen (2018), 'The combined impact of professional role identity and public service motivation on decision-making in dilemma situations', *International Review of Administrative Sciences*, **84** (1), 21–41.

Schwab, K. (2017), *The Fourth Industrial Revolution*, London: Portfolio Penguin.

Scott, W.R. (1981), *Organizations: Rational, Natural, and Open Systems*, Englewood Cliffs, NJ: Prentice Hall.

Scott, W.R. (2008), 'Lords of the dance: professionals as institutional agents', *Organization Studies*, **29** (2), 219–38.

Senge, P.M. (1990), *The Fifth Discipline: The Art and Practice of The Learning Organization*, London: Random House.

Shapiro, S.P. (2005), 'Agency theory', *Annual Review of Sociology*, **31**, 263–84.

Sharma, A. (1997), 'Professional as agent: knowledge asymmetry in agency exchange', *The Academy of Management Review*, **22** (3), 758–98.

Smith, G. (2009), *Democratic Innovations Designing Institutions for Citizen Participation*, New York, NY: Cambridge University Press.

Sørensen, E. and J. Torfing (eds) (2007), *Theories of Democratic Network Governance*, Basingstoke: Palgrave Macmillan.

Sørensen, E. and J. Torfing (2009), 'Making governance networks effective and democratic through metagovernance', *Public Administration*, **87** (2), 234–58.

Sørensen, E. and J. Torfing (2016), 'Political leadership in the age of interactive governance: reflections on the political aspects of metagovernance', in J. Edelenbos and I. van Meerkerk (eds), *Critical Reflections on Interactive Governance: Self-Organization and Participation in Public Governance*, Cheltenham, UK and Northampton, MA, USA: Edward Elgar Publishing, pp. 444–66.

Sørensen, E. and J. Torfing (2017), 'Metagoverning collaborative innovation in governance networks', *The American Review of Public Administration*, **47** (7), 826–39.

Sørensen, E. and J. Torfing (2018), 'Co-initiation of collaborative innovation in urban spaces', *Urban Affairs Review*, **54** (2), 388–418.

Sørensen, E. and P. Triantafillou (eds) (2013), *The Politics of Self-Governance*, London: Ashgate.

Stoker, G. (2006), 'Public Value Management: a new narrative for networked governance?', *The American Review of Public Administration*, **36** (1), 41–57.

Streeck, W. and K. Thelen (eds) (2005), *Beyond Continuity: Institutional Change in Advanced Political Economies*, Oxford: Oxford University Press.

Talbot, C. (2009), 'Public value: the next "big thing" in public management?', *International Journal of Public Administration*, **32** (3–4), 167–70.

Tao, J., A. Cheung, M. Painter and C. Li (eds) (2010), *Governance for Harmony in Asia and Beyond*, Abingdon and New York, NY: Routledge.

Theoharis, G. (2009), *The School Leaders our Children Deserve: Seven Keys to Equity, Social Justice, and School Reform*, New York, NY: Teachers College Press.

Thompson, J.D. (1967 [2003]), *Organizations in Action: Social Science Bases of Administrative Theory*, New York, NY: Routledge.

Tilly, C. (ed.) (1975), *The Formation National States in Europe*, Princeton, NJ: Princeton University Press.

Tonon, J.M. (2008), 'The costs of speaking truth to power: how professionalism facilitates credible communication', *Journal of Public Administration Research and Theory*, **18**, 275–95.

Torfing, J. (2016), *Collaborative Innovation in the Public Sector*, Washington, DC: Georgetown University Press.

Torfing, J. and T.B. Køhler (2016), 'Styringskløft mellem Finans ministeriet og kommuner', *Altinget*, available at www.altinget. dk/embedsvaerk/artikel/styringskloeft-mellem-finansministeriet-og-kommuner (accessed 5 December 2016).

Torfing, J. and A.H. Krogh (2017), 'Institutionsstyring: tillids- og dialogbaseret styring som alternativ til regelstyring og pisk og gulerod', in J. Torfing and P. Triantafillou (eds), *New Public Governance på Dansk*, Copenhagen: Akademisk Forlag, pp. 87–104.

Torfing, J. and P. Triantafillou (2013), 'What's in a name? Grasping new public governance as a political-administrative system', *International Review of Public Administration*, **18** (2), 9–25.

Torfing, J. and P. Triantafillou (eds) (2016), *Enhancing Public Innovation by Transforming Public Governance*, Cambridge: Cambridge University Press.

Torfing, J., B.G. Peters, J. Pierre and E. Sørensen (2012), *Interactive Governance: Advancing the Paradigm*, Oxford: Oxford University Press.

Torfing, J., E. Sørensen and T. Fotel (2009), 'Democratic anchorage of infrastructural governance networks: the case of the Femern Belt forum', *Planning Theory*, **8** (3), 282–308.

Torfing, J., Sørensen, E. and A. Røiseland (2019), 'Transforming the public sector into an arena for co-creation: barriers, drivers, benefits, and ways forward', *Administration and Society*, **51** (5), 795–825.

Trubek, D.M. and L.G. Trubek (2005), 'Hard and soft law in the construction of social Europe: the role of the open method of coordination', *European Law Journal*, **11** (3), 343–64.

United Nations (2018), *E-Government Survey 2018*, New York, NY: United Nations.

van der Wal, Z. (2017), *The 21st Century Public Manager*, London: Routledge.

van der Wal, Z., T. Nabatchi and G. De Graaf (2013), 'From galaxies to universe: a cross-disciplinary review and analysis of public values publications from 1969 to 2012', *The American Review of Public Administration*, **45** (1), 13–28.

van Heffen, O., W.J. Kickert and J. Thomassen (eds) (2000), *Governance in Modern Society: Effects, Change and Formation of Government Institutions*, Dordrecht: Kluwer Academic.

van Witteloostuijn, A. and G. De Jong (2009), 'Ecology of national rule birth: a longitudinal study of Dutch higher education law, 1960–2004', *Journal of Public Administration Research and Theory*, **20** (1), 187–213.

Vinzant, J.C. and L. Crothers (1998), *Street-Level Leadership: Discretion and Legitimacy in Front-Line Public Service*, Washington, DC: Georgetown University Press.

Voon, M.L., M.C. Lo, K.S. Ngui and N.B. Ayob (2011), 'The influence of leadership styles on employees' job satisfaction in public sector organizations in Malaysia', *International Journal of Business, Management and Social Sciences*, **2** (1), 24–32.

Waldo, D. (1948), *The Administrative State: A Study of the Political Theory of American Public Administration*, New York, NY: Ronald Press.

Waldo D. (ed.) (1971), *Public Administration in a Time of Turbulence*, Scranton, PA: Chandler Publishing.

Wamsley, G.L. and M.N. Zald (1973), *The Political Economy of Public Administration: A Critique and Approach to the Study of Public Administration*, Lexington, NY: Lexington Books.

Wamsley, G.L., R.N. Bacher, C.T. Goodsell, P.S. Kronenberg, J.A. Rohr, C.M. Stivers, O.F. White and J.F. Wolf (1990), *Refounding Public Administration*, Newbury Park, CA: Sage.

Warren, M.E. (2002), 'What can democratic participation mean today?', *Political Theory*, **30** (5), 677–701.

Watson, T.J. (1980 [2003]), *Sociology, Work and Industry*, 4th edn, London: Routledge.

Weber, M. (1919 [2015]), *Weber's Rationalism and Modern Society: New Translations on Politics, Bureaucracy, and Social Stratification*, edited and translated by Tony Waters and Dagmar Waters, New York, NY: Palgrave Macmillan.

Weber, M. (1947), *The Theory of Social and Economic Organization*, translated by A.M. Henderson and Talcott Parsons, edited with an introduction by Talcott Parsons, London: The Free Press of Glencoe Collier-Macmillan Limited.

Weibel, A. (2007), 'Formal control and trustworthiness: shall the twain never meet?', *Group & Organization Management*, **32** (4), 500–517.

West, D. (2016), *Megachange*, Washington, DC: Brookings.

Williams, I. and H. Shearer (2011), 'Appraising public value: past, present and futures', *Public Administration*, **89** (4), 1367–84.

Wilson, J.Q. (1989), *Bureaucracy*, New York, NY: Basic Books.

Wilson, W. (1887), 'The study of administration', *Political Science Quarterly*, **2** (2), 197–222.

Wright, B.E., D.P. Moynihan and S.K. Pandey (2012), 'Pulling the levers: transformational leadership, public service motivation, and mission valence', *Public Administration Review*, **72** (2), 206–15.

Wukich, C. and I. Mergel (2016), 'Reusing social media information in government', *Government Information Quarterly*, **33** (2), 305–12.

Xia, M. (2007), *The People's Congresses and Governance in China: Toward a Network Mode of Governance*, London and New York, NY: Routledge.

Yeboah-Assiamah, E., K. Asamoah and T.A. Kyeremeh (2016), 'Therefore, is bureaucracy dead? Making a case for complementarity of paradigms in public administrative thinking and discourse', *International Journal of Public Administration*, **39** (5), 382–94.

Yifen, Y. (2007), 'Network governance: a new framework of public administration', *Journal of Public Management*, **1**, 89–96.

Index